SOLDIERS AND STATESMEN
1914-1918

Photo : Bassano.

To / Sir Wm Robertson
In grateful remembrance of our
work together during the Great War.

D. Haig F.M.

Xmas 1918

SOLDIERS AND STATESMEN
1914-1918

BY
FIELD-MARSHAL
SIR WILLIAM ROBERTSON, BART
G.C.B., G.C.M.G., K.C.V.O., D.S.O.

VOLUME TWO

With Four Plates

CASSELL AND COMPANY, LTD
LONDON, TORONTO, MELBOURNE AND SYDNEY

First Published 1926

CONTENTS

CHAPTER VIII

CHAPTER IX

CHAPTER X

CONTENTS

vi

CONTENTS

vii

LIST OF PLATES

SOLDIERS AND STATESMEN
1914 – 1918

CHAPTER VIII

HOME DEFENCE

Duties Explained—Pre-war Investigation of Invasion Problem—Mr.
Balfour's Views on Possibility of Invasion—Investigation by Lord
Morley's Sub-Committee, 1907—Conclusions reached—Influence
of Possible Invasion on Outbreak of War—Investigation by
Joint Naval and Military Conference, 1916—Troops maintained
for Home Defence—Further Investigation after Battle of Jutland
—Reduction of Home Defence Force, February, 1917—Final
Investigation at end of 1917—Air Raids—Adequate Defence of
Home Country compulsory.

THE duties of Home Defence during the war were
supposed by the general public to consist almost
wholly of measures for securing the country against
invasion, and the War Office was thought to be free
to restrict or enlarge them as it might choose. But, in
fact, they covered a much wider field than mere invasion,
and included a series of obligations which the War Office
was compelled to carry out and had little or no power to
challenge. For example, at the commencement of the
war there were in the United Kingdom a total of twenty-
six " defended ports," the selection of which had from
time to time been made, and their relative importance
fixed, not by the War Office, but by certain inter-departmental bodies who were charged with the consideration
of all coast-defence questions. Some of the ports, such

as Dover, Portsmouth, and Plymouth, were defended because they served as naval bases, while in the case of commercial waterways such as the Mersey, the Tyne and the Clyde, the chief object was to give protection to shipping. The Admiralty was the recognized authority for prescribing what was known as the " scale " of naval attack to which the several localities were deemed liable, and upon that scale the nature and strength of the defences were based. Before being finally adopted the scale was submitted for the sanction of higher authority and it was periodically reviewed, but in practice Admiralty opinion in regard to it was seldom or never questioned. The fortifications and armament required to meet the approved scale, often of an elaborate and expensive kind, were paid for out of Army funds, while the war garrisons allotted varied between 1,000 and 20,000 men each, according to the perimeter of the area to be defended.

In addition to these obligations there were scores of " vulnerable points " scattered about the kingdom, inland as well as on the coast, such as cable landing-places, wireless stations, railway bridges, magazines, factories, and depots which had to be guarded against evilly disposed persons within the country, if not against interference by outsiders. These, also, were selected for defence mainly by public departments other than the War Office —the Admiralty, Post Office, and Home Office, for instance—and absorbed in the aggregate many thousands of men, none of whom were available for repelling organized invasion.

To meet the latter contingency entirely separate and mobile forces were required, and, as already explained, the provision of them was at one time officially regarded as being the " primary " duty for which the

2

military authorities were responsible. The fallacy of this policy was exposed by the South African war, 1899–1902, and three years later the Prime Minister, Mr. Balfour, went to the opposite extreme by stating in the House of Commons, when discussing the problems of Imperial Defence, that the " serious invasion of these islands is not an eventuality which we need seriously consider." [1]

Although " invasion " was thus summarily ruled out as impracticable, " raids " were admitted to be feasible, and these, it was conceded, might be made on two or more places simultaneously and by hostile bodies varying in strength between 500 and 10,000 men each. Further, as they would probably occur, if at all, in the nature of a surprise and would finish within a few hours, it was also agreed that each of the localities exposed to them must in war-time always have a sufficient defence force of its own ready on the spot. The net result, therefore, of accepting the feasibility of raids and rejecting that of invasion was to leave the aggregate number of defence troops required no smaller than before. The only advantage to be derived from the change was the soothing reflection that the raiders would be but a temporary inconvenience, since they would quickly depart of their own free will, whereas the invaders, should they come, would remain in the country until forcibly expelled.

Lord Roberts and other prominent men associated with him drew public attention to the danger incurred by the acceptance of the no-invasion theory, and this, combined with recent changes in the European situation, led the Liberal Government, in 1907, to appoint a subcommittee of the Committee of Imperial Defence, under

[1] " Hansard," May 11, 1905.

the chairmanship of Lord Morley, to examine the question afresh.[1]

The soldiers did not, of course, contest the principle that the first line of defence was the Navy, but they held that the problem was so surrounded with uncertainties that naval protection alone was not an adequate insurance against attack. The Navy had but little first-hand experience of modern war, and as everybody knows, long periods of peace are apt to engender unsound ideas as to what is practicable and what is not. Steam had supplanted sails since Nelson's day; fleets of transport could be dispatched from enemy ports in all weathers, and could effectively combine their action at a fixed time and place; and in various ways invasion had become an easier, and therefore a more attractive, enterprise than in the past, especially to a country like Germany who was saturated with the belief that offensive action was the one and only means by which success in war could be attained.

Feasibility of invasion was, moreover, not the only factor to be considered, nor perhaps the most important one. What the soldiers feared was that when war came the bare *probability* of invasion would compel the Government, in order to allay public anxiety, to detain troops at home at a time when they were urgently needed for employment abroad. They argued that no matter how confidently we might talk in peace, when confronted in war with an enemy possessing millions of troops, abund-

---

[1] In the House of Commons on June 3, 1907, Mr. Balfour corrected the impression created by his speech in 1905. What he maintained in the speech was, he said, "that with the defence forces they then had at home added to the Fleet, they need not fear serious invasion; but the Home defence forces were an absolutely indispensable element of national security."—"Hansard," June 3, 1907.

ant sea-transport, and an undefeated fleet within a few
hours' steaming of our shores, no Government would
dare to rely upon the Navy alone for giving the country
that immunity from insult and injury which it would
expect to enjoy. Our own Fleet must, too, as the sailors
themselves were never tired of asserting, be free at all
times to move about the seas as and where circumstances might require. This it could not do if tied
down by the responsibilities which attach to the duties
of Home Defence.

In short, the soldiers were wholly opposed to dog-
matism in any shape or form on a subject in regard to
which the chances of war might play so great a part.
They suggested that however foolish attempted invasion
might seem to us, if the enemy should decide to run the
risk inseparable from it a limited number of transports
might conceivably succeed in slipping through our first
line—the Navy—and, if that were so, then obviously we
must have a second line—troops—to deal with whatever
force the transports could convey and would be able to
disembark.

Lord Morley's sub-committee occupied several
months during 1907–8 in completing its task, the conclusions eventually reached being announced by the
Prime Minister, Mr. Asquith, in the House of Commons
in 1909.[1] It was considered that " so long as the naval
supremacy of this country is adequately assured invasion
on a large scale . . . is an absolutely impracticable
operation." On the other hand, if we permanently lost
command of the sea then, whatever might be the strength
of our military forces, " the subjugation of the country
to the enemy would be inevitable." The essential thing
therefore was to maintain a Home Army of such strength

---

[1] " Hansard," July 29, 1909.

as " to compel an enemy which contemplates invasion to come with such substantial force as to make it impossible for them to evade our Fleet." Allowing the necessary margin of safety, the maximum strength of the potential invaders was fixed, as a figure upon which to base our own requirements, at 70,000 men, and it thus became " the business of the War Office to see that we have, under all circumstances, a properly organized and properly equipped force capable of dealing effectively with a possible invasion by 70,000 men. If these two conditions are satisfied, that is, the naval condition and the military condition, it is the opinion of the Defence Committee, after the most careful investigation that has ever been made, that this country will be safe from invasion. But both these conditions must be satisfied."

The announcement was made not a day too soon, for our defence arrangements were not only inefficient in themselves, as the result of being pushed into the background by Mr. Balfour's unfortunate statement four years earlier, but they were based on conditions which no longer existed. For more than a century past France had been looked upon as the only possible invader, and our preparations had been chiefly directed towards the defence of the south coast between Dover and Plymouth. With Germany as the most likely enemy circumstances were profoundly changed, and larger naval bases had to be provided on the east coast in order to meet that readjustment of our naval dispositions which the new situation had rendered necessary. This meant, of course, a strengthening of the existing defences, and entailed, besides the provision of larger garrisons and accommodation for them, the erection of much additional armament and a variety of appliances connected therewith—a long and costly process. Not months but years would be needed to complete these measures, and they were in fact far from finished when war broke out.

The Prime Minister's statement did not by any means dispose of the invasion controversy. In one form or another it was constantly being brought before the Committee of Imperial Defence, either by the "blue-water-school," who continued to pour ridicule on all mention of invasion, or by the "bolt-from-the-blue" party, who feared invasion might come upon us as a complete surprise the day after war was declared, if not before it was declared. Fortunately, the discussions seldom led to anything worse than waste of time, but more progress might have been made in giving practical effect to the policy laid down had the latter been less frequently questioned than it was.

The attitude of the General Staff remained unchanged. It was that the enemy, Germany, would have ample troops and ships at her disposal, and therefore the Admiralty must say whether the Navy could in all circumstances prevent her transports from crossing the sea. If they could give a reasonable—not necessarily an absolute —assurance to that effect, there was no more to be said on the part of the War Office. If they could not give it, then the provision of military means of protection would be necessary. So far as I am aware the assurance was never given, and it was not likely to be. "When I was at the Admiralty," said Lord Goschen in 1905, "I was sounded as to whether I would give a guarantee that the Navy would be able to resist every form of invasion. I declined altogether to give that guarantee, because I felt that there was so much of the element of the unforeseen which could not be left out of consideration in a matter of this supreme importance." [1]   That was exactly the soldiers' point.

Exactly what view was taken by the responsible authorities in August, 1914, I am not in a position to say, but whatever it was the Government decided, when the dispatch of the Expeditionary Force to France was being considered, that two of the six divisions must be temporarily held back so as to give the territorial troops more time to get into their places.   Similarly, the later dispatch of territorial troops was made subordinate to the retention of an adequate number at home, and although this policy was slightly modified during 1916–17 the requirements of Home Defence continued to take priority over the reinforcement of the armies abroad until the spring of 1918.   This display of what may seem to be excessive caution on the part of the Government and their professional advisers was due to certain reasons which are not generally known, and some reference to them will now be made.

In January, 1916, shortly after taking up the duties of C.I.G.S., I arranged with the First Sea Lord and Lord French, the newly appointed Commander-in-Chief of the Home Forces, that the question should be systematically examined by a conference of naval and military officers, so as to determine more precisely than hitherto what the strength and composition of the Home Defence army ought to be.   The conclusions reached were that, if the political and military situations made it worth the enemy's while to incur the risks involved, he could collect for the purpose of invading Great Britain, and without our knowledge, approximately ten divisions (having a strength of 160,000 men) and could hope to transport them across

[1] " Hansard," July 10, 1905.

the North Sea and land them at any suitable spot on the east coast south of the Wash. It was further concluded that the British Navy could not ensure effective interruption of the landing operation within a less period than twenty-four hours after the hostile transports were sighted from our shores. This scale of attack was, it will be observed, more than twice as formidable as the pre-war estimate (which was itself pronounced by the blue-water school to be impossible), but the Board of Admiralty nevertheless gave it their official approval.

It may be thought that although a hostile landing could not be absolutely prevented, the enemy's sea-communications would surely be severed in the course of a few days, and the whole enterprise be thereby engulfed in disaster. But, on the other hand, the main German Fleet had not yet been brought to battle, and who was to say, if the Admiralty would not, that the British Fleet was so superior to it that the danger of invasion could be ignored? The General Staff certainly could not say this, for the question was, as it always had been, primarily a naval one, and they could not disregard naval opinions in which the highest Admiralty authorities had expressed their concurrence. Some risks must always be taken in war, and we could afford to take them in regard to operations abroad, for we could hope to retrieve, sooner or later, such military misfortunes as might there occur. At home—the centre of the Empire's strength—the case was quite different, since a set-back there might be fraught with the most serious consequences. The General Staff therefore could do no other than accept the scale of attack approved by the Admiralty as the one with which the Army must be prepared to deal.

Measures for security against invasion entail great dispersion of force because of the uncertainty as to where a landing may be attempted ; hence, the number of troops required usually exceeds by far the anticipated strength of the attack. It was so in 1916, Lord French putting his requirements at no less than 9 territorial divisions, 17 mounted brigades, 10 independent brigades, and 23 cyclist battalions. Besides this " Field Force " of 230,000 men, the estimate included 220,000 men for sedentary duties such as garrisons for " defended ports," detachments for " vulnerable points " and anti-aircraft defence, or 450,000 men in all. Later, after the Dublin rebellion, it became necessary to provide additional troops for Ireland, and in this way the aggregate amounted to no fewer than 500,000 men.

These demands were never fully met—they could not be—and in April, 1916, Lord French formally brought the deficiencies to the notice of the Army Council. He pointed out that his calculations had been based on the assumption that his units would be kept at war strength and be fully equipped, whereas neither of these conditions had been fulfilled. The independent brigades were short of men and were armed with Japanese rifles and carbines for which the reserve of ammunition was so small that none could be spared for practice. The territorial divisions were all much under strength, and had in them a large percentage of recruits ; the rifles with which they were armed were of little use as weapons of war, and were few in numbers ; and, in general, the divisions were, in their present condition, " of very little value as fighting formations." Lord French disclaimed all intention of calling into question the advisability of maintaining so weak a force for Home Defence since that was a matter of policy lying outside his province to discuss, nor did he wish it to be supposed that he desired to hold back troops in this country which were needed for the prosecution of the war abroad. But he nevertheless went on to say that " I think it right to record my opinion that the forces at my disposal to repel invasion are not, at the present moment, adequate for the purpose."

The General Staff were aware of the deficiencies to which Lord French referred, but they considered that the troops available, indifferently trained and equipped as they were, ought to be sufficient to deal effectively with such hostile landings as were likely to be attempted, especially as the Germans already had their hands full at Verdun, and would soon have to meet an Anglo-French attack on the Somme. On the other hand, the General Staff hesitated, in view of naval opinion as indicated above, to make any further reductions in strength, while it can be understood that the Government, to whom Lord French's report was communicated, were equally loath to order reductions on their own responsibility. Instead of doing that, some Ministers expressed great dissatisfaction that the demands of Lord French had not been fully met, holding that he was the best judge as to what was required. The Prime Minister, however, and other members of the Cabinet were content to leave the matter in the hands of the General Staff, realizing that it was impossible to meet the demands of everybody, and that for the moment the essential thing was to be strong on the Western Front.

The question was again reviewed by a joint-conference in August, 1916, after the battle of Jutland had been fought and when the battle of the Somme was in progress. Practically the same conclusions were reached as before. It was recognized that the position at sea was now less favourable to the enemy, and that so long as he was engaged on the Somme and at Verdun there was no possibility of troops being found for the invasion of

Great Britain. On the other hand, the time within which the Navy could ensure interruption of landing operations was not considered to have been shortened, and it was thought that if and when the situation in France changed in favour of the enemy it would still be possible for him to attempt invasion with the same force of 160,000 men.

The conclusions were approved, generally, by the War Committee to whom they were submitted, and it was agreed that as the enemy had sufficient sea-transport to convey 160,000 men, and as no one could say that he would not be able to spare that number at some future date, we must be prepared to meet them, unless the Navy could undertake to prevent them from crossing the sea, and this the Navy would not do. A further reason why the troops at home could not be materially reduced was that the sedentary portion of them was largely composed of draft-finding units which must remain in the United Kingdom in any case, while the mobile portion, in addition to forming part of the Home Defence forces, constituted a necessary, indeed the only, strategical reserve for use when and where required abroad. There was about this period considerable uncertainty regarding the situation in the vicinity of India and elsewhere, and it was only common prudence to keep a few troops in hand with which to meet emergencies.

Early in 1917 the question was again reviewed, as it was desired to strengthen the armies in France which were shortly to take part in the operations designed by General Nivelle. By leaving the United Kingdom without any reserve formations available for service abroad it was possible to provide two additional divisions, and the General Staff were anxious to send them to France provided the Admiralty would modify their previous calculations respecting the transport of enemy troops across the North Sea. After hearing the naval view the War Cabinet (which had just replaced the War Committee of Mr. Asquith's Government) approved of the two divisions being sent.

During the course of the summer the strength of the Defence Forces was gradually reduced from the 500,000 men originally requisitioned to less than 400,000. More than one-half were incapable of performing other than sedentary work, while of the remainder, the mobile portion, 16,000 were stationed in Ireland, 50,000 were lads under the age qualifying for service abroad, and most of the others were classified as medically unfit for service outside the United Kingdom. Thus, there were practically no men retained for the combatant duties of Home Defence who could have been sent to the front.

It was rather commonly supposed during the war that, after making allowance for men on leave from the front, the bulk of those to be seen about the country in uniform—a very large number—were in some way or other connected with Home Defence. This was not the case. For instance, at one time in 1917 there were nearly a million men out of the total 1,400,000 on the home establishment who were not so connected. Of the million, 400,000 were under medical treatment; 50,000 belonged to the Army Medical Corps ; 90,000 to the Army Service Corps ; others to the Pay and Ordnance Corps ; 200,000 to the Labour Corps ; and nearly 50,000 were not engaged on army duty of any kind, but were under the Ministry of Munitions, in agriculture, or in dock and transport work. Men such as these lay outside General Staff control, and at the time were not allowed to be employed in the fighting line either at home or abroad.

Before the end of 1917 the joint-conference was again called together to make another and final review of the position. The entry of America into the war had augmented the available naval resources in both heavy and light ships ; the extension of submarine patrols had increased our chances of obtaining warning of any contemplated invasion ; and the enlargement of British minefields had added to the enemy's difficulties of assembling and moving large convoys without much previous mine-sweeping, which could hardly pass unobserved. On land the arrangements for defence had been improved ; while the development of the Air Force provided us with better facilities for oversea reconnaissance, and with additional means for acting offensively against hostile transports and the troops which might disembark therefrom. Having regard to these and other new factors which told in our favour, the conference recorded the conclusions that the difficulties of transporting a force of 160,000 from Germany to the British coast were practically insuperable, and that the maximum number that could be transported would be limited to that which could be carried in one convoy. This number was now put at 30,000 men.

The Board of Admiralty, however, did not entirely concur, and maintained that it was not possible to calculate with precision the number of transports that the enemy might bring over in one operation. But although they declined to take the responsibility of definitely saying that 160,000 men was an impossible number, they thought that the strongest force that could be transported would probably not exceed 70,000 men. Thus, after three years of war, we got back to the estimate formed eight or nine years before.

There was at the time practically no likelihood of

invasion being attempted by a force of any strength, for apart from the difficulties inherent to it, the enemy, being now relieved of all anxiety with respect to Russia, was engaged in mounting a great attack on the Western Front. The War Cabinet was therefore advised both by the Admiralty and General Staff that such risk as there was regarding invasion by the larger force mentioned, 160,000 men, might safely be accepted. As to the smaller force, 70,000 men, they were told that, in view of the experience of landing operations gained during the war, and of the limited time at the disposal of the enemy before interference with the landing would take place, they might confidently rely upon his being defeated, provided the possible landing-places were suitably entrenched and held by sufficient troops to oppose the landing until naval intervention could take effect. These opinions were accepted, and of the existing eight Home Defence divisions four were broken up, while the remaining four were reconstituted into training battalions. The general result was to leave four divisions for Home Defence and to set free about 40,000 men (mostly belonging to categories below A1) for employment in France.

Looking back it may seem that the possibility of hostile landings was always much too remote to justify the attention which it received. But the General Staff had to deal with the situation as it appeared to them at the time, and they knew that the Government expected that adequate protective measures should always be maintained. The air-raids which took place in 1917 furnished a proof of the importance with which these measures were regarded.

The best defence against air attacks at home is, as everybody knows, to keep the hostile airmen employed abroad, either in defending their own country or on the fronts where the opposing main armies are engaged. But while, in theory, it may be correct to give chief consideration to the maintenance of superior air forces on the fighting fronts, in practice suitable defence against air attack at home must first be provided, and sufficient resources to satisfy both purposes will seldom be forthcoming. They were not in 1916–17, and the General Staff, in deciding what should be done, were sometimes not allowed by the Government to give to the needs of the field armies that priority of treatment which, in their opinion, they should have been accorded. More than once in 1917, when air-raids were made on London, air squadrons were kept back in England which might preferably have been sent to France, and sometimes squadrons already in France were ordered to return.

The following extracts from letters written by me to Sir Douglas Haig will serve to explain how the matter was viewed :—

15th June, 1917.

We have been badly raided by enemy aeroplanes twice during the last fortnight, a third raid not being of much account. There is no panic here and no desire to play the enemy's game by keeping large numbers of good machines in this country, but at the same time it is thought that the raiders must be given one or two sharp lessons, and to do this we have not enough of the right sort of machines in the country. We never know that the raiders are coming until they appear off the coast, and the distance in time from the coast to important places like London is less than the time required by most of the machines we have got to ascend to the necessary height. Consequently, before they can get up the enemy has done his job and is on his way home again. The War Cabinet considered yesterday what should be done: whether reprisals should be undertaken on the southern part of the Western Front, or whether some special effort should be made to deal the raiders a nasty knock. Opinion inclines to the latter, as there are many objections to the former, and the idea is that you should send over for a week or two one or two squadrons of good machines so as to give the enemy a warm reception, and the machines would then return to you. . . .

Two squadrons were accordingly sent back from France and shortly after they had returned to that country a further raid occurred.

9th July, 1917.

The result of the air-raid on Saturday was the calling of a special Cabinet meeting in the afternoon at which much excitement was shown. One would have thought that the world was coming to an end. I could not get in a word edgeways. French was there and gave a long story as to his insufficient forces, and made a great protest because the two squadrons you had lent him were taken away. In spite of all I could say the decision come to was that you were to send two squadrons to England until the Cabinet choose to release them. There is no doubt that French has not got a very good force. It is mainly made up of oddments, and of course oddments will not do. When we received your wire yesterday the Cabinet were inclined to go back on their decision, and agree to ask you for less than two squadrons and perhaps for none. To-day they had another meeting, at which French was again present, and the old ground was re-traversed. The result was that you have now to send back one squadron in place of two. I am afraid I cannot say when the squadron will be returned.

Of course it is necessary that these raids should be put an end to, or at any rate be severely punished. We saw Saturday's raid from the War Office windows. Our anti-aircraft artillery was apparently of no use, and our airmen arrived in driblets and were powerless, but succeeded in getting one machine down. The fact is we have not got enough machines to meet our requirements. I find that I have brought the question before the Cabinet no fewer than six times during the present year. I doubt if any real progress will be made until a different organization is established. The Army and the Navy now say what they want, the Air Board consider their wants, and then Addison (Minister of Munitions) makes the machines. I am inclined to think that we need a separate air service, but that would be a big business. There is a special debate on the subject to-night, and it will probably be followed by a secret session.

The attitude of Ministers responsible for protecting

II   17   C

the homes and lives of the people as here shown is easy
to understand, and attention is drawn to it not by way
of criticism but in order to emphasize the fact that when
war is afoot the requirements of Home Defence whether
on land, on sea, or in the air, will, except perhaps in the
case of a great crisis, such as that which occurred in
March, 1918, invariably have to be given precedence
over requirements connected with operations abroad.[1]

[1] Note, for example, the effect which invasion had on the dispositions
of the French and German armies in 1914–15, *vide* Vol. I, pages 65–66.

CHAPTER IX

THE MESOPOTAMIA CAMPAIGN

Origin of Campaign—Operations in 1914—General Nixon appointed to Command, March, 1915—Extension of Operations to Kut—Imperial General Staff called upon to advise for first time, October, 1915—Confusing Methods of Communication between London and Simla—Question of Advance to Baghdad—Irregular Manner in which the Question was considered—Failure of the Advance and Investment of Kut—Operations placed under Direction of Imperial General Staff—Unsuccessful Attempts to relieve Kut—Reorganization of Force and Communications—General Maude appointed to Command—Renewed Desire of Ministers to capture Baghdad—General Staff's Objections—Offensive Operations undertaken—Baghdad occupied—Subsequent Events.

AS recalled in a previous chapter, the campaign in Mesopotamia was at first conducted by the India Office, not by the War Office. The Secretary of State for India looked for military advice to his Military Secretary, a senior General Officer of the Indian Army, whose department was in no sense organized for the purpose of planning or directing operations in the field. Occasionally the War Office or Admiralty would be asked by the Cabinet or the India Office to give their views on isolated questions, but as they had no direct relations with the commander in Mesopotamia, or with the military authorities in India, their knowledge of the situation was imperfect and their advice was accordingly of limited value. As to administrative matters, reliance had necessarily to be placed on the War Office for the supply of

19

British personnel, and of such war material and other resources as India herself was unable to provide. Of these requirements the War Office might or might not have adequate previous notice ; being unacquainted with the situation, it was not in a position to assess their urgency as compared with the needs of other theatres ; and the result was that the latter might be given preferential treatment when it ought to have been given to Mesopotamia. In circumstances such as these the operations were bound to come to grief, as they did, irrespective of the difficulties created either by the action of the enemy or by topographical conditions.

The inception of the campaign may be said to date from September 26, 1914, with the submission by the Military Secretary, India Office, of a memorandum entitled " The rôle of India in a Turkish War." The possibility of Turkey joining the Central Powers had produced a crop of rumours and reports to the effect that she was making preparations for hostile action in Egypt ; was spreading Pan-Islamic propaganda in Mesopotamia, Persia, Afghanistan, and India ; trying to win over the Arabs to her side ; sending arms and ammunition to different places in her Asiatic possessions ; and about to proclaim a *Jehad*, with the object of causing Afghanistan and the Indian frontier tribes to rise against us. Germany's ambitions in the Middle East, as shown by her proceedings during the previous fifteen years in connexion with the Baghdad railway and other enterprises, had also to be remembered, and there was the further point that the British Navy obtained a considerable portion of its oil supplies from the Anglo-Persian Oil Company's refineries in the island of Abadan at the head of the Persian Gulf. The Admiralty urged upon the India Office the necessity of troops being dispatched to defend these oil works ; the Viceroy expressed doubts as to the efficiency of our naval strength in the Gulf ; while the Political Secretary at the India Office, dealing with the question on political grounds, wrote :—

Though it may be true that so far as Turkey's power of offence in Europe is concerned we can safely leave her till a later stage in the war . . . in the meantime the political effect in the Persian Gulf and in India of leaving the head of the Gulf derelict will be disastrous, and we cannot afford, politically, to acquiesce in such a thing for an indefinite period while the main issues are being settled elsewhere.

Thus, the authorities of the Admiralty, India and the India Office were all of opinion that action of some kind at the head of the Gulf ought to be taken, but apparently India, though favouring an increase of naval strength, was not impressed with the proposal to employ troops. The First Lord of the Admiralty, Mr. Winston Churchill, held much the same view, and noted on a naval staff minute asking for troops, that :—

There is little likelihood of any troops being available for this purpose. Indian forces must be used at the decisive point. We shall have to buy our oil from elsewhere. The Turks also can be dealt with better at the centre.

In his memorandum the Military Secretary expressed grave concern at the prospect of a Turco-Arab coalition which, if it materialized, " might be a serious danger to India and would most certainly add enormously to our difficulties and responsibilities." These were strong words, and it was suggested that a force from India should be sent at once to land " on Persian soil at Muhammareh or Abadan Island, ostensibly to protect the oil installations but in reality to notify to the Turks that we meant business and to the Arabs that we were ready to support them." The force was to consist in the first place of one infantry brigade, with some artillery and engineers, of the 6th Indian Division, the remainder of the division to follow later. The advantages claimed for the plan were :—

1. It would check Turkish intrigues and demonstrate our ability to strike.
2. It would encourage the Arabs to rally to us and confirm the local sheiks in their friendly attitude.
3. It would safeguard Egypt, as without Arab support a Turkish invasion was impossible.
4. We would effectually protect the oil installations at Abadan.

The memorandum was apparently seen by Lord Kitchener, but the opinion of the Imperial General Staff was neither asked for nor given—a typical instance of the system of making war by departments which prevailed during 1914 and the early part of 1915.

On the evening of September 26 the India Office warned the Viceroy that the 6th Division (which was one of the three to be found by India for service in Egypt or Europe) might be wanted " to demonstrate at the head of the Persian Gulf." As time went on the news received regarding Turco-German proceedings both in Europe and the Middle East became more and more disquieting, and on October 2 the situation was considered so unsatisfactory that it was decided to carry out the Military Secretary's recommendation. Instructions were accordingly sent to India to dispatch the leading brigade of the 6th Division at once, the remainder to be held in readiness. Further instructions were issued on October 3, but in neither case was the mission of the force clearly laid down, and before the second message had been received India telegraphed to the India Office saying :—

We assume you are sure this advanced brigade is strong enough for its purpose. We cannot judge of this without knowing its instructions and objective. Do you intend that we should manage this expedition or do you mean to run it direct from the India Office ?

There could be no stronger proof of mismanagement than this telegram, for what could be more conducive to trouble than to order the dispatch of an expedition without specifying what it was required to do and who was to " run " it ?

The reply sent by the India Office, on October 5, was as follows :—

The force under orders is only intended to occupy Abadan, protect oil-tanks and pipe-line, cover landing of reinforcements if this should be necessary, and show Arabs that we intend to support them against Turks. With warships at Muhammareh the troops detailed are considered ample for above purposes. Should Turkey become a belligerent management of expedition will devolve on you, but instructions as to scope of operations will, of course, come from me. Meanwhile you should prepare the remainder of division for dispatch. . . .

It would be easy to argue that neither the protection of the oil-supply nor the acquisition of Arab assistance was of sufficient importance to justify opening up a new campaign. There were, however, strong objections to a policy of passive inactivity, and criticism can more fairly be directed against the omission properly to lay down what the expedition was expected to do rather than against the decision to dispatch it. Had the Government been clear in their minds on this point, the telegram of October 5 would perhaps have been worded in a manner more helpful to those for whose guidance it was intended. Active operations, once started, would be certain to provoke strong opposition, and it was absurd to suppose that one brigade or even one division could adequately protect the pipe-line extending for some 130 miles into Persian territory, and in addition so impress the Arabs with our power as to induce them to co-operate with us against the Turks. Before taking that step they would want visible proof that Turkish rule was broken and gone for good, and meanwhile their aim would be to keep on the winning side, extracting from winner and loser alike every advantage possible. Doubtless, it was difficult to say exactly what should be done, as we were not yet at war with Turkey. But problems of this kind usually are difficult and the duty of the High Command is to face them at the outset, for if they are postponed in the hope that they will solve themselves an unfair burden will be put upon commanders in the field and sooner or later trouble will ensue.

As there was no well-thought-out policy upon which a plan of campaign could be intelligently constructed, the operations which followed were mainly determined by the local situation of the moment, and with no proper regard either to their possible consequences in Mesopotamia or to their effect on the position in other theatres of war. A further result of the haphazard methods employed was that the High Command (in the shape of the India Office) sometimes gave orders on matters which ought to have been left to the discretion of the local commander, and at others imposed upon him the responsibility of deciding questions which ought to have been decided by themselves.

The transports conveying the advanced brigade anchored off Bahrain Island in the Persian Gulf on October 23. A few days later Turkey took hostile action against Russia in the Black Sea, and on November 1 the Viceroy was told by the India Office that the brigade should proceed at once to the Shatt-al Arab, and " concert measures with the naval authorities for immediate attack on Fao. Force will then clear Turks out of the Shatt and its vicinity as far as Shamshamiya (about eight miles short of Muhammareh) if possible. After which it will await arrival of reinforcements from India."

These instructions, it will be noticed, gave no better clue to the policy of the Government now that Turkey was a declared enemy than those of October 5 had done. The immediate object seemed to be the occupation of Muhammareh and Basrah, as soon as the remainder of the 6th Division had been brought up, and the instructions might well have been confined to saying so in as many words, and have left the military commander himself to decide how the object was to be attained. How could the authorities in London say, before the brigade had resumed its voyage, what distance up the Shatt it might usefully and safely go without awaiting reinforcements, or, on the other hand, whether it might not usefully go beyond Shamshamiya ? Obviously, details like these could only be settled by the commanders on the spot, after they had conferred together and when it was seen how the operation progressed.

What in fact happened was, the action of the enemy and the unfavourable weather combined to prevent the brigade from reaching Shamshamiya until other units of the division began to arrive in the Shatt on November 13. They were accompanied by the Divisional Commander, General Barrett, who had been instructed before leaving India that his " objective " would be telegraphed to him later. He received it on November 14 in the following order : " Your objective is Basrah. If after discussion with and taking over from Delamain [commander of the advanced brigade] you consider your force strong enough you will move on Basrah." The General decided to advance with as little delay as possible. On November 17 a hostile gathering some 5,000 strong, of which 3,500 were Turkish infantry and 1,000 Arabs, was engaged about 4 miles south of Muhammareh and dispersed. Basrah was occupied without further opposition on November 22, having been evacuated by the enemy after the action of the 17th.

His instructions not going beyond the occupation of Basrah, General Barrett now felt himself, as the official history describes, " at rather a disadvantage in not having received before leaving India some indication of our probable future policy." The Commander-in-Chief in India, on his part, insisted before the Mesopotamia Commission that he had furnished the General with copies of the whole correspondence with the India Office, which afforded all the information that the Government of India themselves possessed. But the General —who had a host of other things to think about— ought not to have been left to deduce the nature of his mission from files of correspondence ! As already suggested, the fault lay with the Home authorities, who, when they decided to employ the expedition, did not specifically and comprehensively state what its mission was to be.

Hoping to elicit some information on the point which might be of help to him, the General approved, on November 23, of a telegram being sent to the Indian Government in which the Political Officer attached to his head-quarters reviewed the situation, and recommended that the campaign should be extended to include the occupation of Baghdad. This astonishing proposal was promptly rejected, as it deserved to be. Baghdad was more than 500 miles distant from Basrah by river, and the employment of only one division was at present contemplated, no other being readily available. In reply, the General was requested to consolidate the position he had won, and report what means he required to hold it and keep control of the river as far up as was necessary for that purpose.

The Political Officer's telegram was repeated by India to the India Office as soon as received, and was there considered, according to custom, by the Military Secretary, who also took the view that it was premature to embark on any such ambitious project as that suggested. He maintained, however, that we could not hope to make the necessary impression on the Arabs unless the forward movement was continued, and he considered that Kurna, 50 miles above Basrah, at the junction of the Tigris and Euphrates, would be a suitable objective to take as the next step. He thought that by the time we were fully established there, more would be known about the attitude of the Arabs, the strength and intentions of the enemy, and the situation in general. We could then decide on the next move, with Baghdad as the ultimate objective. The advantages of the Kurna position were claimed to be its " commanding military value," its control over the " whole navigable waterway to the Gulf," the possession of the " rich cultivated area from Kurna to the sea," the safeguards it provided against Turkish intrigues in Persia, the " moral effect on the Arabs," and the " control of the telegraph up to this point." Some at least of these " advantages " can be so described only by a stretch of the imagination.

On November 27 the Secretary of State for India (Lord Crewe), informed the Viceroy that " we are not disposed to authorize an advance to Baghdad at present as there are grave international considerations involved, but, as soon as General Barrett is ready to do so, we sanction an advance to Kurna with a brigade or such portion of his force as may be necessary for the operation. . . . It will probably be desirable to keep the bulk of the division at Basrah, which should for the present be regarded as the head-quarters." The last sentence is quoted as another example of departmental interference with the commander, for who but he could possibly say where his head-quarters or the bulk of his troops ought to be?

The operations against Kurna concluded on December 9 with the surrender of the town and about 1,000 Turkish troops, and the question again arose what was to be done next. It transpired that the troops defeated in the fighting for Basrah and Kurna had retired to Nasiriya on the Euphrates, and when this became known in London inquiry was made of the Government of India whether a force could be sent to eject them and occupy Nasiriya so as to close that line of approach from the north. General Barrett was in favour of moving up the Tigris to Amara, but circumstances caused him later to acquiesce that it would be best to move on Nasiriya. Eventually, on January 4, 1915, the Government of India and the India Office together agreed that, owing to the uncertainty of the situation, no advance should be made on either place.

About this time news began to be received of a Turkish concentration for an attack on Basrah, the pipe-line up the Karun valley was threatened, and many of the Arabs instead of rallying to us as had been hoped were joining the Turks. These events necessitated the dispatch of an additional brigade, much against the wishes of the Indian Government, who had many anxieties at the moment owing to unrest in Afghanistan and on the north-west frontier. This reinforcement, sent off early in February, proved insufficient; the India Office considered that the expedition ought to be given a strength of two divisions; and the Indian Government, while agreeing, contended that the requisite additional troops ought to be found by the War Office, as India could spare no more.

In March there was an unsuccessful skirmish up the Karun river near Ahwaz, against a numerically superior force of Turks and Arabs, and the situation became so unsatisfactory that on March 5 the Indian Government was peremptorily ordered by the India Office to dispatch a second brigade, the Viceroy and Commander-in-Chief being relieved of responsibility for the consequences in India. A few days later a third brigade was sent from Egypt, and the expedition thus attained the strength of two divisions in infantry, though not in all other arms. It was also given the organization of an army corps, and on April 9 General Sir John Nixon, a more senior officer, arrived at Basrah to take over the command from General Barrett.

This appointment marked the beginning of an entirely new phase in the campaign. The initiative no longer came from the India Office but from General Nixon, acting in conformity with the instructions of the Indian Government and sustained by their concurrence.[1] One reason for this may have been that the India Office, being nearer to events in Europe (which were not favourable to us during 1915), realized the necessity for not committing ourselves too deeply in Mesopotamia, whereas the Indian Government, absorbed in its own, and comparatively insignificant, problems, felt little of the ever-increasing anxieties with which the Government at home was beset.

The instructions given to General Nixon by Indian army head-quarters when he was about to proceed to

[1] Report of Mesopotamia Commission.

Mesopotamia to assume command, and dated March 24, contained the following paragraph :—

OPERATIONS

(1) Your force is intended to retain complete control of the lower portion of Mesopotamia, comprising the Basrah Vilayet and including all outlets to the sea and such portions of the neighbouring territories as may affect your operations.

(2) So far as you may find feasible, without prejudicing your main operations, you should endeavour to secure the safety of the oil-fields, pipe-line, and refineries of the Anglo-Persian Oil Company.

(3) After acquainting yourself on the spot with the present situation you will submit :—

(I) A plan for the effective occupation of the Basrah Vilayet.

(II) A plan for a subsequent advance on Baghdad.

(4) In all operations you will respect the neutrality of Persia so far as military and political exigencies permit.

These instructions it will be seen went very far beyond anything which had yet received the sanction of either the Indian or the Home Government. To quote the Mesopotamia Commission, they " revolutionized the whole foundation and organization of an expedition initiated and founded for much smaller and more limited objects, and this was neither recognized by Sir John Nixon nor those who so instructed him." The Basrah Vilayet, whose " effective " occupation was foreshadowed, extended up the Tigris to the vicinity of Kut, 250 miles from Kurna, while the idea of advancing on Baghdad, another 200 miles by river, had already been deprecated by the Home authorities although not specifically rejected. When questioned on the subject by the Mesopotamia Commission, the Commander-in-Chief in India explained that the instruction regarding the occupation of the Basrah Vilayet was meant to apply only to the occupation of Nasiriya and Amara ; that General Nixon had been so

informed] while at army head-quarters on March 24 ;
and that the desirability of occupying both these places
having frequently been referred to in the communications
exchanged between India and the India Office, it was
only prudent that a plan should be made ready for use if
wanted. For much the same reasons it was thought
necessary to be prepared with a plan for an advance on
Baghdad.

The explanation was hardly adequate. The plans
might, for instance, have preferably been called for in
a separate document and not in these particular instructions under the heading of " Operations," since the
latter course might, and in fact did, lead General Nixon
to think that an offensive policy was to be adopted forthwith. The instructions ought, moreover, as on all occasions when a commander in the field first takes up his
duties, to have been drafted, or at any rate approved,
by the Government. Instead of that they were issued
without being referred either to the Viceroy or to the
India Office, who were therefore at first in ignorance of
what General Nixon had been told to do. This astonishing procedure led to infinite misunderstanding, the
India Office sometimes thinking that the General was
bent on pursuing a more forward policy than had been
authorized or was expedient, while he on his side could
not reconcile their complaints with his instructions. A
copy of the latter was forwarded to the India Office by
post a fortnight after they had been issued, but their
meaning and possible developments do not seem to have
been realized by that department any more than they
had been by the authorities in India. As the Mesopotamia Commission reported, " Simla and Whitehall were
not pulling well together. Up to this date no full and
frank exchange of opinion seems to have taken place

either as to the scope and aim of the expedition, or as to the preparation and expenditure necessary to ensure its success."

Immediately on arrival in the country, General Nixon set to work to give effect to the offensive policy with which he considered himself charged to carry out. The hostile forces collected in the neighbourhood of Basrah, and composed of some 10,000 Turks and about the same number of Arabs, were defeated at Shaiba on April 14, and driven off in disorder to the north-west. A week later the newly-formed 12th Division was sent eastward to deal with the Turco-Arab forces in Persian Arabistan, where their interference with the oil supply was causing some anxiety. By the middle of May this mission also had been successfully completed and the safety of the pipe-line assured.

Nixon, still acting, as he thought, in accordance with the tenor of his instructions, now proposed to direct the 6th Division, under General Townshend, to move up the Tigris to Amara. The Viceroy was in favour of the operation, but Lord Crewe was not, though he gave it his sanction in a telegram of May 23 provided the General was satisfied that he could hold the place during the summer against any attack that might be made against it, and without the aid of reinforcements from other theatres. Here, again, one must interpolate the remark that to sanction the operation on the conditions specified, was to follow no policy really worth the name. The first question to be settled was not whether Amara could be garrisoned after being occupied, but whether, having regard to our war plans as a whole, its occupation would be consistent with sound strategy and administrative possibilities. Lord Crewe apparently had some doubt on the subject, and with good reason, but as he stood alone he could perhaps have done no more than he did—make it clear that no additional troops could be found. The question (one of policy) ought, of course, to have been settled not by him but by the Cabinet.

A day or two later he was succeeded at the India Office by Mr. Austen Chamberlain, who telegraphed to the Viceroy on May 28 :—

Till I know the immediate objects contemplated and the force with which General Nixon is advancing I am unable to give further instructions. Our policy must depend partly on local factors, forces available, and partly on situation elsewhere. I should like to be informed what force General Nixon considers necessary for garrisoning Amara, and how generally he proposes to distribute his troops during the summer if the occupation of that town is contemplated.[1]

The Viceroy replied reiterating the advantages claimed for the forward movement, and saying that he did not propose for the present to alter Nixon's instructions of March 24. After this statement the Home Government could no longer be in doubt that an aggressive policy was being pursued, notwithstanding their injunction that " a safe game must be played," and as they did not modify it they must be considered to have accepted it.

Meanwhile Townshend's force had occupied Amara, taking 1,700 prisoners and 12 guns, and immediately afterwards Nixon commenced making arrangements for the dispatch of the 12th Division up the Euphrates to Nasiriya. This operation also was supported by the Viceroy, and acquiesced in by the Secretary of State. It was successfully completed by July 25, 950 prisoners, 15 guns, and much war material being captured.

This succession of victories—much overrated in real

---

[1] This telegram was not well adapted to put matters on a better footing. For that Mr. Chamberlain should have said definitely what the policy was to be, and then left the Indian authorities to settle with the General the " immediate objects " and distribution of the troops.

importance—had the unfortunate effect of stimulating the authorities in India to a fresh advance. In a memorandum of June 24, General Nixon had emphasized the advantages that would be gained by occupying Kut, and two days after Nasiriya had been taken the Viceroy telegraphed to the India Office asking for approval, and saying, " Now that Nasiriya has been occupied the occupation of Kut-el-Amara is considered by us to be a strategic necessity." Other telegrams on the subject passed, and on August 6 approval was given. On September 1 General Townshend set his forces in movement ; on the 28th he defeated the enemy's main forces at Kut ; and then pursued them to Aziziya about 50 miles beyond Kut (by road) and half-way between that place and Baghdad. Being unable with his limited means to accomplish more, he decided to halt and communicate with Nixon as to future plans.

The latter officer, acting upon his instructions of March 24, had already forwarded to Indian army headquarters on August 30 a " Memorandum on an advance to Baghdad " in which he dwelt upon the desirability of following up the hostile forces at Kut when defeated, and said that although in favourable circumstances one division might suffice to take Baghdad, two would be required to hold it for the duration of the war. The General's view is not easy to comprehend, for if Baghdad were of such importance to us, and therefore to the enemy, as his proposal implied, much more than two divisions might eventually be needed to retain possession of it. The memorandum seems to have been well received by the Indian General Staff, while, judging from his correspondence with the India Office, the Viceroy was also impressed with the idea of bringing Baghdad within the scope of the operations, provided sufficient troops were available.

There was, however, still no clear understanding between the different authorities as to what the general policy really was. For instance, General Nixon was warned by the Commander-in-Chief early in September not to extend his operations above Kut without reference to India, and yet he afterwards complained that he received no indication of Government policy until October 6, and that if he had done so Townshend would not have been allowed to go as far beyond Kut as Aziziya.

Matters were brought to a head on October 3 by a telegram from the General saying that although there was no longer any chance of surprising the retreating enemy, who would probably stand and fight at Ctesiphon, he considered that he was strong enough to open the road to Baghdad, which from a military point of view [1] it was highly desirable to do. With that intention he proposed to concentrate at Aziziya. Next day he asked India whether he might expect to be reinforced by a division in order that his position at Baghdad might be maintained. As India could not provide the division he was told that no advance in strength beyond Kut was to be made until it was certain that the requisite reinforcement could be supplied by withdrawing troops from France, and this was said to be " very doubtful."

General Nixon's telegram was brought before the Cabinet on October 4, and a special inter-departmental committee, comprising representatives of the Foreign Office, India Office, War Office, and Admiralty, was appointed to consider what should be done. Its terms of reference were to consider :—

(1) Whether there should be an advance to Baghdad.

---

[1] One cannot help being struck by the loose way in which phrases such as " military point of view," " strategic necessity," etc., were bandied about at this period without any practical connexion with hard facts.

(2) The defensive positions near Baghdad that could be used to oppose a possible Turkish attack.

(3) Whether without Baghdad any offensive operations on a large scale could be undertaken by the Turks in the neighbourhood.

(4) The general effect which the occupation of Baghdad would have on the Turkish forces engaged against Russia and against ourselves in the Dardanelles.

The committee reported that both on military and political grounds an early occupation of Baghdad was most desirable ; but that the attempt should not be made unless the place could afterwards be held. One additional division, to arrive at Basrah within four weeks of the order to advance, was the minimum reinforcement considered necessary. The answers to the remaining questions need not be repeated, for they were to a great extent beyond the competency of the committee to supply, as the committee itself more or less said.

It is not understood what assistance the Government expected to derive from the appointment of the committee. As the Mesopotamia Commission recorded, the chairman, Sir Thomas Holderness, " though a distinguished civilian, had no special experience or training in the class of questions submitted to the committee," while the naval and military representatives had not the necessary official status to enable them to speak with the authority required in a case of such high importance. Throughout the campaign the Military Secretary of the India Office had been the official adviser of the Government, and if the latter had relied upon him for the advice they wanted responsibility would have remained clearly fixed, and would not have become, as it did, divided.

The General Staff at the War Office were also

called in to advise, and in a memorandum dated October 12 they reported that a reinforcement of not less than *two* divisions would be necessary. They made the further important statement that, in view of certain large Allied movements in the Mediterranean (due to the situation in the Balkans and Dardanelles), it was impossible to foresee how soon it might be practicable to transport troops from Europe to the Persian Gulf, and that unless one of the two divisions could be found by India no advance on Baghdad should be sanctioned until one or more divisions from France had left Egypt *en route* for Mesopotamia.

Together with various telegrams exchanged between the India Office and India, this memorandum and the report of the Holderness Committee were considered by the Cabinet on October 14, and it was agreed that the War Staff of the Admiralty and the General Staff should now join together in preparing a further report on the whole situation. This was done in a memorandum dated October 19, the pith of which was that, whereas there might be no difficulty in seizing Baghdad there might be a great deal in holding it, since it was possible that the 9,000 Turks then supposed to be in front of Townshend might be increased by the end of January to as many as 60,000. Later, even more than this number might be assembled, in which case the two additional divisions recommended would not be sufficient. The final conclusion was that it would be unwise " to occupy Baghdad with the intention of staying there until the end of the war." A raid was favoured, however, even if the raiding force was not withdrawn immediately, provided that the military authorities had unrestricted power to withdraw it at will. The argument used in support of this temporary occupation was that the failure to push on at once from Kut might create as bad an impression in the East as would be caused by a withdrawal from Baghdad after occupation.

The combined staffs further recommended that, whatever the main decision might be, the force employed " should continue to be a purely Indian force, and that India should accept all responsibility for its reinforcement, which is certain to prove a very serious drain on resources in personnel, and for its maintenance until such time as peace has been proclaimed. They realize that this is an Indian affair, and they realize that troops can be devoted to the purpose which could not be profitably employed elsewhere." They insisted " that under no circumstances must troops which might otherwise be employed in Europe be diverted from the primary theatre of war for the purpose of conducting a campaign which cannot appreciably influence the decision as between the armies of the Allied and those of the Central Powers."

But this important principle was almost certain to be violated, and perhaps seriously, for no one could say for certain what number of troops and drafts might be wanted once the advance on Baghdad was started. Moreover, the campaign could not possibly be regarded as an " Indian affair " : it was an " Imperial affair," for the question to be settled was not one of going to Baghdad or even of holding that place after getting there, but, as in the case of all the other advances that had been proposed and made, whether such an extension of the operations would materially help towards the winning of the war. The combined staffs themselves said distinctly that it would not, and therefore one wonders why they did not recommend outright that defensive policy which appears to have been at the back of their mind. It may

THE MESOPOTAMIA CAMPAIGN

be that they were reluctant to oppose a project which they knew the Government was eager to see undertaken, and therefore adopted the middle course of suggesting a raid, and saying that the troops employed should be limited to those which could not suitably be used in Europe. If this were the reason, it was not a very good one. Gallipoli had already proved that " limited liability " is a fatal principle upon which to base offensive projects, and the lesson was to be repeated in Mesopotamia. When Townshend's force was besieged in Kut, after the advance on Baghdad had failed, troops *had* to be sent to his assistance which *were* suitable for employment elsewhere.

The combined staffs would have been wise to refrain from expressing any opinion at all on the subject, unless first allowed to obtain direct from India and Mesopotamia such information as they might wish to have. Not having previously directed the campaign, they could not be sufficiently acquainted with local affairs to be able to say how the situation should be met. Had they, for instance, been aware of the very defective line of communication, they would doubtless have condemned the Baghdad advance on those grounds alone.

Confusion was aggravated by irregular methods of procedure as between India and the India Office. Sometimes the India Office would telegraph to General Nixon direct, and at others through the Viceroy ; while the Viceroy would sometimes send home his opinions on military matters without consulting the Commander-in-Chief, or would present the views of the latter in such a way as he deemed fit and not necessarily as given to him. On October 7, for example, the Commander-in-Chief proposed that the Viceroy should telegraph to the India Office as follows :—

I have consulted the Commander-in-Chief, who has no doubt that as things stand at present we could capture Baghdad, but that our available troops would not be sufficient to hold it should the Turks mass troops for a counter-attack, and that the effect of entering Baghdad and subsequently having to retire would be disastrous. Moreover, he doubts whether in the present state of the river, combined with our present insufficient number of light-draught steamers, we could adequately supply our troops there. As a military operation, therefore, he holds that to occupy Baghdad with our present force would be most unwise.

This was a highly important telegram on a military matter, but the Viceroy preferred to send another in its place. To some extent the subject matter of the draft had already been covered in a "private" telegram sent by him to the India Office the day before, in which he deprecated the occupation of Baghdad unless reinforcements were provided, and apparently he did not consider that the Commander-in-Chief's apprehensions in regard to transport and supply (of which the "private" telegram had said nothing) were of sufficient importance to be specially brought to notice. He merely wired that the Commander-in-Chief agreed with what had been said in the "private" telegram, namely, "that it would be unwise to occupy Baghdad with our present forces." The Commander-in-Chief on his side had no knowledge of the "private" telegram when he submitted his draft, and afterwards he did not insist that his doubts regarding the adequacy of the supply arrangements should be reported. They therefore remained unrepresented, and the system which made such an omission possible stands for ever condemned by the disasters which, in consequence of the transport and supply arrangements being so deplorably bad, culminated later in the surrender of Kut. The way in which the scope of the operations was allowed to be extended, without reasonable care being taken to see that the capabilities of the line of communication were increased in like proportion, is, indeed, quite incomprehensible. The Mesopotamia Commission considered that the original plan of the British Government in sending the expedition had been realized by the occupation of Kurna and the victory at Shaiba, save that something remained to be done to complete the protection of the supply of oil. Most people would agree, and certainly the plan had been sufficiently realized by the subsequent occupation of Amara and Nasiriya without going on for still another 150 miles to Kut. The line of communication, unreliable and ill-organized, was now 300 miles in length, while Basrah was peculiarly ill-suited as a base. It had practically no quays or wharfage, and vessels were unloaded in mid-stream by primitive methods into native sailing-craft. There were no warehouses available for the storage of goods, and accommodation for troops was also lacking. Moreover, the troops at and in front of Kut had been worked hard for several months past and were greatly in need of rest. Units were much below strength, and drafts for them had to come from India or Europe, whereas the enemy had much nearer resources upon which to draw. The climate was trying and wastage from sickness was heavy, and in numerous ways the situation was already most unsatisfactory and precarious. To attempt in these circumstances to go forward for another 100 miles (200 miles by river) to Baghdad would be not merely bad strategy but bad sense, and therefore could not be good policy.

It so happened that I was present at some of the meetings of the War Committee when the project was being discussed, having been summoned from France in connexion with other matters. At one of these Lord

Kitchener described the difficulties which he himself had encountered when moving up the Nile to Khartoum, and pointed out the risks that would be incurred if Townshend were sent on unsupported and with a defective line of communication. Lord Curzon also dissented, even in stronger terms than Lord Kitchener, but although they were the only members of the Committee who had first-hand knowledge of the East, they were over-ruled. The question was no affair of mine, but I subsequently took advantage of an informal conversation with other Ministers present to support what Lords Kitchener and Curzon had said. Most Ministers seemed much too anxious to present the country with what they called a " striking victory," as a set-off to the failure in Gallipoli and the German invasion of Serbia. " Baghdad," said one of them, was " the one bright spot on the military horizon," while telegrams sent by the India Office to the Viceroy about this time contained such passages as these[1] :—

The Cabinet are so impressed with great political and military advantages of occupation of Baghdad that every effort will be made by us to supply the force that is necessary. We do not wish to attempt it with insufficient forces. I shall be glad to know whether you are satisfied that one division will suffice. . . .

We continue to attach the greatest importance to the capture of Baghdad if we can hold it securely. . . .

Arabs are wavering and will probably join Turks unless we can offer them greater inducement. We are therefore in great need of a striking success in the East.

From first to last, both in London and India, the advantages to be derived were overrated, and were too often allowed to obscure the practical difficulties that stood in the way of their attainment. The Indian General Staff in a memorandum of October 5 said that the possession

[1] Mesopotamia Commission Report, pages 23–24.

of Baghdad would deprive the enemy of a well-equipped base, would place us in a good position to defeat him in detail as he moved down the rivers from Asia Minor and Syria, would increase our prestige, offset the failure in the Dardanelles, and interrupt the enemy's communications with Persia and Afghanistan. The Viceroy also, in his telegram of October 6 previously mentioned, held that it " would create an immense impression in Middle East, especially in Persia, Afghanistan, and on our frontier." But in point of fact it would have no such effects as these unless it were accompanied by complete domination of the surrounding country—that is, unless we were capable of thoroughly defeating all and sundry hostile forces that might eventually be employed either for the defence or recapture of the city. There was no prospect of our being in a position to do this for an indefinite time to come, if only because of bad communications, and, as the Commander-in-Chief himself had pointed out, a withdrawal after occupation might be disastrous. Nor would the occupation be, as some asserted, much of an encouragement to the people at home. For a few days the newspapers would be provided with sensational head-lines, but the idea created in the public mind that a great success had been won would soon be followed by disappointment when the barren results became manifest.

From a purely military standpoint there was still less to be gained, for even if it were good strategy to push deeper into the country the fact remained that the capture of towns is seldom of real value unless it is in some way to the detriment of the enemy's main armies, such as the interruption of their communications, dislocation of the civil administration, overthrow of the government, and so forth. Regarded from this aspect the domination of Constantinople, the enemy's capital and centre of communications, aimed at by the Dardanelles Expedition, was a legitimate operation ; the capture of Baghdad was not. In the South African war we occupied town after town in the advance from the Modder to Pretoria, but as the hostile forces remained at large the war dragged on for nearly two years after the capitals of both Republics and every other important town had been seized.

The question came before the War Committee for final decision on October 21, and amongst the papers then considered were the following :—

The Report of the Holderness Committee.

The Joint Staff memorandum of October 19.

A minute by the Military Secretary of the India Office, dated October 15.

A telegram from the Viceroy of October 21 suggesting one of three alternatives—occupation of Baghdad, raid on Baghdad, or no advance beyond Kut—the first being considered the most satisfactory solution.

The Committee thus had the assistance of an abundance of counsellors, but not one of them was acquainted with all the factors involved, and therefore the advice they were able to give was necessarily wanting in value. The General Staff knew little about the *local* situation, for they had not previously dealt with it. For the same reason the Viceroy and Military Secretary were no authority on the *general* situation. The Holderness Committee was no authority on anything, while responsibility for carrying out the advice tendered—the most important element in the whole case—was divided up between the Military Secretary (the military spokesman of the India Office), the Viceroy (the military spokesman of India), and the Commander-in-Chief (the chief executive officer of the Indian Army). Similarly, not one of the Ministers on the War Committee, with the exception of Lord Kitchener, was qualified to form an opinion on such technical matters as were involved. In these circumstances the choice of a right decision, and the successful execution of that decision, must evidently be a matter of chance.

The decision reached was that the advantages of occupying Baghdad outweighed the disadvantages of possible eventual withdrawal, and that, subject to the concurrence of the Government of India, occupation should be ordered forthwith. It was conveyed to India the same day in a " private " telegram drafted by Mr. Chamberlain and three of his ministerial colleagues. The information was added that, in the opinion of the combined staffs, the Turkish forces in front of Nixon might attain a strength of 60,000 men by the end of January, and even a larger figure later on.

Lord Kitchener, opposed to the project from the beginning, did not altogether concur in the telegram, and sent to Mr. Chamberlain a supplementary draft of what he thought the Viceroy should be told. Mr. Chamberlain considered that the essential points in the draft were suitably covered by the telegram, and that to repeat them would confuse the Viceroy rather than help him. Consequently the supplementary draft was not included. Lord Kitchener again insisted that the tone of the telegram was misleading, in that it gave the impression that everyone in London was in favour of permanently occupying Baghdad. The difficulty was adjusted by compromise, Lord Kitchener being allowed to send his message, and any other information which he thought the Viceroy should have, in the form of an Intelligence report to the Commander-in-Chief.

These reports, it may be explained, were periodically forwarded by the War Office to India as a matter of routine, and in all probability the information here referred to was regarded by India merely as an item of intelligence, and not as having any specific connexion with the War Committee's decision conveyed in Mr. Chamberlain's telegram. At any rate the official history records that the Commander-in-Chief did not read into the Intelligence report the meaning which Lord Kitchener apparently intended, namely, that he doubted the wisdom of attempting against Baghdad anything more than a raid. The incident was not unlike the one that had occurred in India a fortnight before when the Viceroy did not send home the draft prepared by the Commander-in-Chief about transport and supply.

The Viceroy replied to Mr. Chamberlain's telegram on October 23 that the calculation of the combined staffs was accepted,

but with reinforcement of two Indian divisions from France we believe that Sir J. Nixon has a fair prospect of being able to hold his own against 60,000 or 70,000 Turks, provided he occupies Baghdad as soon as he is ready. Although I realize that the occupation of Baghdad is a provocation that will probably determine the Turks to send large forces to attack us, which, however, will not be easy for them to do, and although the bad effect of a possible withdrawal in the future cannot be ignored, I am confident right policy at present time is to take the risk and to occupy Baghdad with the least possible delay, relying upon you to send two divisions from France as quickly as possible to Mesopotamia. On this understanding I propose, unless I hear from you before Monday (two days later) to the contrary, to order Nixon to march on Baghdad at once.

On the same day the Cabinet authorized the India Office to inform the Viceroy that :—

Nixon may march on Baghdad if he is satisfied that the force he has available is sufficient for the operation. Reinforcements will take time owing to the relief and transport arrangements, but two divisions will be sent as soon as possible.

This telegram, says the official report, was repeated by India on October 24 to General Nixon, " who was instructed to take action accordingly."

Thus it came about that, eleven months after the question was first mooted, and including the three weeks' continuous investigation just terminated, the Home Government placed upon General Nixon the sole responsibility for deciding whether the scope of the campaign was or was not to embrace the capture of Baghdad—an operation which the Viceroy had said would " probably determine the Turks to send large forces to attack us." The General's burden remained, moreover, unshared by either the Indian Government or Indian army headquarters, since the latter merely told him " to take action accordingly." Having from the first been unduly confident of success, and not in agreement with the representations of his Divisional Commander, General Townshend, as to the difficulties ahead, the action Nixon unfortunately took was to direct him on October 24 to begin the advance on Baghdad by November 14, by which date the transport and supply arrangements for the movement would, he thought, be completed.

To the layman it may appear that as Nixon was left with a free hand he had only himself to blame for what followed, and to some extent that must be admitted. But there was much to be said on the other side, for, as already suggested, the question was not merely one of going to Baghdad or even of remaining there. Much wider issues were involved. The question was essentially one of policy and general strategy, and not merely one of tactics. Therefore it was beyond the power of any local commander properly to decide.

Another reason for this was that General Nixon was

without good information either as to the probable
strength of the enemy's reinforcements or the date of
arrival of his own. He no doubt had received from time
to time Intelligence reports which enabled him to make
an estimate of the enemy's strength for himself. But that
could not pretend to have anything like the same accuracy
and completeness as one prepared in the Intelligence
department of the War Office, which had all the intelligence sources of the world upon which to draw. If
the War Committee considered, as they did, that the
estimate of the combined staffs that the 9,000 Turks in
front of Townshend might soon be increased to 60,000,
was sufficiently important to necessitate sending it to the
Viceroy, surely the latter should have seen that it was
communicated to Nixon, upon whose shoulders the
responsibility for making the final decision was to rest.
One can hardly believe that Cabinet instructions such as
those of October 21 should have been transmitted to
India in a " private " telegram ; or that the Commander-
in-Chief, to whom the telegram was shown by the Viceroy,
did not forward to Nixon the information it contained
about the enemy's strength because, being marked
" private," he considered that he had no official cognizance
of its contents ! In referring to this matter the Mesopotamia Commission very justly remarked that " the neglect
to convey to him (Nixon) so vital a piece of information
reflects seriously on the system which allowed such
inadvertence to be possible."

Again, the eagerness of the Government to gain
possession of Baghdad, and the confusion caused by the
employment of so many different counsellors, had tended
to obscure the necessity of getting the two reinforcing
divisions into the country sufficiently early to be ready
for use when wanted. Nearly a month had elapsed

since the Turks were defeated at Kut, and it was only common sense to suppose that they had since been sending towards Baghdad all the additional troops they could scrape together. We, on our side, had as yet done nothing but talk and telegraph, and the provision of the additional divisions recommended by all the authorities consulted was never treated, as it should have been, as the linch-pin of the whole operation. To tell Nixon, as the Cabinet did on October 23, that the two divisions would " be sent as soon as possible " was not of the least assistance to him.

The Indian General Staff had said that he ought not to be permitted to advance until an assurance was received that a division would be dispatched from France " before, say, the end of October." The Holderness Committee had said that at least one division " should without fail begin to arrive at Basrah within four weeks of the issue of orders for the advance." The General Staff in London had said that *two* divisions were needed, and that the advance should not be sanctioned until one or both had passed Egypt *en route* to Basrah. The Viceroy had asked to be guaranteed the receipt of one division by December 21, and afterwards, as already shown, he had asked for two " as quickly as possible." But, on October 23, when the advance was sanctioned, the divisions were still in the trenches in Flanders ; shipping for their transport had not yet been collected ; and how many weeks would be required in which to complete the move could be calculated by no one—least of all by General Nixon.

So far as any particular department in London could be regarded as responsible for seeing that the right thing was done, it was the business of the India Office, in consultation with the War Office (who would liberate the divisions), and the Admiralty (who would transport them), to make sure that they were on the spot when required. In the circumstances of the case the only practical way of achieving this was not to allow the advance to begin until the divisions had, at least, arrived at Basrah, and transport for the onward journey was known to be forthcoming.

Another important point overlooked was that the reinforcements might be wanted for something more than merely to garrison Baghdad after that place had been taken. The official history says that " none of the military authorities concerned had seriously questioned General Nixon's assurance that he had sufficient troops to defeat the beaten remnant of Nur-ud-Din's army— the only apparent barrier between him and Baghdad." Seeing the confusion which prevailed at the time, the omission is not surprising. On the other hand, and as the history itself records, Townshend telegraphed to Nixon as early as October 3, saying,

if Government desire to occupy Baghdad then I am of opinion that methodical advance from Kut by road by two divisions or one army corps, or one division closely supported by another entire, exclusive of line of communication troops . . . is absolutely necessary unless great risk is to be incurred.

Later in the day, on learning that a division might be sent from France, he telegraphed in a somewhat less pessimistic tone, but on the whole it would appear that he did all that a subordinate commander properly could do to show to his superior that he felt grave doubts as to the wisdom of the advance being continued with his weak division alone.

His reports may or may not have gone further than Nixon, but on November 2 he wrote unofficially to the Viceroy saying,

These troops of mine are tired and their tails are not up, but slightly down ; the Mohammedans are not pleased at approaching the sacred precincts of Suleiman Pak at Ctesiphon—the troops are not confident and have had enough ; as it is now, the British soldier and the sepoy, as the Roman soldiers did under Belisarius, look over their shoulders and are fearful of the distance from the sea, and go down in consequence with every imaginable disease.[1]

These were not the words of a confident General, as the Mesopotamia Commission pointed out.

Quite apart from what Townshend or any other military authority may have said, it is astonishing to find that no arrangements were made for having suitable reserves at hand before the division began its advance. Everybody agreed that, sooner or later, strong opposition would be encountered, and it was possible, of course, that the combined staffs' estimate of the rate at which the enemy could bring up fresh troops might prove to be under and not over the mark. Further, as the force employed was comparatively small, quite a few additional enemy troops would suffice to turn the scale against us, and common prudence demanded that a proper margin of safety should be provided to meet this contingency. In short, to allow such a force as one division, or indeed any force, to go 50 or 100 miles deeper into hostile territory unsupported by adequate reserves, and to depend for ultimate success upon the punctual arrival of reinforcements which were still thousands of miles away, was to incur a risk for which there was no justification whatsoever. That such a transgression of elementary military principles should have been committed proves how hopelessly defective were the methods by which the war was then conducted. According to the official history no one could have tried harder or more consistently than

[1] Mesopotamia Commission Report, page 27.

Mr. Chamberlain to obtain the best advice and to ensure that suitable precautions were taken, but good results were not to be obtained by him or anyone else so long as the system of management at Government headquarters remained unchanged.

The consequences of these imperfect arrangements speedily made themselves felt. Early in November reports began to come in from different sources indicating that strong enemy reinforcements were on their way to Baghdad, and by the 17th of the month so much evidence of this kind had accumulated that the Chief of the Indian General Staff proposed to dispatch to Nixon's assistance at once the " Emergency Force " of two infantry brigades and other troops which had just been formed to take the place temporarily, if required, of the divisions coming from France. The Viceroy, however, deeming the reports to be unreliable, took it upon himself to decide that the Force should not go.

Meanwhile Townshend's column, numbering about 14,000 combatants, was continuing to move forward, and on November 22 the enemy's main forces, over 18,000 strong, were engaged at Ctesiphon, eighteen miles short of Baghdad. After three days' hard fighting, in which the column suffered a loss of about thirty per cent. of its strength, Townshend was obliged to fall back on Kut. By the time that place was reached, December 3, his troops were too exhausted to go farther, and he decided, in communication with Nixon, to remain at Kut until the reinforcements expected from France could come to his relief. By December 7 the Turkish investment was complete and the siege of Kut had begun.

As soon as the result of the Ctesiphon fighting became known the Viceroy withdrew his objection to the Emergency Force leaving India, and the Commander-in-Chief, disregarding the usual roundabout procedure of communicating with the War Office through the Viceroy and India Office, telegraphed direct to say that the immediate dispatch of the two divisions from France was " absolutely essential." Only one was as yet in process of transfer, and the other, leaving about a month later, did not arrive in Mesopotamia until the middle of January, or more than three months after its transfer had first been spoken about. There was nothing to be surprised at in this delay. It was chiefly due to the sea-transport being wanted for other duties, as the General Staff had said early in October it probably would be.

The situation was reviewed almost daily by the War Committee from the time that the failure at Ctesiphon was reported until the end of the year. At first the hope was entertained that nothing worse than a temporary set-back had been experienced, and that offensive operations would be resumed as soon as the reinforcements under orders had arrived. Nixon, himself, in answer to a War Committee inquiry, stated on November 26 that he expected to be in a position to capture and hold Baghdad by the middle of March without any additional troops. A few days later, however, when Townshend was about to be invested, he asked to be given another division, while on December 14 he reported that, in view of the strength of the hostile concentration that might possibly be brought against him within the next two or three months, he ought to be given two additional divisions " as soon as possible, otherwise I may have to fight again without any reserve."

As invariably happens when the military machine is not of the right model, or is not in good running order, the stress of events commenced to set up friction, and the mutual confidence that ought to subsist between Ministers and commanders in the field soon began to weaken. The War Committee, feeling the weight of their responsibility, would sometimes make considerable, if not excessive, demands upon Nixon for information about his plans, dispositions, defences, transport, and similar matters, to supply which might tax both his time and temper at a moment when his undivided attention ought to be devoted to urgent affairs at the front. This was shown by a telegram sent home on December 11 in which he said that it was impossible to forecast developments until he knew when his reinforcements would actually arrive.

> Even now I have no definite information as to departures from Egypt except in the case of three units, nor of the order in which units will arrive. . . . Want of adequate river transport is more acute than ever. The net result of my demands in this direction since July last is one ship from India promised at the end of this month.

About a week later the Home authorities again intervened, as they were apparently not satisfied that measures for the relief of Kut were being pushed on with sufficient vigour. They thought, too, that troops ought to be sent to the Karun valley so as to anticipate possible enemy designs in that quarter. Nixon's frame of mind on receiving these suggestions can be understood from his reply :—

> There is no question about the relief of Townshend being my first object, and every unit that can be spared is being sent up the Tigris as soon as ever it arrives. But you will remember that I was originally promised the whole of the 3rd and 7th Divisions by the end of December, and it now looks as if it would be the end of January before they will arrive. As regards Karun, I am well alive to possibility of a hostile movement in that direction, and it was with this eventuality in view that I have already asked for and will require two more divisions. The Secretary of State, I presume, grasps the fact that it takes nearly two months to transfer a force like a division from one line to another under conditions as they exist here.

Deplorable as the situation was, and especially so because of the further sufferings and losses which it was fated to impose upon Townshend's unfortunate force, it had at least one compensating factor : it helped to show in a way about which there could be no dispute that India could no longer be allowed to conduct war on its own account, and that the campaign in Mesopotamia must be prosecuted in conjunction with, and not separately from, all others in which we were engaged. In the telegrams exchanged India demanded that British battalions in Mesopotamia should be given 500 men each as drafts, and no doubt they needed them. But so did battalions on other fronts, the total shortage at this time being 200,000 men. The provision of the two extra divisions requisitioned was equally difficult to arrange, for there was bad news from the Balkans as well as from Mesopotamia ; Egypt, according to Lord Kitchener, was also in need of reinforcements ; while there was always the necessity for concentrating the greatest strength possible on the Western Front. As the official history puts it : " The demands from every quarter were such that it was necessary to weigh very carefully our available resources in men in relation to our different commitments and probable requirements."

The fact now had to be faced that the " one bright spot on the military horizon " (the capture of Baghdad), which Ministers had hoped would bring a " striking success," had completely vanished from sight—for the present at any rate—and in Mesopotamia as elsewhere difficulties loomed high and forbidding in every direction. There was only one practicable way over them—the one which the War Committee took—and that was to recognize that no good could be done anywhere until a definite policy had been formulated and a comprehensive plan dealing with the war as a whole had been agreed upon. It was at this juncture that I took up the duties of C.I.G.S. and laid before the Committee the proposals for " The future conduct of the war " to which reference has previously been made.[1]   In accordance with them Nixon was informed on December 29 that he could not be given the additional two divisions for which he had asked, and that after relieving Townshend he was to adopt a defensive policy.   For the time being, therefore, the Baghdad project was abandoned, and the main purpose of the operations was the defeat of the enemy investing Kut.

The relief force, known as the Tigris Corps and commanded by General Aylmer, an officer fresh from India, was at first composed of the two divisions from France and certain reinforcements recently arrived from India and Egypt.   Later, the 13th Division was brought from Egypt, as well as various units from other places.   Three attempts were made to extricate the besieged garrison— in January, March, and April respectively—but in the circumstances success was not possible.   Different reasons have been given to account for the failures, such as premature attacks, abnormal conditions of weather, and floods, but there is no doubt that the truth lies in the report of the Mesopotamia Commission : " The evidence shows conclusively that shortage of river transport was the chief cause of the failure to relieve Kut."

The first attempt was made long before suitable preparations for it could be completed.   The hurry was due to no fault of either Nixon or Aylmer, but to the fact that all the information which they had, whether about the length of time that Townshend's supplies would last, or about the impending arrival of enemy reinforcements, led them to conclude that the place must

[1] See Vol. I, page 254.

be relieved without further delay. Consequently, as the official history reveals, the operation was carried out "with an improvised staff, makeshift organization, and inadequate transport, medical, and other resources." The weather, moreover, was atrocious, while the troops "had no trench mortars, no heavy howitzers, and but a few light ones, no heavy guns or Véry lights, and a limited number of machine guns. . . . The force was very short of aircraft and there were no balloons for observation of fire." The deficiencies of river transport were especially felt, and as an instance of this "there were at Basrah on the 21st January [when the operations were suspended because the troops were too exhausted and weak to do any more], 10,000 infantry and 12 guns which could not be sent upstream owing to the lack of shipping" to keep them supplied on arrival at the front!

When the news of the failure reached England the War Committee called upon the General Staff to review the situation afresh, and also to report upon the system by which the operations were being controlled. As to the first of these questions nothing need be said here except that I asked for authority to consult the Commander-in-Chief in India direct before submitting the review. The request was granted, and thus for the first time in the war an unrestricted official exchange of views between the senior military authority at the War Office and the executive head of the Army in India was permitted.

As to the second question, the desirability of placing the operations under the General Staff, as in the case of all other campaigns, had several times been discussed between Lord Kitchener and myself during the four weeks that I had been at the War Office, but without result. One reason was that I did not wish to become embroiled in a discredited undertaking unless allowed complete freedom of action in the endeavour to put it right, and of that there was at the moment not sufficient prospect. Nor was it quite wise to swap horses when crossing the stream—the stream being the task of saving the garrison of Kut before it was compelled by starvation to surrender. Had there been a reasonable possibility of General Staff intervention being of any practical use in the accomplishment of that task the position would have been different. But there was little or none, for at the time it was thought that all would be over one way or the other by February, when Townshend's supplies would, so far as the General Staff knew, be exhausted. The fact that they would last for a much longer period, i.e. to the middle of April, was not reported by Townshend until after the attempted relief had failed.

The other side of the question was that the state of affairs was growing worse every day rather than better, and if permitted to remain unremedied its effect on the operations elsewhere, already somewhat tiresome, might become serious. Moreover, for the Government to continue to call upon one department (the General Staff) for military advice, as they had latterly been doing, while leaving executive action in the hands of another (the India Office), was, however well-intentioned, no real improvement on the previous practice of not making use of the General Staff at all.

I accordingly recommended that control of the operations should in future be vested in the General Staff, who would replace the India Office as the responsible authority for seeing that the policy of the Government was carried into effect. All instructions relating to the operations would issue from the C.I.G.S. to the Com-

mander-in-Chief in India, under the authority of the
Secretary of State for War, in exactly the same manner
as to the Commanders-in-Chief in other theatres. As
the bulk of the Mesopotamia force belonged to India,
that country would necessarily remain the main base,
which the Commander-in-Chief in India would continue
to administer. It followed that the operations must be
controlled through him, and not in direct communication
with the Force Commander.

I further pointed out that the proposed system could

only work effectively if it is accepted whole-heartedly by the Government of India, and if precedent and established custom are, for the
nonce, set aside in the general interest. No compromise or half-
measure will lead to any improvement on the existing arrangement;
while given goodwill on both sides, central control over all the forces
of the Empire in the field will lead both to greater efficiency and economy
of force. . . . The cause of the Entente has suffered greatly from
the want of co-ordinated action, and this lack of co-ordination is increased by the existing system under which India is outside the control
of the Imperial General Staff.

The recommendations were considered by the War
Committee on February 3, accepted as they stood, and
put into effect the same day. " This assumption of
control by the War Office forms," says the official account,
" a landmark in the history of the campaign in Mesopotamia. Greatly welcomed by Mr. Chamberlain, Lord
Hardinge, and all the military authorities, it was evident
that, owing to the greater interest taken in the operations
by the War Office, this change of system would add greatly
to the efficient conduct of the campaign." The statement may be amplified by the addition that hitherto
it had not been possible for the War Office to take
interest, great or small, in the operations, because that
department had no means of knowing anything about

them beyond what the India Office chose to tell. Increased efficiency was to be expected for quite another reason than the one mentioned. The operations would henceforward be controlled by a body of officers specially organized and trained for the purpose, instead of by two civilians (the Viceroy and the Secretary of State for India) and a department (Military Secretary's, India Office) having none of the organization that the proper discharge of the duty demanded.

The transfer to the War Office of administrative as distinct from operative control was expressly excluded from the above arrangement because it was more difficult to adjust, and there was a probability that it might give rise to objections which would tend to hang up the whole question. I hoped, too, that the more essential improvements might be obtained without it, but in this I was wrong. The operations continued to be hampered by defective communications, notwithstanding the strenuous efforts and wide experience brought to bear upon them by General Sir Percy Lake, who had taken over the chief command when General Nixon returned to India about the middle of January owing to a break-down in health. Under pressure of the General Staff the Government of India at last assented to the construction of certain railways that had been asked for by the Force Commander many months before and refused, but the progress made was nevertheless slow and unsatisfactory. Eventually, in July, 1916, the War Office took over administrative as well as operative control and, as the Mesopotamia Commission reported, it was not until then " that the railways were really pressed forward with the vigour which the situation demanded." Supreme responsibility for the two functions of operations and administration ought, in fact, never to be separated, and it was a mistake on my part not to have asked for War Office control of both at the same time.

The next attempt to relieve Kut began on March 7 and was discontinued as a failure within forty-eight hours. Again there were at Basrah some 12,000 infantry, 26 guns, and a large amount of animal transport (urgently needed at the front) which could not be sent up in time for the operation. In reply to a telegram of mine calling attention to reinforcements being idle at Basrah while relief operations were in progress, General Lake suggested that the General Staff did not seem to realize the paralysing effect on his operations that shortage of river transport still exercised. To some extent he was right, for as transport and all other administrative duties were then in the hands of India and the India Office, the General Staff had not the means of ascertaining what the position was. It was, moreover, so utterly bad as to be incredible to anyone not on the spot. So inadequate was Basrah to support the traffic passing through that at one time Lake begged me to send no more reinforcements owing to the congestion of men and stores then waiting to go up country. The river transport available when the second failure occurred gave an average daily delivery at the front of only 300 tons as against a requirement of 468 tons, without allowing anything for the conveyance of troop personnel.

General Aylmer having twice failed, it was decided to give command of the relief force to General Gorringe, and the change took place on March 11. In coming to this decision the authorities in London were by no means unmindful of the difficulties against which General Aylmer had had to contend, but the position was extremely critical and in the discharge of their responsibilities the

Government agreed with the War Office that another General should be given an opportunity of showing whether he could obtain any better results.

The third attempt commenced on April 5 and continued until the 22nd. The force had a strength of 30,000 rifles and 127 guns as compared with 24,000 rifles and 92 guns in the second attempt. Concentration of the maximum strength available was again prevented by the shortage of river transport, 3,000 rifles and sabres, 32 guns, and a large amount of road transport not being able to arrive in time, by road, owing to heavy rain and floods, while river transport to convey them could not be spared without further interference with food supplies already cut down below the margin of safety. The actual operations were also greatly hampered by floods, which restricted the avenues of attack and made movement across country, already embarrassed by insufficient land transport, very difficult.

Learning on April 23 that the troops had reached the limit of their offensive powers, I telegraphed to Lake, after consultation with Lord Kitchener and Mr. Asquith, asking whether the time had not come to open negotiations to prevent the Kut garrison starving. The telegram crossed one from Lake saying that Gorringe was no longer hopeful of success, and that Townshend had asked whether he should open negotiations. The tenor of Lake's reply to my telegram was such that he was informed on the 25th by Lord Kitchener that the Government did not feel justified in calling upon his troops for a further effort, and he was authorized to open negotiations unless he and Gorringe had reason to change the opinion they had already expressed as to the prospects of success.

A gallant, but unsuccessful, attempt having first been made by the Navy to revictual Kut by the *Julnar*, Townshend was directed by Lake to start negotiations. They ended on April 25 with the surrender of the garrison— a sad termination, as the official history says, to the project which had originally contemplated the capture of Baghdad and which, from first to last, had cost the Empire over 40,000 casualties.

A total of close on 12,000 men, British and Indian, went into captivity,[1] where over 4,000 of them died. Of the British, more than 1,700, or over 70 per cent., died or have never been traced. On May 6, when already 300 had died since the surrender as a result of their privations, the rank and file were marched off to Baghdad. The officers were not allowed to remain with the men, but they extracted a promise from the Turks that the columns should not be required to march for more than eight miles a day. The promise was not kept, the men being made to cover the last 100 miles in $8\frac{1}{2}$ days. They arrived at Baghdad on May 15 where " they were marched through crowded streets for some hours. The march itself was a nightmare. The Arab soldiers freely used sticks and whips to flog the stragglers on, and although in some cases they kept the promise given to the British officers that men who fell out from sickness would be put on camels and donkeys, many died by the roadside." The subsequent dispatch of the unfortunate prisoners up country was referred to in a Parliamentary report as follows :—

Their state of preparation for a march of 500 miles, the health and strength and equipment which they possessed for withstanding one of the fiercest summers of the globe, can be pictured from what has been described already. . . . The truth . . . in all its details will never be known, for those who could tell the worst are long ago dead. But

---

[1] They are included in the 40,000.

it is certain that this desert journey rests upon those responsible for it as a crime of the kind which we call historic, so long and terrible was the torture it meant for thousands of helpless men.

The same report stated that while some of the prisoners were treated with almost theatrical politeness and consideration, others were " left to starve and die through simple neglect and incompetence," while others again were " driven and tormented like beasts."

Such was the price that had to be paid in soldiers' lives for the ill-starred advance on Baghdad. In referring to the high officials responsible for the advance being undertaken the Mesopotamia Commission reported that—

The weightiest share of responsibility lies with Sir John Nixon, whose confident optimism was the main cause of the decision to advance. The other persons responsible were : in India, the Viceroy and the Commander-in-Chief ; in England, the Military Secretary of the India Office, the Secretary of State for India, and the War Committee of the Cabinet. We put these names in order and sequence of responsibility.[1]

It is a question whether the order should not be reversed, and for the reasons given by the Commission themselves in previous paragraphs of their report where they say—

The division of responsibility between the India Office and the Indian Government, the former undertaking policy and the latter the management of the expedition, was, in the circumstances, unworkable. The Secretary of State, who controlled the policy, did not have cognizance of the capacity of the expedition to carry out the policy. The Indian Government, who managed the expedition, did not accompany developments of policy with the necessary preparations, even when they themselves proposed those developments.

The scope of the objective of the expedition was never sufficiently defined in advance, so as to make each successive move part of a well-thought-out and matured plan.[2]

---

[1] Mesopotamia Commission Report, page 111.
[2] *Ibid.*

In other words, and as suggested at the beginning of this chapter, the chief cause of the trouble was a thoroughly bad system of High Command. This could be remedied only by the action of the Cabinet, and therefore the latter should be placed first and not last in order of responsibility for the consequences that ensued. The India Office, as the State department responsible to the Cabinet for the control of the operations, also seems to come much higher up in the order of responsibility, and before any of the authorities in India. As these views may seem to have a military bias, the opinion of a war historian[1] may be quoted :—

The whole of the preliminaries to the Baghdad advance were a melancholy example of imperfect consideration and confused thinking due to bustle. The primary fact was that the Cabinet wanted a striking success on political grounds, and were not disposed to inquire too rigorously into details, and this spirit of haste infected also the Government of India. The root question, the chance of transporting the reinforcements rapidly to the fighting front, was never seriously considered. The Generals on the spot were not unnaturally confident after their experiences of the summer, but they were not put in possession of facts known to the Home Government, and they were manœuvred into a position where it was very difficult for a soldier to decline the venture. No one of the authorities concerned can be exonerated from blame, but the chief responsibility for the Baghdad advance must rest with the British Cabinet.

With the fall of Kut the position in the Middle East had again to be reviewed. At Aden the British garrison had been more or less besieged on the land side by Turkish troops since the autumn of 1915, and, not being able to protect our friends in the hinterland, a loss of prestige was incurred which enemy agents naturally tried to exploit. Southern Persia and the " neutral zone," or that part of Persia lying between the so-called British and Russian spheres of influence, were dominated by rebel gendarmerie and German-led bands of Persian

[1] " A History of the Great War," by John Buchan, Vol. II, page 402.

insurgents, some of whom had worked their way down south as far as Kirman, about two hundred miles from the Baluchistan border. From the day that Turkey allied herself with the Central Powers every German consulate in Persia had become a centre of intrigue, propaganda, and organized attacks against British residents and British interests in general. No effective action to counter the mischief was taken until the spring of 1916, when the Indian Government dispatched Sir Percy Sykes to Bandar Abbas to raise a force of levies for expelling the German adherents from the various places of which they had taken possession. This measure, like others having the same object, was valuable in itself but had not yet had time properly to restore British authority or to prevent hostile propaganda from increasing and spreading.

In Afghanistan, the Amir seemed anxious to avoid a collision with us, but circumstances might any day become too strong for him, and they were not made easier by the arrival of German emissaries at Kabul. On the north-west frontier of India the tribes were waiting to see what the Amir would do, and also had their eyes turned towards Egypt—an attack upon which had been loudly proclaimed. Germany's endeavours to set alight these inflammable countries had, moreover, been simplified by the access she had gained to Constantinople ; our evacuation of Gallipoli was another event that told in her favour ; and now the surrender of Kut would be quoted as a final proof of the decline of British power.

This state of affairs not unnaturally led to many demands being made for the provision of troops. The authorities in India asked for them because the normal garrison had, they considered, been unduly weakened by the calls of Mesopotamia and other theatres. The position at Aden was described by the Secretary of

State for India as an intolerable indignity which ought to be removed. Persia, it was said, required military detachments at various places, either to " show the flag," to expel hostile intruders, or to protect friendly chiefs.

Conditions were not, however, so unfavourable as they appeared to be, and steps to meet them had already been taken. In February, two months before Kut fell, two divisions in Egypt, where disposable reserves for eastern requirements were kept, had been earmarked by the General Staff for dispatch to India, if wanted, and ships to convey them were held ready in the Mediterranean. These reinforcements would suffice for some time to meet India's needs in the event of a rising on the frontier, or in Afghanistan, or a combination of both. The active policy recently initiated in Southern Persia could, if vigorously applied, be depended upon to check enemy propaganda and defeat the aims of German filibusters in that region. Northern Persia had just been cleared of all hostile parties by a Russian division and a body of cavalry commanded by General Baratoff, which had entered the country from the north in December and by the end of April was within 50 miles of the Mesopotamia frontier. (It arrived there a fortnight later, and connected with the British near Kut.) The Tigris Corps was quite capable of holding its own against any Turkish force likely to interfere with it for several weeks to come. The position at Aden was annoying but not in the least dangerous, and must be accepted.

For the present, therefore, the situation was well in hand, and it only remained for the Government to decide what the future policy in Mesopotamia was to be. On April 30, the day after Kut fell, the views of the General Staff on this point were laid before the War Committee, with the recommendation that we should revert to the defensive, abandon, for the time, all idea of going to Baghdad, and, in general, keep our commitments in the Middle East as low as possible. The Committee agreed, and approved of the following instructions being sent to India for transmission to Sir Percy Lake :—

At present our policy in Mesopotamia is defensive, and we do not attach any importance to the possession of Kut or to the occupation of Baghdad. It is, of course, impracticable to prescribe policy for a long time ahead. Lake would probably be directed to fall back on Amara, or even to Kurna, if no other considerations were involved, but it is important to minimize and counteract the effect of the fall of Kut and in order to assist the Russians to keep occupied the Turks now opposed to the Tigris Corps. For these reasons Lake should, for the present, maintain as forward a position as can be made secure tactically and be ready to take advantage of any weakening of the Turks on his front so long as this can be effected without incurring heavy loss, whether caused by the enemy or by unhealthy conditions. It is undesirable and impossible to reinforce Lake owing to the conditions in other theatres of war, but he will be kept adequately supplied with drafts and munitions. His forces are superior to those of the enemy, according to our information, and he should therefore have no difficulty in carrying out the above policy unless the Turks are strongly reinforced. In that event he should be given full discretion to fall back ; at any rate he must be clearly shown that the security of his force is of primary importance, and that neither now nor at any time is he required to maintain a more forward position than he thinks he can hold with reasonable safety. Lake should inform you if he considers he cannot carry out his assigned rôle with the forces at his disposal.

When these tentative instructions were issued I hoped that after the effects of the set-back at Kut had blown over it would be possible to withdraw to Amara. This would ease the strain on the communications, and the force would be more suitably placed than at Kut for carrying out its original mission of protecting the oil-fields and preventing hostile access to southern Persia. For various reasons, however, some months elapsed before I felt justified in asking the Government to approve of the change being made. Early in June a Turkish force, based on Baghdad, pressed Baratoff's troops back through northern Persia as far as Hamadan, a distance of about 300 miles, thus causing renewed unrest in that country. In August other Turkish forces attacked the left wing of the army of the Grand Duke Nicholas in Armenia, driving it back 40 miles and recapturing Mush and Bitlis which the Russians had occupied only a month before. These successes threatened to lead to a recrudescence of Turco-German activities in both Persia and Afghanistan, and if followed by a withdrawal on our part down the Tigris might create an embarrassing situation in these and other Middle Eastern countries. The General Staff therefore came to the conclusion that for the time being there was nothing to be done but to remain at Kut, and meanwhile to continue improving the communications and the fighting efficiency of the troops in every possible way, so as to be better prepared for whatever emergency might arise. Instructions to that effect were sent to the Commander-in-Chief.

About the middle of September it became evident that certain members of the War Committee were as eager as ever to acquire possession of Baghdad, notwithstanding the policy agreed to on April 30. The inclination to aim in practice at a goal which had in principle been rejected was disquieting, and in order that it might cease I brought the question forward for reconsideration and definite settlement.

General Baratoff had not been able to regain the ground he had lost in northern Persia, and the Russian authorities, having their hands full in Caucasia and Europe, were paying little attention to his proceedings. Everything pointed to the conclusion that such prospect as there had been of arranging combined Anglo-Russian operations was rapidly disappearing. The Turks, still at Hamadan, were pushing troops down south towards Isfahan, an enterprise which we could do little to check from the existing positions on the Tigris. Progress on the communications was disappointingly slow, and the strain on the supply services was such that one division and most of the cavalry had already been sent downstream to Amara. The troops were suffering severely from the climate, and the large drafts required to make good wastage caused by the high sick-rate entailed sensible reductions in the reserves available for other theatres. By sending the whole force back to Amara more healthy camping grounds could be obtained, and we could more readily deal with the Turkish detachments and hostile troops roaming about south-west Persia.

There was the further point, as I constantly reminded the Committee, that to continue expending our energies in operations against the Turks in Asia instead of against the main hostile armies in Europe was to do exactly what the Central Powers wished us to do. This obvious conclusion has since been confirmed by General Ludendorff, who, in referring to the situation in the summer of 1916 and the probability of our resuming the advance on Baghdad, says :—[1]

The stouter the Turkish resistance the larger the force they [the English] would have to employ. For that reason the fighting value of the Turkish army was a matter of the greatest importance to us. The stiffer the Turkish defence in Palestine and Mesopotamia, and the larger the force absorbed in the English effort to achieve their object, the more our burden in the West would be lightened. Of course, in their Indian contingents the English had troops at their disposal which they did not care to use in France, so that their employment in Asiatic Turkey did not benefit our situation in the West All the same it increased the military demands of the British.

[1] " My War Memories," page 255.

The principal arguments against withdrawal were its injury to our prestige, and the fact that it would diminish the threat on Baghdad and so set free the Turkish troops protecting that city for employment elsewhere. On the other hand, we were apparently not holding more than 20,000 or 30,000 of these troops, while as to prestige it had constantly been an overrated factor throughout the Eastern operations. Because of the drain on our resources and the poor return promised, the campaign had always caused me great concern and anxiety, and I was anxious to restrict it, once and for all, to the narrowest possible limits. The costly and objectiveless plan upon which we were working must, I felt, be changed.

General Maude (now Commander-in-Chief in Mesopotamia), whom I consulted, agreed that to resume the advance on Baghdad was at present impracticable, but he was not in favour of withdrawal. He suggested that further improvement of the communications and the possibility of a Russian offensive later on might enable us to go forward with advantage, and that meanwhile we should stay where we were. He gave other reasons in support of this plan, but although I had great confidence in his judgment I felt it necessary to advise the War Committee that, from a military standpoint, immediate withdrawal to Amara was the right course to adopt ; and that, politically, also, it seemed preferable to resuming a policy of aggression offering no adequate return for the price we might have to pay for it. If the Committee would agree to this view I would instruct Maude that his mission was to protect the oil-fields and to deny hostile access to the Gulf and south-west Persia ; that he must not expect to be given reinforcements, but might on the contrary have to release

71

the 13th Division sent to assist in the relief operations at Kut; and that, with these considerations in mind, he should occupy as forward a position as the state of his communications, climatic conditions, and tactical requirements would permit.

Some members of the Committee were willing to approve these instructions, while those who were attracted by the glamour of Baghdad strongly opposed them. They turned a deaf ear to my representation that the troops available were not sufficient to carry out the project they wished to see undertaken, and that if they had been the communications were not well enough organized to maintain them. It was essential, as I impressed upon the Committee, that a decision one way or the other should be reached, as a new Commander-in-Chief in India (General Monro) as well as the Commander-in-Chief in Mesopotamia had just been appointed, and required to be told what they were expected to do. As the advocates for going to Baghdad would not yield, while other Ministers were not prepared to override my advice on what was largely a military question, the result was a compromise. On September 28 it was decided that the mission of the force should remain unchanged, but the commander was to continue to improve the communications "in view of a possible future advance on Baghdad, which is, however, not at present contemplated." This decision necessarily led to a further period of inactivity and uncertainty. The force was unable to go forward and was not allowed to go back, while the enemy on his part was disinclined to attempt more than the passive defence of the positions he was holding on both banks of the Tigris.

I conveyed the above policy to the Commander-in-

Chief in India in the following telegram dated September 30 :

The mission of the Mesopotamia Expeditionary Force is to protect the oil-fields and pipe-lines in the vicinity of the Karun river, to maintain our occupation and control of the Basrah Vilayet, and to deny hostile access to the Persian Gulf and Southern Persia. At present no fresh advance to Baghdad can be contemplated, but it is the desire of His Majesty's Government, if and when possible, to establish British influence in the Baghdad Vilayet. This further advance should not be undertaken unless and until sanction for it is given, but in the meantime the General Officer Commanding should continue to improve the river and railway communications and maintain as forward a position as the state of his communications will allow and as can be made secure tactically without incurring heavy losses, whether caused by the enemy or by climatic conditions. Military and political considerations connected with Nasiriya, the Muntafik and Bani Lam tribes and the Pusht-i-Kuh-Bakhtiari country suggest that our present positions should be maintained if this can be achieved without undue sacrifices but we desire your views as to the feasibility of this course. Doubtless you will consult Sir P. Cox as to the effect on the Arabs of any withdrawal. Further, the Mesopotamia Expeditionary Force should ensure that hostile parties do not work down south across the line Shushtar-Isfahan. No further reinforcements for the force must be expected. On the contrary, it may become necessary to withdraw the 13th Division which was sent to Mesopotamia in order to assist in the attempted relief of Kut-el-Amara.

It will be observed that it is the wish of His Majesty's Government that the force should be kept as far forward as feasible, and in this connexion I wish you to understand that so far as I am personally concerned the proposal as to the dispositions of the force is a matter which I leave entirely to your judgment.

Before General Monro left England, on September 14, we discussed the operations together, and I asked him to send me his views. He called at Basrah on the way to India, and on October 19 he reported in answer to my telegram of September 30 that :—

I consider that our present position on the Tigris is the one best calculated to carry out the instructions of H.M. Government and to

uphold our prestige. In sending you this reply I have earnestly
weighed your directions in respect of exercising all economy of force
in this theatre of war, and I hold the opinion that no economy would
be effected by withdrawal at the present juncture.

On October 26, just before leaving Mesopotamia for
India, he sent me a further telegram saying that :—

An entirely passive attitude would in my judgment be unprofitable
and bad for the troops. I realize fully that visions of Baghdad are
beyond our sphere, and hold out no special advantages. But whilst
dismissing such a project, much might be done here which would
enhance our prestige to a great degree, ease the supply question, and
hearten the troops.

Maude would deprive the Turks of the supplies coming from the
vicinity of the Hai, if he were to move forward his left on to that
river, and very likely would manoeuvre them out of their position on the
right bank of the Tigris. Having settled the Hai, a forward movement
to Samawa from Nasiriya could be made with very little risk. From
Samawa greater control would be exercised by us over all tribesmen,
and confidence in our prestige and intention to stay would be greatly
increased. This outline could be accomplished, I think, with insignificant losses, and at any rate it is fully realized by Maude that severe
losses must not be incurred.

I had no objection to these suggestions, and on October
27 a telegram expressing general acceptance of them was
dispatched. They entailed no alteration of the instructions of September 30. My desire was to subordinate
everything to the necessity of maintaining the utmost possible pressure upon the German armies on the Western
Front, so as to take full advantage of the exhausted
and dispirited condition into which those armies had
been brought by the operations on the Somme. This
necessity, coupled with the situation in other theatres of
war—the Russian Front, the Balkans, Egypt, and East
Africa—made the continuance of a modest and cautious
policy in Mesopotamia imperative.

By the month of December the improvements made in the communications and in the health, training, transport, and equipment of his force were sufficient to satisfy General Maude that he could assume the offensive in conformity with the instruction to maintain " as forward a position " as could be secured. Setting his divisions in motion on December 13 he proceeded by systematic and progressive stages to dislodge the Turkish forces from each of their positions in turn until, on February 24, their defence finally broke down and they fled, in disorder, towards Baghdad. They were pursued, as after the first battle of Kut, to Aziziya, their losses amounting to about three-fourths of the whole force, and including 7,500 prisoners. The operations were skilfully planned, were carried out in complete accord with the spirit of the General Staff instructions under which Maude was acting, and may be regarded as a masterpiece of tactics in fighting astride a formidable river.

When the telegram reporting the rout of the enemy reached London the first question which Mr. Lloyd George, now Prime Minister, asked me was : " Will Maude get to Baghdad ? " I replied in rather guarded terms that it depended upon the condition of the transport and supply services ; that although he was unlikely for some time to come to have any anxiety regarding the enemy, he might have a great deal about the food, ammunition, sick and wounded of his own army ; and that we must be careful not to burn our fingers a second time in trying to reach Baghdad before we were properly ready. " But you must give us Baghdad if you possibly can," he said, urging that the people had so far experienced nothing but disappointments, and that it was important to present them with a victory that would forcibly appeal to their imagination. The capture of

Baghdad would have, he said, a tremendous effect not only in England but throughout the world. I promised to do my best to meet his wishes, but asked for time to consider matters.

The enemy's defeat certainly offered a strong inducement to wipe out the slur of the Kut surrender, and the possession of Baghdad would moreover be of some military advantage to us. It would deprive the Turks of their best base for operations both in Mesopotamia and Persia ; we would be better placed there than at Kut for co-operating with the Russians ; and we could more easily frustrate any attempt made down the Euphrates with the object of turning our positions on the Tigris, since the former river is only about 20 miles from the latter at Baghdad as against three times that distance at Kut.

Maude, of course, was keen to go on, and reported that the opportunity seemed

favourable for further advance, if this accords with policy of H.M. Government. Scope of such advance would depend on information received as to further enemy reinforcements being diverted in this direction.

He pronounced himself satisfied that his communications would be equal to the additional strain that would be put upon them.

Owing to the absence of Mr. Lloyd George and myself at Calais, where a conference was being held with the French in regard to the forthcoming campaign under General Nivelle, the decision as to future policy in Mesopotamia was deferred until our return to London on February 28. As before, the feasibility of reaching Baghdad was not the main question. This remained unchanged, namely, would the extension of operations to northern Mesopotamia, even if successful, increase our chances of winning the war ? Personally I could never see that it would, and felt that it might conceivably reduce them. It was evident, too, that the advance could not be limited to Baghdad itself. Our authority must be established throughout the whole of the Baghdad district, some 50 miles beyond the city. Moreover, as our gain would be the enemy's loss, he might be expected to try to get the place back, and this might compel us (as in fact it eventually did) to pour still more troops and munitions into the country. For these reasons I was no more desirous of permanently occupying Baghdad now than when the Turks were defeated at Kut in 1915, but I knew that the War Cabinet were in favour of going on and were not likely to listen to any other proposal. After explaining the case to them, therefore, I asked if I was right in assuming that it was still their policy to establish British influence in the Baghdad Vilayet, subject to the security of the force and the capacity of its communications. The answer was in the affirmative, and I was requested to instruct Maude in that sense, on the understanding that, while he should have regard to the proviso just mentioned, he was expected to exploit his recent success to the "fullest possible extent." The instructions were sent the same day, February 28, and were as follows :—

It has been decided by the War Cabinet that their instructions of the 28th September [1] last shall be modified as follows :—" Subject to the security of your force and to the capacity of your communications, it is the policy of H.M. Government to establish British influence in the Baghdad Vilayet."

You are required by this decision to press enemy in direction of Baghdad, and so exploit your recent success to full extent which you judge to be useful and feasible, having regard to your communications, to enemy reinforcements, and to importance of your main body not being compelled later to fall back for any reason. Such a retirement,

---

[1] Dispatched on September 30.

although it might not be a direct military disadvantage, might indirectly be so because of its objectionable political effect.

From information in my possession I am given no grounds for supposing that Turks can assemble sufficient force to imperil your safety south of Baghdad before Grand Duke is ready to take the offensive, which should be in about four or five weeks' time. He is being pressed by me to begin as soon as possible, but date depends largely upon the disappearance of the snows, which are this year exceptionally heavy.

The superiority of the Allies when the Grand Duke advances should be such as to make it safe for you to occupy and hold Baghdad, but it appears to me to be premature and possibly dangerous to attempt this until we see definitely what the Russians can do.

There would be every advantage in your cavalry raiding Baghdad if that becomes feasible, in order to destroy the important depots which the enemy has there. The capacity of your communications must be the chief factor in the situation at the present time. Further, I understand that Baghdad can be rendered untenable during the flood season, and that its effective possession would meanwhile necessitate making extended dispositions beyond the town.

You say, in your telegram of 6th February, that you do not expect to be able to maintain three divisions and a cavalry division at Baghdad before 1st April, and I doubt if you should enter Baghdad with your main body until you can maintain four divisions and a cavalry division.

Question of withdrawing 13th Division from you will for the present be in abeyance in the altered circumstances, and fresh troops coming from India will provide for your lengthened communications.

Inform me if the War Cabinet decision and the foregoing instructions do not explain your mission sufficiently. Further, I hope you will continue to give me your views as the subsequent development of the situation may require, as it is difficult for me correctly to appreciate local circumstances. . . .

Information received from Maude later showed that the Turkish defeat was more complete than I had supposed when dispatching the above instructions, and on March 3 I accordingly telegraphed to him saying that the

feasibility of occupying Baghdad forthwith is probably greater than I then concluded. I hope, therefore, you understand that, subject to due regard being paid to security and communications and to the other points mentioned therein, my telegram of 28th left matters to your own judgment. In brief, our object should be to attain greatest possible result from your recent victory and at the same time to avoid overdoing things to such an extent as to incur repetition of the old communication trouble, or, after a definite occupation of Baghdad, to be compelled to withdraw.[1]

These instructions crossed a telegram dispatched by Maude to me the same day, saying that he proposed to move forward from Aziziya on March 5 if his supply arrangements were satisfactory. To this I at once agreed, the Russians having promised to launch an offensive in co-operation with the movement. Maude entered Baghdad, after some sharp fighting *en route*, on March 11, and to that extent the Mesopotamia Army was at last rewarded for the exertions it had made during the past two and a half years under extremely trying and disheartening conditions.

Maude forthwith proceeded to clear the Vilayet of the enemy's troops. These offered a stouter resistance than had been expected, while Russia failed to render the assistance she had promised. The Grand Duke Nicholas had assured me in February that his troops would take the offensive in the direction of Mosul as soon as climatic conditions would allow, but the Russian revolution occurred a few days after Baghdad was reached, and although a junction was temporarily made with General Baratoff's force on April 2, General Alexeieff, Chief of the Russian General Staff, informed me before the month was out that there was now no chance of his troops co-operating unless we could feed

---

[1] Liberty of action was deliberately given to Maude because the question was, subject to the conditions specified, local in character. The position was quite different from that which confronted General Nixon in October, 1915, when the decision to go on to Baghdad was left to him. See page 46.

them. We undertook to do this, but it was of no avail. In Asia as in Europe the Russian armies were rapidly falling to pieces, and instead of combining with us against the Turks their defection left the Turks free in Caucasia to send additional troops against us in both Mesopotamia and Palestine.

As anticipated, the Turks made preparations for regaining what they had lost, and General Falkenhayn assumed charge of the operations, with head-quarters at Aleppo. Many reports were current during the summer as to the strength of the threatened attack, some of them being true and others deliberately exaggerated so as to induce us to reinforce the Mesopotamia army at the expense of the Western Front. One report emanating from Berne—a place often used by the enemy for starting false rumours—was that 400,000 men would be employed, of whom 160,000 would be German. This story, pronounced by the General Staff to be quite impracticable, caused considerable alarm in the War Cabinet, and those members of it who, in February, had been the most eager to push on to Baghdad, were now, in July, the most nervous about our being there.

In order to reassure them and to prevent extravagant counter-measures being demanded, I explained that the possibility of attack had received attention since the day on which the occupation of Baghdad had been decided ; that additional infantry, artillery, aeroplanes, munitions, and transport had been sent out ; that Maude had been asked to say if he was satisfied that the measures taken were adequate ; and that he had replied : " If our outstanding demands, especially as regards mechanical transport, are fully met and, as casualties occur, ranks of our units here are promptly filled, I feel no anxiety as to our ability to meet successfully considerably superior number of Turks." To this statement I added another : " On the whole I feel confident in General Maude's power to hold his own in Mesopotamia. In giving this assurance I am relying on his proved skill as a leader, the high morale of his troops, the time he has had to make his preparations, and the equipment of his forces." I was also able to say that, by taking suitable action in Palestine, we could compel the enemy to divert for the defence of that front some of the troops he was collecting for us in Mesopotamia.

This action was subsequently taken to such purpose that the enemy's projected counter-offensive in Mesopotamia was abandoned, while Maude, by a series of brilliant and daring manœuvres, defeated and dispersed one Turkish force after another, and by the first week of November, a few days before being fatally struck down by cholera, his allotted task of consolidating British authority in the Baghdad district was fast approaching completion. At the time of his death, according to the report of his successor, General Marshall, " the Turkish army was low in morale, and desertions from it were numerous and frequent. On the Tigris and Euphrates they had retreated out of rapid striking distance, and only on our right flank was there a good opportunity of hitting them." To work with Maude was as easy as it was pleasant, and his death was a great loss to the Army and the Empire.

The threat on Baghdad having disappeared, the War Cabinet at once became eager to push on to Mosul, about 200 miles farther north. As there was nothing to be gained and something to be risked (in view of the Russian collapse) from this extension, the General Staff objected to it and for the moment it was dropped. It was, however, several times revived, being supported by loose talk about the advantage of " joining hands " with Allenby in Palestine, but fortunately I was able to prevent it from materializing. Towards the end of the war it was carried out, though with what object I cannot say.

The total numbers employed in the Mesopotamia campaign amounted to about 400,000 combatants and 490,000 non-combatants. The casualties sustained were 31,758 killed, 15,350 missing and prisoners, and 51,156 wounded, besides a very heavy wastage due to sickness. Considered as a military measure, and in its relation to the war as a whole, the campaign greatly exceeded in scope the requirements of the situation, and left us a legacy of increased military liabilities of which the full consequences cannot yet be seen. When, previous to the Great War, our land frontier in Asia was covered by the deserts of Persia and the mountains of Afghanistan we could rely upon being able to reinforce the Indian garrison and complete our other defensive arrangements before any serious military force coming from Russian territory could arrive sufficiently near to be dangerous. In the event of hostilities by Russia to-day, especially if she were allied with Turkey, the safety of the British troops located in the remote regions of Mesopotamia might be the cause of anxiety and compel us to undertake military action there at a considerable disadvantage. The uncivilized tribes inhabiting the districts traversed by our line of communications, about 800 miles long, are another possible source of trouble, and should disturbances occur the reinforcement of these outlying troops might be difficult. Those who condemn the policy which has tied us to Mesopotamia usually do so on the plea that we cannot find the money to pay for it. It is also not without disadvantages on military grounds.

CHAPTER X

THE SALONIKA EXPEDITION

Mr. Lloyd George's Proposed Campaign in the Balkans, January, 1915—Diplomatic Action during the Year—Events following Invasion of Serbia—Views of British G.H.Q. in France—French Proposals—Dispatch of French and British Divisions—Joffre interviews British Cabinet—The Kitchener Stipulations as to British Co-operation—Failure to save Serbia—British Proposal to withdraw from Salonika is negatived—French Proposals in 1916 for Offensive Action—British General Staff, supported by Cabinet, advise against it—Rumania joins the Entente—Action of Salonika Forces to assist her—Embarrassing Attitude of Greece during 1916—Military Policy considered at Rome and Calais, in 1917—Sarrail appointed Allied Commander-in-Chief—Events during 1917–18.

OF all the problems which brought soldiers and statesmen into conference during the years 1915–17 the Salonika Expedition was at once the most persistent, exasperating, and unfruitful. The chief causes of this were the animosities and rivalries, domestic and foreign, with which for centuries past Balkan diplomatic affairs had been interwoven ; the differences of opinion between the two Entente Governments mainly concerned, the French and our own, as to the policy to be pursued ; and the political undercurrents in Paris by which the attitude of France was too often determined. Policy, such as it was, had in it too much of compromise and opportunism, and too little of decision and permanence. It was never in accord with sound strategy, and seldom

83

within the limits of available resources. In general, the Army and Navy chiefs, of Britain at any rate, were constantly being pushed or persuaded into courses of action to which they were opposed, and from which no useful result, political or military, could possibly be derived.

As previously mentioned,[1] the first proposal for engaging in military operations in this quarter of Europe originated with Mr. Lloyd George early in January, 1915, after which date it periodically competed against and eventually supplanted the expedition to the Dardanelles. Mr. Lloyd George's view was that the continued employment of the British Expeditionary Force in France would be a mistake, since the attempt to force the German lines there would only end in failure and great losses. He maintained that there was a danger of the people becoming weary of long casualty lists explained by " monotonous " and rather " banal " telegrams from G.H.Q. about " heavy cannonades " and " recovering trenches." A definite and visible victory in the shape of captured guns and prisoners, retreats of the enemy's armies, and the occupation of large areas of the enemy's territory would, he considered, alone satisfy the British public, and decide neutrals that the time had come for them to throw in their lot with us. The winning of a real victory " somewhere " was, he argued, imperative, and as there was no prospect of winning it on the Western Front it must be sought for in another place. He accordingly proposed that the Expeditionary Force should be withdrawn from France and, followed by the territorial divisions and New Armies as they became ready, be transferred to the Balkans. This would thereafter become our main theatre of war, and the operations could be based on Salonika or on the Dalmatian coast, or on both.

[1] *Vide* Vol. I, page 82.

Mr. Lloyd George hoped that this new strategy would cause Bulgaria to remain neutral, and would secure for us the active alliance of Greece and Rumania. With the forces of these two countries, the British and Serbian armies would then combine in a great attack against Austria. Mr. Lloyd George estimated that in this way one and a half million men could be assembled, and subsequently be increased in proportion as the British New Armies took the field. Austria, he considered, could not find sufficient troops to meet the attack and at the same time hold her existing front against Russia. Hence, she would require German assistance either on that front or on the new one. If Germany supplied it, she herself would become vulnerable to a Russian attack. If she did not supply it, Austria would be crushed by the Entente armies coming from the Balkans, who would afterwards unite with Russia in turning against the Germans. The weakening of the Western Front by the withdrawal of the Expeditionary Force was not considered to entail any serious danger since, in Mr. Lloyd George's view, the French and Belgian armies could " easily " hold their own against any force that the enemy could assemble after the Austrians had been withdrawn to defend their Balkan frontier. Should there be any doubt about this, before the Balkan diversion had produced its full effect, France could be reinforced as required by troops from England, and if that were not deemed a sufficient safeguard part of the troops could be kept in reserve at Boulogne. These various measures would, it was claimed, bring within our reach " something which could be called a victory."

A second operation was to be simultaneously undertaken with the object of gaining a " dramatic victory " over the Turks, who were reported to be concentrating an army of 80,000 men for the invasion of Egypt. Mr. Lloyd George proposed to let them " entangle themselves in this venture," and whilst so engaged to land 100,000 men " in Syria " so as to " cut them off." He considered that they could not long maintain themselves once their communications with Constantinople were severed ; they would therefore have to fight or surrender ; reinforcements from Europe could not arrive in sufficient time to help them ; and (on these assumptions) they would eventually be " wiped out and the whole of Syria would fall into our hands." Incidentally, pressure on the Russians in Caucasia would be relieved. Taking the two operations together, Mr. Lloyd George held that they would serve the common purpose of bringing Germany down by the process of " knocking the props under her," and of compelling her so to lengthen her lines of defence as to make them more easily penetrable. Failing the adoption of some such scheme as the above he could see no chance of our ever winning the war.

In putting forward these proposals Mr. Lloyd George said that " the French Generals " were confident that even if the whole German army then in Poland were transferred to the Western Front the French and British troops would still be able to hold their own. Who these Generals were, and what their responsibility in the management of the war was, I do not know, but I should doubt if General Joffre, the French Commander-in-Chief, was one of them. He knew it to be the fact that the Western Front was not safe against what the Germans might conceivably bring against it, and, as already suggested,[1] had they, before our armies and munitions were ready, done in 1915 what they did in March, 1918 they might have gone far to win the war.

[1] See Vol. I, page 148.

Mr. Lloyd George's strategy did not appeal to the Government, and there was no reason why it should. Its fallacies were too numerous and self-evident. Undoubtedly we were in need of a victory " somewhere," but before it could be won we must raise the armies with which to win it. Undoubtedly, too, we were confronted with formidable difficulties on the Western Front, but there was not the least justification for supposing that things would be made any easier by going to the Balkans, for we could not alter the geography of Europe which conferred upon the enemy the advantage of a central position, and thereby enabled him to keep one of his opponents in check with a part of his armies while he threw the bulk of them into a decisive blow against another. Mr. Lloyd George's plan would gratuitously provide an additional means of utilizing this advantage, since the enemy could transfer troops by rail to the new front in, say, two or three days, whereas we, condemned to move on the outside of the circle by sea, would for the same operation take as many weeks.

Again, the armies sent to the Balkans would have to be supplied with the special clothing, equipment, and transport needed for mountain warfare—a matter of several months—and after disembarkation more time would be absorbed in establishing the requisite communications through the three to four hundred miles of intricate country to be traversed before the Austrian frontier would be reached. Meanwhile, the enemy would be afforded the invaluable opportunity of attacking either the French or the Russians at a time when the British could render no assistance to either, direct or indirect.

Even if the new line of advance were opened without serious mishap of this or any other kind, and if we succeeded in reaching the Danube, further progress would be just as difficult as on the Western Front, for go where we might, we could not evade the entrenchments, wire entanglements, machine guns, and similar obstructions from which we were running away. In some shape or form they are a feature of all wars ; their value had been specially manifested on the Western Front ; and there was not the least doubt that they would be extensively used on all other fronts, as in fact they were. Writing from Gallipoli in June, 1915, Sir Ian Hamilton said :—

> We are becoming tied up—knotted up, I might say—in this cursed trench warfare, just as much as the British and Germans seem to be tied hand and foot by it in France. Every day I see the growth of the system—machine guns, barbed wire, redoubts.

Finally, what, as a matter of practical politics and quite apart from strategical considerations, would our French and Belgian Allies have thought had the Expeditionary Force been taken away from France in the wholesale manner suggested ? The proposition has only to be stated in this way to show how impracticable it was. Mr. Lloyd George once said that he had explained his plan to me when on a visit to G.H.Q. in France in January, 1915, and that I had agreed with it. If so, I must have entirely misunderstood the account he gave me of it, for besides being consistently of opinion that the war would be decided on the Western Front and nowhere else, a tour made in the Balkans in 1906 had convinced me that of all countries in Europe none was defensively stronger, and therefore none less favourable to the offensive, than the Balkan Peninsula.

Diplomatic action designed to secure the friendship of Greece and Bulgaria continued throughout the summer of 1915, but met with no success. In time of war the arts of the diplomatist are of little avail unless backed up by military victories, and these the Entente were not yet able to produce.[1] Hence, Greece remained an uncertain neutral, while Bulgaria, or at any rate her king, moved by subterranean paths more and more in the direction not of the Entente but of the Central Powers. By the last week of September all doubts as to her hostile intentions had vanished, and only the formal declaration of war was wanting. Serbia therefore proposed to attack her before she could complete mobilization, but was advised to hold her hand so as to give diplomacy another chance. The opportunity of falling upon Bulgaria before she was ready, and before the Austro-German armies had crossed the Save, was thus lost, but the result would probably have been much the same had Serbia struck when she wished, for she could not have achieved anything decisive against the large forces that were eventually sent against her.

As to Greece, it was thought that, under the guidance of M. Venizelos, the Prime Minister, she would fulfil her treaty obligations and go to Serbia's assistance. To enable her to do this France and Britain acceded to her request to furnish a contingent of 150,000 troops, and one British and one French division were ordered to proceed to Salonika from Gallipoli, the nearest place from which troops could be obtained. On October 2 the French Minister at Athens informed the Greek authorities of their arrival, and assumed that Greece would not object to this or any other measure taken in

[1] " As far as Europe was concerned diplomacy in the war counted for little. When it appeared to fail most, it was when the Allies were having military reverses ; when it seemed to succeed, it was because the Allies were having military success."—" Twenty-five Years, 1892–1916," page 154.

the interest of her ally. But King Constantine, who had approved of the request for troops, now maintained that the treaty could not come into force until Serbia was actually attacked by Bulgaria, and therefore until that moment the landing of the divisions would be a violation of Greek neutrality.

M. Venizelos accordingly felt it necessary formally to protest against the landing, which was nevertheless facilitated in every possible way. On October 4 he informed the Greek Chamber of his intention to respect the treaty and to protect the Serbian flank with the Greek army, whose mobilization had been ordered some days before. He received the confidence of the Chamber by a large majority, but on the following morning was told by the king that his policy could not be endorsed. He resigned the same day, and his successor, M. Zaimis, then proclaimed a policy of " armed neutrality," to be characterized, so far as the Entente were concerned, " by the most complete and sincere benevolence." Of this the tacit concurrence in the landing at Salonika may be regarded as a proof. A few days later, however, M. Zaimis developed the argument that the treaty had a " purely Balkan character " and referred only to an attack on Serbia by Bulgaria and not to an invasion by other Powers. These quibbles showed that the Government, oppressed by the fear of German vengeance, was determined to go no further than neutrality, and that being so the fulfilment of the promise to send 150,000 Anglo-French troops necessarily fell in abeyance.

On October 7 and following days Serbia was invaded by some 200,000 Austro-German troops from the north and by the Bulgarian army of about 250,000 men from the east. Attacked in front and flank in this manner, the Serbian army of less than 200,000 men found itself in a hopeless situation. Meanwhile the French division, the first to arrive at Salonika, had commenced to move forward, the commander, General Sarrail, being instructed by his Government to hold the railway between Salonika and Uskub so as to protect the Serbian communications to the south. Followed by the British division, General Sarrail reached Krivolak, 90 miles north of Salonika, on October 27. He there found his path barred by the enemy, into whose possession Uskub had already fallen, while the Serbian army was in course of being thrown back through the mountains on his left, the greater part of it retiring to Durazzo on the Adriatic coast and the remainder southwards to the Greek frontier. These events naturally led to the question of sending more troops to Serbia's aid, and it proved to be a very thorny one to decide, for although the Governments of both England and France were anxious to help her, it was not possible to do so in sufficient time and strength to be of any practical use.

There were other objections to committing ourselves further in this quarter. Already the operations in Gallipoli were at a standstill for lack of reinforcements, and it was feared that the army there might not be able to hold its own unless kept better supplied with drafts and other reinforcements than had recently been the case. The only alternative was to withdraw it, and this the Government was not prepared to sanction. In Mesopotamia, again, we were contemplating the capture of Baghdad, some 500 miles from the Persian Gulf. Two divisions were being withdrawn from the Western Front to take part in the advance, and others might be needed later on. A threatened Turkish attack on Egypt might lead to a new campaign there, unless pressure elsewhere could be exerted to prevent it. On the Western Front, at the expense of which all troops for other theatres must be found, the armies had just emerged from the battle of Loos and were in no condition to furnish divisions for new enterprises. Finally, the employment of more troops in distant countries meant the provision of more shipping, and in this respect the strain was already acutely felt.

On the other hand, we were under a moral obligation to help Serbia—an ally in distress—however evident it might be that nothing could be done to save her. She probably thought, too, that to some extent her plight was due to following our advice not to attack Bulgaria while the latter was still unready ; and in addition there was some misunderstanding about the 150,000 troops promised to Greece. Serbia seemed to expect that they would be sent into the country although the attached condition of Greece taking the field was not fulfilled.

As elsewhere explained,[1] some members of the Cabinet wished to solve the difficulty by the indirect method of reinforcing the Gallipoli Expedition and pushing home there ; others preferred the direct plan of developing the Balkan operations ; while the General Staff, in a memorandum of October 9, pronounced in favour of the former course and recommended that eight reinforcing divisions should be taken from France. In the end it was decided to send six divisions (later reduced to four) to Egypt, and settle where they should go after they had arrived there and been re-equipped.

Writing to the C.I.G.S. from G.H.Q. in France on October 21 with reference to the memorandum of October 9, I said :—

The more I think of it the more I am convinced that it would be absolutely playing Germany's game to embark on a campaign in the Balkans. She can do nothing there to hurt us. Everybody who

---

[1] See Vol. I, page 129.

knows anything about the history of the Balkans is of this opinion. The Balkan States will never, as a whole, be on Germany's side or on the side of any other Great Power, and Germany will never be so foolish as to make her main effort there. And even if we assume that she does make it there, what then ? She cannot possibly do anything in Asiatic Turkey for years to come, as your recent paper so well shows. I have for long studied the Middle Eastern question and am absolutely in agreement with your paper. It is the height of folly to take away troops from here, as the General Staff have so well shown, unless we are compelled to do so, and the only compelling factor, if it is compelling, is Gallipoli. As you know, I go further than you, and would not withdraw any troops from here unless they could be back in time for the offensive, and this they certainly could not be. Moreover there is the question of loss of efficiency. Pulling troops away from France and sending them to the East and then bringing them back to France would involve delay and also loss in the fighting value of the force.

I do not for a moment wish to interfere with General Staff work at the War Office, and I do not at present propose ever writing again on this subject, but I cannot help urging you to adhere to the principles laid down in your memorandum. If the eight divisions are for Gallipoli I have no more to say. You think they should go there, and war is a one-man business. But if they are for use in the Balkans I am most strongly of opinion that the General Staff should stick to their views and do all in their power to prevent the eight divisions being sent there. Two are just leaving, but that is no reason why the whole eight should go. It is no argument to say that they will be replaced by the 4th New Army. As you know, the 4th New Army will not be nearly as good as the troops composing the eight divisions, it will require a considerable amount of training, and it is not possible in this country to give much training in the winter months. Besides every fool knows that you cannot be too strong at the decisive point, and therefore the 4th New Army should be in addition to and not in substitution for any troops now here. I am not at all moved by the fact that France is sending troops to Salonika. That is largely a matter of political intrigue, and so far as the military are concerned the question has not been properly studied by the French G.H.Q., and I feel sure that the two French divisions just sent will accomplish very little.

Meanwhile French Ministers were wrestling with the

same problem. Hitherto they had taken their military advice on Eastern affairs from the General Staff of the War Ministry as distinct from General Joffre and G.H.Q., and the first proposal was to send to Salonika four French divisions which had previously been earmarked for employment on the Asiatic side of the Dardanelles under General Sarrail.[1] But to this General Joffre objected, and although General Sarrail was sent out the divisions were held back. Instead of them, the second of the two French divisions already serving in the Dardanelles was utilized, and the British Government was asked to supply the balance needed to complete the contingent up to the 150,000 men mentioned.

The request was referred by the Cabinet to the General Staff, who again declared themselves opposed to all operations in the Balkans. They reported that the French plan had not been carefully examined ; that both the size of the force needed and the time required to carry out the plan had been underestimated ; and, in general, that the results likely to be gained were greatly outweighed by the disadvantages incurred. Fortified by this opinion, the Cabinet, or a majority of it, declined to accede to the French request.

The French Government did not allow the matter to drop, and on October 25, after several communications had passed between London and Paris, the C.I.G.S., Sir Archibald Murray, proceeded to Chantilly to interview General Joffre, whose staff had now taken over the management of the Eastern operations from the War Ministry. The intention was to arrange that British participation should be confined to the one division already in Macedonia, or at any rate be kept within the smallest possible limits. The C.I.G.S. had with him

[1] *Vide* Vol. I, page 128.

two representatives from the Admiralty to assist in stating the British case. Sir John French, accompanied by myself, also attended from British G.H.Q., but we took little or no part in the proceedings as we were concerned only in so far as the Western Front might be affected.

Hitherto General Joffre had objected as strongly as anyone to the diversion of troops from France to secondary theatres, and two months before had stood out against the wishes of the combined British and French Governments to reinforce the Gallipoli Expedition and postpone the attacks which he was then preparing in Champagne and at Loos. Now, his attitude was entirely different, and instead of consenting to the British rôle being circumscribed as desired by the C.I.G.S., he insisted upon enlarging it.

This change may be attributed to political rather than to military causes. At the moment the French Government was in imminent danger of being overthrown, owing to the dilatory manner in which it was considered to have handled the Serbian question. If it was to be saved something definite and imposing must be done, and done quickly. General Joffre was alive to the necessity of alleviating these internal troubles, and even if he had wished to resist his Ministers in their Eastern tendencies he was hardly in a position to do so. They, like some of our own, were critical of his recent operations in Champagne, which they classed as a failure, and dissatisfaction was not confined to ministerial circles alone.

General Joffre therefore had resort to a plan which, on the one hand, promised to meet the wishes of his Government, and, on the other, to admit of a resumption of the offensive on the Western Front as soon as a suitable time for such action arrived. It would also put an end

to the Gallipoli Expedition of which he had never been
in favour. All things considered, his solution was perhaps the best that could be evolved from his point of
view, but it was unfortunate that he should have felt
impelled, mainly for reasons of domestic politics, to
propose a plan of which, in his heart, he could hardly
approve. Briefly stated, his plan as described in a French
General Staff memorandum was as follows :—

By means of skilful diplomacy, backed by an army of
less than 180,000 men, which had been put in at the right
moment, Germany had immediately drawn in to her side
350,000 Bulgarians, and might soon bring in 200,000
Greeks and 500,000 Rumanians. Decisive attacks on
the main Western and Eastern Fronts would annul
these German successes, but for various reasons the
Entente were not at the time able to undertake them.
They could do no more than " hinder " Germany's aims
in the East, whilst keeping on the two main fronts the
resources necessary for decisive operations at a later
date. Hitherto Entente diplomacy had failed because
it was unsupported by force. The element of force
must be produced : in the north, a Russian army concentrated in Bessarabia, would give confidence to Rumania
and bring her in on our side ; in the south, a strong army
of British, French, and Italians, assembled at Salonika,
would lay down the law for Greece, and force her into
the Entente. Further, the concentration of these two
armies on the flanks of the German-Bulgar movement
would constitute too serious a threat to be disregarded,
and would consequently immobilize part of the enemy
force then attacking Serbia.

To give effect to these views it was recommended
that the two Russian army corps then assembling in
Bessarabia should be increased to 150,000 men, " as

soon as the rifles which have been sent by France and Italy arrive at their destination." This strength was considered sufficient to force the hand of Rumania, without depriving Russia of the means required for prosecuting her operations in Poland and Galicia.

For the purpose of bringing the necessary pressure to bear upon Greece, and for undertaking offensive action later in conjunction with the Russo-Rumanian armies, it was estimated that the group to be assembled at Salonika should have a strength of 250,000 men. At the moment there were only one British and two French divisions in the country, or about 65,000 men, and in order not to deprive the Western Front of divisions which would be needed later it was proposed to bring to Salonika the whole or greater part of the troops then in Gallipoli. These, plus one French and two British divisions then on the sea *en route* from France to the East, together with an Italian contingent, would provide the 250,000 men required. The whole were to be placed under the command of a British General, with a French General as Chief of the General Staff. As soon as concentration was sufficiently completed the Greek question was to be settled by giving King Constantine the option of joining the Entente or " submitting to the immediate execution of Greece."

From the beginning of the proceedings General Joffre was not disposed to listen to any arguments of the C.I.G.S. against this plan, and the conference accordingly terminated without an agreement being reached. The same evening General Joffre left for London with instructions from M. Viviani, the Prime Minister, to obtain from the British Cabinet the promise of co-operation which he had failed to secure from the C.I.G.S. The latter meanwhile proceeded to Amiens for the night, where he heard for the first time of General Joffre's mission.

General Joffre was seen on the 29th by the principal members of the Cabinet, and the discussions were continued the following day. I was present at some of them, having been brought over from France in connexion with another matter. General Joffre, still a stranger to several British Ministers, impressed the Cabinet as a man who knew his own mind, but his proposals nevertheless met with a cool reception. Some Ministers were eager to welcome almost any plan provided that it obviated fighting on the Western Front, but few of them cared to ignore the advice which they had solicited from their own General Staff only ten days before. General Joffre reduced his first demand for 250,000 to 150,000 men, and realizing that even then he was making no headway he suddenly announced that unless British co-operation was sanctioned he would resign his position of Commander-in-Chief of the French armies. This threat was the cause of some consternation, and the French representatives withdrew from the room so that the British might consider amongst themselves what should be done. Eventually they accepted the French plan and undertook to send to Salonika the four British divisions proceeding from France to Egypt, thus making five in all, which, with the three French divisions, would bring the total strength up to the 150,000 men required. Being uneasy apparently at the thought that they were accepting a plan which, after full consideration, they had previously rejected, and were acting contrary to the advice of their own naval and military staffs, the Cabinet made the following stipulations to which General Joffre agreed:—

In view of the French statement dated 28 October, 1915, including definite calculations of the capacity of the port of Salonika and of the carrying-power of the railways into Serbia (for which the British head-quarters staff do not make themselves responsible), and in view of the strictly limited rôle that General Joffre and the French General Staff desire British troops to fulfil, viz :—To ensure the position of Salonika to Krivolak inclusive, in order to support the French Army, which assumes the duty of protecting the railway between Krivolak and Veles, and of ensuring communication with the Serbian army (the whole operations not to be conducted beyond the line Monastir-Uskub-Istif-Salonika, and solely with the purpose of maintaining communication with the Serbian army), and with the full understanding that if communication with the Serbian army cannot be opened and maintained, the whole Allied Forces will be withdrawn to be used as circumstances may require, the British Government are prepared to co-operate energetically in the manner proposed by the French Government.

KITCHENER.

30th October, 1915.

Having accomplished his mission, General Joffre returned to France, but before he arrived back the Viviani administration, which he had set out to save, had fallen, and a new Government had been formed with M. Briand as Prime Minister. The latter had always been attracted by the Balkan adventure, and his rise to the Premiership largely on the Serbian issue shows how French political affairs had their influence on the strategy of the Entente at this period.

A few days later a conference was held at Paris to consider the position afresh, the British Government being represented by Mr. Asquith, Sir Edward Grey, Mr. Balfour, and Mr. Lloyd George. I was again directed to attend, and on being asked for my views replied that the Balkans were for us an impossible theatre of war, and that we ought to concentrate our strength against the real enemy on the Western Front and not waste energy in fighting Bulgars and Turks. Generals Joffre and Galliéni, the War Minister, seemed to concur although

99

they did not say so, nor did they commit themselves to a definite opinion of any kind. M. Briand naturally dissented, and in the end the arrangement made in London the week before was confirmed.

Without calling into question the right of the British Government to reject the advice of its own experts and to be guided by that of the French staff, it may be observed that the decision to send to Macedonia the only four divisions available was entirely inconsistent with the Government's desire to continue the operations in Gallipoli, since existing means were insufficient for the prosecution of both projects, and the acceptance of one must automatically entail, sooner or later, the abandonment of the other. It did. A few weeks later the troops in Gallipoli had to be withdrawn, and for several months afterwards they remained in Egypt unemployed. They were eventually transferred to France, whence the four divisions sent to the Balkans had been brought. In this way both troops and shipping were wasted for the want of a firm decision in the first instance.

Nor was the position made any easier by the stipulations of the Kitchener agreement, for in practice these would be no safeguard against our being drawn into action of which we did not approve. If the French troops beyond Krivolak should find themselves in difficulties the British troops would be compelled to go to their assistance, and it was futile to lay down conditions to the contrary. Similarly with respect to withdrawal, should the attempt to save Serbia fail. Once troops were sent into the country many different circumstances might arise which would necessitate keeping them there, irrespective of what the fate of Serbia might be. These views were put forward by the General Staff at the time and before the Paris conference took place, but apparently Ministers

AFTER BREAKFAST AT THE QUAI D'ORSAY.

Left to right : 1. Gen. Jilinski (Russia); 2. Gen. Cadorna (Italy); 3. M. Salandra (Italian Prime Minister); 4. M. Briand; 5. M. de Broqueville (Belgian Minister); 6. M. Pachitch (Serbian Prime Minister); 7. Mr. Asquith.

believed, or hoped, that co-operation could be limited in the manner prescribed in the agreement. Subsequent events proved that it could not be.

General Sarrail remained with the French contingent near Krivolak until the last week of November. By that time Serbia had been overthrown and there was nothing he could do but retrace his steps by the way he had come. He rejoined the British contingent on December 10, and two days later the combined forces withdrew inside Greek territory and there proceeded to prepare a defensive position covering Salonika, 30 miles distant in rear.

The endeavour to save Serbia having failed, the British General Staff proposed that, in accordance with the Kitchener agreement, the whole Entente force should be brought away. Its strength would be only eight divisions after all had arrived, and against them the enemy was reported to have the equivalent of between twenty-five and thirty divisions. Moreover, there was nothing to be gained by the occupation of Salonika for, as the General Staff said [1] :—

The only argument for holding it that is worth considering is to deprive the enemy of a submarine base. We cannot for a moment consider that as a sufficient justification for locking up an army of 150,000 men. Even if we thereby prevented altogether the use of submarines in the Ægean, which would not be so, we cannot afford to employ a large force for that purpose. The weight of military arguments against holding Salonika is overwhelming, and, in addition to these arguments, there are other considerations : we might make Greece actively hostile, and offend the conscience of Americans and other neutrals by attempting to hold it. To evacuate Gallipoli and Salonika simultaneously is, of course, an immense undertaking, and must entail a severe blow to our prestige. But the evacuation of Galli-

---

[1] General Staff memorandum, dated November 23, 1915.

poli has already been recommended, and whatever room for doubt there may be as to the wisdom of that decision the General Staff can see no doubt whatever as regards Salonika. We must hope that topographical difficulties will delay the enemy's advance sufficiently to simplify our withdrawal from both places, but in any case the General Staff are convinced that we should withdraw. It is accordingly recommended that all further transport of troops to Salonika should be instantly stopped ; that all troops in Serbia should at once be withdrawn to Salonika and none should be left north of that place ; and that evacuation from Salonika should then proceed as fast as is possible without detriment to the more difficult operation of withdrawing from Gallipoli.

At first the War Committee were disposed to accept this advice, but as the French Government objected to it the question was brought before a ministerial conference at Calais on December 4, no decision being reached. It also found a place in the military conference then being held under the presidency of General Joffre at Chantilly to consider plans for 1916. The conclusion there recorded was, as already described,[1] that the force ought to remain where it was.

Following this recommendation the matter was finally dealt with by another ministerial conference held at Paris between December 6 and 8. There, as in London at the end of October, British Ministers thought it necessary to fall in with the French view. It was decided to set aside the Kitchener agreement of October 30, to retain in Greece the eight divisions then in and *en route* to that country, and to assign to them the mission of defending the town and harbour of Salonika. What real purpose, military or political, this policy was intended to serve was neither specified nor properly considered, and it was upon this negative and ambiguous basis that the Expedition assumed a permanence destined to last till the end of the war. It was also agreed that the general

[1] See Vol. I, page 246.

command of the combined contingents should be vested in General Sarrail.

Various reasons have been suggested to account for the French wishing to keep troops at Salonika at a time when ten of their richest provinces were still in German hands, and when Serbia was beyond the possibility of help, but none of them is convincing. The one most frequently given at the time was that the Government desired to find employment for General Sarrail, who was associated with certain political leaders of the Left whom it was advisable to placate. A more correct explanation probably is that, having become committed to the campaign, the Government was reluctant to abandon it because of the criticism to which that course would give rise. As to military opinion, practically all the leading French Generals with whom I was brought into contact, including Joffre, Foch, and Pétain, showed, in manner if not in actual words, that they intensely disliked the project from the start and would be glad to see the end of it.

From the middle of December a period of stagnation commenced. The Entente forces were condemned by their orders and local conditions to a passive defence, while the enemy, having gained all that he had set out to achieve, was satisfied with leaving matters as they were and remaining outside the Greek borders. He had secured the active alliance of Bulgaria, occupied Serbia and Montenegro, scared Rumania away from any idea of joining the Entente, and reopened the railway to Constantinople. He had thus covered the Austrian frontier and its communications with Turkey by a broad belt of difficult country extending from the Adriatic to the Marmora, and the armies occupying it could be readily reinforced should the necessity for that step arise. He was not only well protected, but had acquired a strong position from which to prosecute such Middle Eastern enterprises as he might desire. He had, too, compelled his adversaries to weaken their forces on the Western Front and to open up another remote theatre of war, thus enhancing the value of that central position which he possessed.

This was the situation at the end of 1915 when I became C.I.G.S., and it was a very difficult one to deal with. Strategically, the right course was to bring the whole of the troops away, but there was never any hope that the French Government would agree to this, and in any case the matter could not be settled on grounds of strategy alone. The attempt to gain a decision on the Western Front had so far failed ; Russia had suffered heavy defeats ; Gallipoli was in process of being evacuated ; Townshend's force had just been shut up in Kut ; and in the general interests of the Entente it was not possible in these circumstances to confess to still another failure in the Balkans. The only practical plan was to defer action for the moment, and later on, if the two Governments persisted in remaining, to seek approval for the withdrawal of the British portion of the force. The Expedition would thus become entirely French, and its employment, resting solely in French hands, would be simplified.

I was never able to bring about this change, and feel sure that, if made, it would have spared Ministers of both countries an infinite amount of trouble, loss of time, and not a little unpleasantness. On several occasions when Salonika affairs came before allied conferences I hoped, from what had previously been said at meetings of the War Committee, that British Ministers would insist upon the British contingent being either withdrawn or reduced. Mr. Asquith and Sir Edward Grey in particular were anxious to support the General Staff in this respect, but as other members of the Committee had other ideas, which they declined to waive, British ministerial opinion at the conferences was seldom either determined or unanimous.

French Ministers, on the other hand, invariably presented a united front, and came to the conferences well prepared not only to meet British arguments against continuing the Expedition, but to produce new ones for enlarging it. When, as was often the case, these arguments were of a political character it would be claimed that they were so important as to necessitate *military* considerations being overridden. This claim British Ministers might feel obliged to accept, though not entirely agreeing with it, since it was essential, especially at those periods when German propagandists were the most active, that good relations between the Allies should be carefully preserved. Only those who shared in the supreme direction of the war can have any idea of the complexity of the obstacles through which Ministers sometimes had to find a way, and therefore one hesitates to criticize the action they took. Still, if French internal politics had been less obtrusive, and if certain British Ministers had been less indifferent to British professional advice and more ready to take a line of their own instead of always following the French lead, it might have been possible to come to an arrangement mutually satisfactory to both Governments, as well as more beneficial to the Entente cause. Almost any plan would have been better than that of keeping, in a malaria-infected country, hundreds of thousands of troops who could never give an adequate return for the expenditure of man-power and shipping which their retention involved.

Early in February, 1916, General Joffre reverted to his previous plan of strengthening the Expedition and asked me to provide 100,000 men from Egypt, where the divisions recently withdrawn from Gallipoli, drafts from home, Australia, and New Zealand, and detachments of various other kinds amounted to some 300,000 men or more. It was the intention of the British General Staff, after this unwieldy accumulation had been overhauled and reorganized, to send as many divisions as possible to France where, in conformity with General Joffre's wishes, preparations were being made for the offensive which later became known as the battle of the Somme. No more troops were to be retained in Egypt than the security of that country and the Suez Canal required, plus the provision of a small strategical reserve of two or three divisions to meet emergencies in Mesopotamia and India. The dispatch of troops to Salonika was the last thing that the General Staff desired, since it would aggravate the dispersion of force which they were striving to correct.

General Joffre's request could not therefore be complied with, and whilst it was still being discussed between us the German attack on Verdun began. A fortnight later, when the situation there had become serious, the General asked me to think no more about reinforcing Salonika but to proceed with the arrangements already initiated for transferring all available divisions from Egypt to France. This policy was confirmed at an allied military conference held at French G.H.Q. in the middle of March, and it was then agreed that, for the present, the constitution of the Salonika forces should remain unchanged. They were to be organized as far as possible for mountain warfare, and, with the Italian forces in Albania, were to keep the enemy under threat of an attack, but no offensive was to be undertaken until the question had been reconsidered by the staffs concerned.

The question was next brought forward on April 25. Some six months had elapsed since M. Briand and his colleagues had replaced Ministers who were accused of being slack in the treatment of Near Eastern affairs, and meanwhile the position had become, in French eyes, worse rather than better. Considerable pessimism also prevailed as a result of the fighting at Verdun. Something vigorous and striking had therefore to be done, as in the previous autumn, in order to appease the critics, and on the grounds that the recent withdrawal of the greater part of the German troops from the Balkans had created a favourable situation for offensive action, General Sarrail was instructed by French head-quarters as follows :—

Au moment jugé opportun, l'Armée d'Orient attaquera toutes forces réunies, les armées ennemies à la frontière grecque et, en cas de succès, les poursuivra en direction générale de Sofia. La direction de Sofia fixée par le Général en Chef a pour but de permettre au Général Sarrail d'orienter son dispositif pour livrer bataille aux forces germano-bulgares à la frontière grecque, et de les poursuivre, en cas de succès.

At the time the Salonika forces consisted of five British, four French, and six Serbian divisions, aggregating about 350,000 men, as against some 300,000 Bulgarians and a few Germans. (The Serbian divisions had just arrived from Corfu, where they had gone from Durazzo to refit after their defeat.)

Although the instructions to General Sarrail, with the reasons for them, were sent to me direct by General Joffre in accordance with the custom by which our business together was conducted, the proposed operations at once became the subject of correspondence between the two Governments, and were afterwards dealt with through the medium of the Foreign Offices and Ambassadors in London and Paris, and not by the General Staffs. The French Government began by asking that General Sarrail might be given two divisions from Egypt, using the same arguments to support their request as in the previous autumn. Offensive action, they said, would bring in Greece and Rumania ; if not, important tactical successes could at least be gained ; at worst, large Bulgarian forces would be " contained " which would otherwise be employed against us elsewhere ; and, finally, the Salonika forces ought not to be idle when the armies on all other fronts were active.

The General Staff were again compelled to differ—not, of course, because of any particular difficulty in finding the two divisions but on the broader grounds of general military policy. Everyone agreed that Greece and Rumania should, if possible, be induced to join the Entente, but the former seemed less inclined to do so than before, while the latter was not likely to join unless military action on her behalf included an offensive from the southern part of the Russian front as well as one from Salonika. Russia, however, was not able to undertake such an offensive, as she was preparing (in accordance with the general Entente plans) to attack in the north towards Vilna, with a subsidiary attack only in the south, in Bukovina.[1]

The chances of Sofia being reached from Salonika were equally small. Being composed of several nationalities having different methods, temperaments, organizations, and languages, the Entente forces were at a great

---

[1] It was not until June, when Italy was hard pressed by Austria in the Trentino, that Russia, in response to an appeal for help, consented to ante-date the Bukovina attack and so brought about Brussiloff's unexpected successes.

disadvantage as compared with the more homogeneous enemy, and their fighting value was far less than their numbers indicated. The Serbians had suffered in morale as a result of their defeats in the previous autumn, and as yet had little experience of the new rifles and guns with which they had since been equipped. The French contingent comprised many native troops who were not well adapted to withstand the rigours of the European climate, and both French and British troops were for the most part unaccustomed to and untrained for mountain warfare. A much more efficient army than this was needed to break through the entrenched positions which the enemy was known to have prepared north of the Greek frontier.

With respect to the argument that the operations would serve to " contain " Bulgarian troops who might be employed elsewhere, it would have been a distinct advantage to the Entente to engage them " elsewhere " rather than on ground close to their own country, with which they were familiar. As a matter of fact they were only too pleased to stay where they were, so as to keep their grip on Macedonia, and it was practically certain that they would never consent to fight either on the Russian or Western Front. Hence, by attacking them the Entente would be doing the very thing which the Central Powers wished to see done, for they would be expending their energies against an enemy who, if left alone, would be glad to remain inactive.

Shipping remained another difficulty. Experts calculated that the British contingent, if reinforced as suggested, would require for drafts, wounded, ammunition, and for other purposes, 250,000 tons above its existing allowance. More tonnage would also be wanted for the French and Serbians, and already the shipping available barely sufficed to supply ourselves, France, and Italy, with the food, munitions, and raw materials that were needed. French Ministers never seemed to understand that British sea-power was one of the most important factors in the war, and that the security of the seas and the financial position of the Entente might be seriously jeopardized if oversea expeditions were allowed to entail too great a dispersion of naval and maritime effort.

Finally, the General Staff had to take into account the views of the British commander, who reported that the " chances of carrying the operations to a successful conclusion are small." Later he reported that his contingent would require 11,000 transport mules to make it properly mobile, and that it ought not to be employed in the manner proposed unless first reinforced by fourteen infantry battalions and thirteen batteries of heavy and mounted artillery. Some of these units could not be provided from any source for several months to come, and others could only be found at the expense of the Western Front.

The question to be decided was not unlike that of launching the Gallipoli Expedition in 1915, and it was necessary to guard against a repetition of the mistake then committed of beginning a task without first making sure that the means required to carry it out would be forthcoming. As in that case, the advantages that would be gained, should the plan prove successful, were obvious to everybody and were not in dispute. The doubtful point was the provision of the requisite means, and in this connexion it was essential to keep in mind the trend of events on the Western Front. However feasible it might have been in 1915, there was in 1916 no possibility of suspending offensive action on that front in order to provide greater resources for use in the East. The French armies were being " bled white " at Verdun, it was said ; the French Government and nation were impatiently looking to the British armies to afford relief by undertaking extensive operations on the Somme ; and these, as General Joffre had recently suggested, must be " *de continuité et de durée prolongée*," requiring " *le renouvellement sans cesse des grands unites engagées.*"

Having regard to these considerations, the nature of the terrain, and the superior communications at the enemy's disposal for reinforcing purposes, there was no alternative but to tell the War Committee that the French proposals were unlikely to be productive of any useful results, and that, so far as the British armies were concerned, our resources, though greater than in 1915, were still unable to sustain the double effort of a long offensive in France and an ambitious campaign in the Balkans. It was, of course, essential to keep on good terms with our Ally, but it was equally essential to do what was best in the general interests of the Entente cause. That the Salonika forces should remain indefinitely idle was unfortunate, but after all it was better so than to attempt something which could lead to nothing. Short of bringing the forces away, or reducing their strength to the requirements of passive defence, the situation could never be improved. My advice therefore was that " we ought not to undertake the proposed campaign, and I must add, with full respect to the Committee, that I can take no responsibility in regard to it. I consider the project entirely unsound from every military point of view." [1]

[1] General Staff memorandum, May 16, 1916, in which the whole question was dealt with at considerable length. The fact that a thoroughly successful advance was made in September, 1918, in no

I reminded the Committee that on previous occasions they had given way on the Salonika question to no purpose, and I suggested that the time had arrived to make a stand for the policy which they believed to be right. In defiance of sound strategy, and in order to conform to French wishes, we had concentrated too far forward on the outbreak of war. We stood to fight at Mons, again to please the French, in defiance of sound tactics. At Loos, again, we fought on a difficult section of the front when we would have preferred to fight elsewhere. The present question offered the Committee an opportunity of showing that they could no longer consent to follow a course of which they disapproved, and I suggested that, if they agreed with me, they should

wise detracts, it is thought, from the accuracy of the views given in the memorandum, for the circumstances were totally different in 1918 from what they had previously been. Referring to the opening attack on September 15, 1918, Ludendorff says :—" The Bulgarian 2nd and 3rd Divisions offered no resistance ; they simply surrendered the position. No other explanation exists for the rapid advance of the Entente troops over that wild broken country, eminently suited for defence."—" My War Memories," page 712.

General Falkenhayn, too, in referring to the situation in the autumn of 1915, when pressed by his allies to extend the scope of the Balkan operations, says on page 183 of " General Head-quarters, 1914–1916, and Its Critical Decisions " :—

" If the opportunity arose incidentally to do military or moral harm to the Entente, it should, of course, not be missed. The idea, however, of seeking the decision of the war in the Balkans was wholly unsound. . . . The employment in that inhospitable region of even a single German soldier more than was necessary, or for a moment longer than was necessary, to achieve our aim (i.e. the conquest of Serbia) could only be justified by some advantage of far-reaching importance to the decision of the war."

Nothing pleased the German General Staff more than that the Entente forces should remain at Salonika, for if they had been expelled or withdrawn they would have become " available for employment in other theatres of war, while the Bulgarians would not. They were not fitted reject the proposal absolutely, since half-measures would only create fresh difficulties later on.

The War Committee took my advice, and on May 17 sent a memorandum to the French Government expressing their inability to agree with the plan put forward. The Committee recalled that General Joffre had himself at previous discussions with the British military authorities laid special stress on the adverse effect produced on French man-power by the fighting at Verdun, and the consequent need for strengthening the Western Front, and they urged that this should be done by troops taken from Salonika. Reference

for such employment, nor was their Government bound to supply them " (page 190).

The same authority, in referring to the position in the spring of 1916, says (page 258) : " From the point of view of the war as a whole, it remained more advantageous to know that between two and three hundred thousand men were being chained to that distant region (Salonika) than to drive them from the Balkan Peninsula, and thence to the French theatre of war. That any serious danger could arise to our defence on the Macedonian front was regarded as outside the bounds of possibility. The German-Bulgar positions were favoured in a quite unusual way by the nature of the country, and in accordance with the circumstances were fortified with exceptional strength. . . . An enemy offensive had no hope of success unless it were followed up in great strength. If, however, the necessary masses were thrown in, the difficulties of supply must become insuperable. In both cases there was no clear objective within reasonable reach for an enemy offensive. It could only have become effective if it were pressed as far as the interruption of the Nish-Sofia-Constantinople railway. To reach this, more than 150 miles of most difficult and pathless mountain country had to be crossed. It was out of the question that the enemy would embark on such an enterprise. As a matter of fact they did not seriously venture on it for more than two and a half years. When, in September, 1918, they at last advanced to the attack they knew quite well that no resistance would be offered. The German troops had been withdrawn from the Macedonian front and the Bulgarians had meanwhile been completely demoralized by political propaganda."

was also made to the strain which oversea expeditions were already throwing upon the mercantile marine, and to the consequent necessity for reducing the duties of that service and not adding to them. Several other reasons against the plan were mentioned, the memorandum concluding with the statement that, while desirous of co-operating to the fullest possible extent, the Committee were convinced that it was not feasible to undertake a campaign in the Balkans at a time when the Entente armies had such heavy responsibilities on the main fronts, and were also engaged in Egypt, East Africa, Caucasia, Persia, and Mesopotamia. They suggested that, as in Egypt and Mesopotamia, the general policy should be defensive in character ; that the Entente troops then at Salonika should be reduced to the number required for defence purposes ; and that the Entente should seek to re-establish their influence in the Balkans by direct attack on the Austro-German armies instead of trying to defeat those Powers indirectly by taking the offensive against the Bulgarians. The Committee deprecated even what might be termed a limited offensive, since the power of restricting it would probably get beyond control once the Greek frontier was crossed. In short, they pronounced themselves to be " definitely and unanimously opposed to any offensive operations from Salonika."

The French Government did not allow the matter to rest where the Committee had left it, and as a result of further communications between the two Foreign Offices a conference was held in London on June 9 to consider afresh what should be done. The French advanced no new arguments except that their plan had received the support of both Russian and Italian head-quarters, and consequently that the British General Staff stood alone in opposing it. This introduction of the opinions of Allied officers who had no first-hand knowledge of the situation, and bore no responsibility for the management of the campaign under discussion, led to fresh complications, and those members of the War Committee who preferred to fight anywhere rather than on the Western Front, took the view that as the British General Staff were in a minority of one their objections could no longer be upheld. I had to explain, therefore, that the case was not quite what the French represented it to be. Only a few days before General Alexeieff had asked me to send divisions from Salonika or Egypt to Alexandretta so as to assist the Russian operations in the Caucasus, which showed that he attached no special importance to the Balkans. At Italian headquarters, again, the opinion had for long been that " it would be unwise to use any troops in the Balkans which could be better employed in the main theatres of operations," while only the day before General Cadorna had sent me a message to the effect that, in supporting the French plan, he had formed his judgment on theoretical grounds only, since he was not well informed of the local situation.

The results of the conference, as summarized in a Foreign Office Note sent to the French Government, were that the British Government remained of opinion that an offensive from Salonika could not " be taken at present with any prospect of success," and that, if attempted, it would " probably lead to grave embarrassments that must be prejudical to the offensive in France, and may even be fatal to the Allied chances of success in the whole war." Unfortunately, the summary then went on to say that the British Government would not refuse at a future date to examine the question of an offensive as soon as circumstances would allow, and meanwhile they would hasten the equipment of the British contingent as much as possible.

This addition knocked the bottom out of the memorandum of May 17. According to the latter the War Committee objected to the proposed offensive on general grounds, and because they thought it to be unsound fundamentally, whereas the new decision merely deferred it and for technical reasons, and conveyed the impression that we would be willing to take part in it as soon as the troops could be suitably equipped. The Committee seemed to think that they had only expressed their readiness, in a non-committal sort of way, to review the question later on, and that matters still stood practically the same as before. As the French Government were likely to place quite a different construction on the communication, and as General Joffre would shortly wish to know when our preparations would be complete, I had to ask the Committee to say definitely which of the two policies—that of May 17 or June 9—they desired should be carried out. Unless all ambiguity were removed misunderstandings might arise in the War Office, with the Generals in the field, and also between ourselves and the French.

On the same day, June 14, as I made this report the French reply to the Foreign Office Note was received, and it showed that the communication of June 9 had been interpreted exactly as I had feared that it might be. The French Government signified their acceptance of the British suggestion to defer " for technical reasons the Salonika offensive " and noted the " double promise " that we would examine the question afresh as soon as circumstances permitted, and would meanwhile " hasten as much as possible the equipment of the English Eastern Army," so as to enable it to co-operate with the French when the offensive was eventually undertaken. They, on their part, would arrange to have their troops fully equipped and ready during the course of July. Instructions would be sent to General Sarrail informing him of the agreement reached at the recent conference, so that the offensive should only take place when the state of the troops and the material rendered it possible.

The War Committee thus saw themselves involved in a plan to which, only three weeks before, they had stated that they were " definitely and unanimously opposed," and nothing of sufficient importance had occurred in the meantime to justify going back on that opinion. A further memorandum was accordingly handed to the French Ambassador on June 21, reiterating that the British Government could not agree to make any preparations for an offensive in the Balkans which would have the effect of depriving the British armies in France of the men, munitions, or other material which they might require in the Somme operations due to commence in a fortnight's time. After these operations had taken place the Government would not refuse to reconsider the Balkan project, and such preparations for it as could be made would be put in hand, but they were not likely to be completed before November, and it was by no means certain that even then the difficulties in regard to shipping would permit of the project being carried out.

The French Government replied on June 30 that some of these statements were quite inconsistent with the decisions taken at the conference of June 9, and that if they had then been made the French Ministers and Generals would have protested against them. More-

over, since the conference events had occurred which, in
their opinion, profoundly modified the whole situation,
making it " absolutely different " from the one examined
three weeks ago. The Russians under Brussiloff were
prosecuting a vigorous campaign against the Austrians,
and had captured over 200,000 prisoners. Italy, relieved
by this blow, had repulsed the Austrian armies which
had been attacking her. The Germans were about to
be attacked on the Somme. The Bulgarians were thus
abandoned by their Austro-German allies, from whom
they could at present expect no help. Further, one of
the original objects of the Salonika Expedition had been
to neutralize the Bulgarians, so as to assist Rumania
to take the field, and in the opinion of French Ministers
the situation had never been so favourable for obtaining
Rumanian intervention. The offensive on the main
fronts would so fully absorb the activities of the Central
Powers that Rumania would be quite safe from attack,
while France would undertake to supply her, via Russia,
with what her army needed. It only remained for the
Salonika army " to take action against the Bulgarians,"
and all the principal conditions formulated by Rumania
for joining the Entente would then be fulfilled.

When giving the memorandum containing this reply
to Sir Edward Grey, M. Cambon remarked that as I was
the chief opponent of the French proposal, General
Joffre and I ought to settle the matter between us. To
this Sir Edward demurred, pointing out that while it
was quite true that I objected to the plan, it was also
opposed by the shipping authorities and Board of Trade,
and that it was these two sets of opinions that had really
determined the War Committee's views.

As on other occasions when Salonika affairs were
under consideration, French Ministers looked too much

at the good points of their case and too little at the
weak ones. No one denied that Brussiloff's operations
had wrought, at any rate temporarily, an important
change in the situation, of which every possible advantage
should be taken. But it was still an open question
whether his successes could be developed or even secured,
for they had been a complete surprise to everybody and
to no one more than to the Russians themselves. Certainly it was much too soon to assume, as the French
Government did, that the Central Powers would be unable
either to reinforce the Bulgarians or to provide a force
sufficiently powerful to attack Rumania.

Moreover, the Salonika army was no stronger and
the Bulgarians were no weaker than before. The
defences between the Greek frontier and Sofia were no
less formidable. The British contingent was still un-
equipped with suitable artillery, and the shipping position
had become not better but worse. Thus the question
still was, could we take part in aggressive operations in
the Balkans simultaneously with the prosecution of the
offensive expected from us in France? The correct
answer was not to be found by ignoring the difficulties to be surmounted, any more than it was by over-
looking the advantages which told in favour of the
project.

The General Staff remained of opinion that they could
do no more than agree to co-operate with the other
Entente contingents in detaining on the Greek frontier
as many enemy troops as possible, so as to prevent
them from being used against Rumania if and when the
latter decided to take the field. To hold out to her the
hope of being able to achieve more than this would only
lead to disappointment. For further help, and help of a
direct kind, she must look to her immediate neighbour,

Russia. The War Committee did not question these views, and on July 12 the French Government was informed that as soon as Rumania declared herself on the side of the Entente the British contingent would be directed to co-operate in the manner and to the extent just indicated. The nature and amount of British assistance were thus made quite clear to the French authorities, by whom the Entente negotiations with Rumania were mainly conducted.

While the negotiations were still proceeding I sent the following letter to the Foreign Secretary so as to make doubly sure that there should be no misunderstanding with respect to the assistance that could be given to Rumania :—

1st August, 1916.

DEAR LORD GREY,

I am as keen as anyone to get in Rumania, but for that very reason I think we must be careful in regard to promising to undertake offensive action against the Bulgars before Rumania definitely comes in. Until the Bulgars reduce their forces we have no prospect of doing any good, and if we came to grief or failed to achieve sufficient success to satisfy Rumania she might after all not come in. Briefly, I fear we may, by promising to undertake an unduly early offensive, bring about the very opposite of what we wish. Joffre, like myself, sees no hope of our breaking the Bulgarian line, and he never really intended trying to do so until a Russo-Rumanian force entered Bulgaria on the north. May I ask you to keep the above very important point in view ? No answer is expected.

Yours truly,
W. R. ROBERTSON.

P.S. Above is with reference to what was said at the War Committee this morning. As a matter of fact we shall not be ready to make a *general attack* before the last week of this month—we can hold the Bulgars but cannot do more than that.

A few days later Mr. Lloyd George (now War Minister) went to Paris, on behalf of the Government, to complete arrangements with M. Briand for bringing Rumania in, and again in order that misunderstanding should be prevented I sent with him my Director of Military Operations (Major-General Maurice) to keep before him the General Staff views as to the extent to which British military co-operation would be forthcoming. The agreement reached by the two Ministers was that the " first object of the Franco-British forces (at Salonika) will be to contain the Bulgarian forces so as to facilitate the action of the Rumanian army, without prejudice to any further objectives which may present themselves for consideration during that operation."

In further proof of the consistency of the views expressed by the British General Staff I may quote from a letter which I received from Lord Hardinge [1] on August 15, two days before the Rumanian military convention was signed :—

MY DEAR GENERAL,

After your very clear explanation at the War Committee a few days ago of the extent of offensive that our forces are prepared to take at Salonika as their immediate objective, Lord Grey and I both considered that the Rumanian text [2] " offensive affermié " expresses sufficiently clearly the intentions of our military authorities. . . . The agreement, which you quote, signed last week by Mr. Lloyd George and M. Briand, is an additional safeguard to protect our forces from having to undertake operations beyond the " material means at their disposal." . . .

As early as the middle of July it was thought in French circles that Rumania would take the decisive step at once, and that a military convention would be signed on the basis of an offensive starting from Macedonia on August 1

[1] Under-Secretary of State, Foreign Office.
[2] i.e., of the military convention.

to cover the final preparations of the Rumanian army, to be followed by a Russo-Rumanian offensive against Bulgaria on August 8. Being less sanguine as to when, if ever, Rumania would actually join the Entente, as she had already been nearly two years in making up her mind, and determined that the life of a single British soldier should not be uselessly sacrificed, I instructed the British commander at Salonika that he was not expected to commence operations until " Rumania definitely came into the field."

A hitch in the negotiations did, in fact, occur just before the date on which the operations were due to begin, and it was then arranged that they should start on August 4 instead of the 1st, the Rumanian forces to move on the 14th instead of on the 8th. On August 3 the convention was still unsigned and French G.H.Q. were accordingly obliged to change General Sarrail's instructions from " attacking " to " harassing " the enemy, and to defer fixing the date of commencing even this modified form of action until the situation became clearer. The convention was at last signed on August 17, Rumania engaging to take the field against Austria-Hungary not later than August 28, but without being in any way bound to declare war against Germany, Bulgaria, or Turkey, though she undertook to sever diplomatic relations with them. . Apparently she thought that this limitation of her commitments would be feasible, and on August 27 she declared war on Austria-Hungary alone. The next day Germany declared war against her, and Bulgaria followed suit on September 1.

While these delays were occurring the military situation underwent a further change, making it quite different from what it had been in the month of June when the question of Rumania's intervention first began to assume a definite shape. The Austrian collapse had been checked ; the British attack on the Somme had been delivered without achieving any decisive rupture of the German front ; and Hindenburg, always in favour of striking on the Eastern in preference to the Western Front, had replaced Falkenhayn in the High Command. Rumania's alliance with the Entente at this juncture rendered it practically certain that she would be singled out for attack, and the British General Staff calculated that at least fifty-six enemy divisions could be assembled for that purpose. The attack, if successful, would be an encouraging compensation for the German people for the failure at Verdun ; it would remove the new menace to Hungary ; assure the continued support of Bulgaria ; keep open communication between Central Europe and Constantinople ; and place the enemy on the flank of the Russian army, possibly compelling the latter to evacuate Galicia. In short, the Entente task now was not to assist Rumania in order that she might the better attack Austria or Bulgaria, but to help her to ward off the attack with which, as a consequence of her own indecision, she herself was threatened.

In bringing these facts to the notice of the War Committee on September 9, I observed that there were only two ways of meeting the situation which need be considered. One, to concentrate sufficient troops in the Balkans effectively to oppose the enemy in that theatre, and the other to threaten the security of his lines on the main fronts to such an extent as would prevent him from successfully carrying out his Balkan plan. The first method was not practicable, as had already been explained many times, and even if it were it would have meant the abandonment of our own plan of campaign in France. The second method must therefore be followed, and with the approval of the War Committee it was put into execution. The British and French High Commands, acting in agreement, arranged that the Somme offensive should be continued with energy ; General Sarrail was instructed to exert the full powers of his force so as to prevent the diversion of Bulgarian troops from Macedonia ; Russia was asked to increase the amount of her assistance to Rumania, and General Alexeieff promised to provide, if possible, six divisions additional to the four already sent.

Operations on the Salonika front commenced in the middle of September and were continued at intervals until early in December. They fulfilled their object of preventing Bulgarian troops from being withdrawn for use in the north, and a certain amount of Serbian territory, including Monastir, was reconquered. On the Western and Italian fronts the enemy forces were also effectively held, the general result being that those employed in the Rumanian campaign were always numerically inferior to the forces of Rumania and Russia combined.

General Sarrail was criticized for not achieving more than he did, and it must be admitted that the operations were not as effective as the resources at his disposal rendered possible. Amongst the reasons for this was the lack of co-operation between the Allied contingents, which in its turn was largely due to the failure of General Head-quarters properly to co-ordinate the actions of the different bodies. There was also friction between General Sarrail and some of the Allied commanders, and this became so acute that it had to be inquired into by the French Minister of War who visited Salonika for the purpose. On the other hand, it must be remembered that some of the contingents were indifferently trained and equipped, and there were several difficulties of a special kind by which General Sarrail was greatly hampered. First, for some weeks before the convention was signed, the indecision of Rumania and the persistent endeavours of France to bring her into the war led to his receiving many perplexing orders and counter-orders, entailing constant changes in his plans with all the complications which invariably attend alterations of this kind. Secondly, affairs in Greece were in such a state of chaos and uncertainty that Sarrail never knew from hour to hour what might happen next, or what policy the Entente Governments might adopt for dealing with the situation. His actions can only be properly understood by bearing these awkward features in mind.

As measures for assisting Rumania were arranged almost entirely between French and Russian head-quarters and not by the British General Staff, I cannot say whether she misunderstood in any way what the Entente armies could and would do on her behalf. But subject to this, her misfortunes may be attributed to her own mistakes rather than to want of foresight and lack of support on the part of her Allies. Had she intervened in the month of June, as she was advised to do, when the Austrian armies were in full retreat before Brussiloff, and the Somme offensive was about to begin, she would have been in little danger of attack and the Austrian defeat might have been turned into disaster. But instead of seizing the favourable opportunity offered she lost it by continuing to haggle about the territory she was to receive as the price of her intervention, and when at last she decided on war the German High Command had got the situation elsewhere well in hand and were in a position to assemble a considerable force with which to attack her.

Moreover, her strategical dispositions at the outset of

the campaign were faulty. As early as the first week of September I telegraphed to the British Military Attaché at Bucharest calling attention to them, in the hope that he might have a chance of suggesting their reconsideration. So far as our information showed they seemed to invite defeat. Rumanian head-quarters apparently based their plan of campaign on the supposition that Bulgaria would not fight, a belief into which they were tricked by King Ferdinand, and that they would be free to concentrate the bulk of their troops for the conquest of Transylvania, where they expected to encounter no serious resistance. Having discovered their error, they proceeded from one change of plan to another, but still adhered to their original intention of invading Transylvania by all the routes leading into that country. The result was that their forces were dispersed over a front of some 650 miles, and, as usually happens in such cases, they were beaten one after another.

The above account of what took place shows that the Entente authorities did not, as was alleged at the time, force Rumania into the war without making arrangement to support her, and that they were not taken by surprise when she was attacked. There was little doubt, from July onwards, as to the danger in which she stood should an attack be made upon her. The difficulty was to know how to assist her in meeting it, and, as in the case of Serbia a year before, direct assistance could not possibly be given either by the French or ourselves—a statement that was made over and over again by the British General Staff during the negotiations. Only Russia could render this assistance, and she was confronted with many difficulties of her own, while the value of her help was further reduced owing to constant disagreement between the Russian and Rumanian staffs.[1] It must unfortunately be said, too, that Rumania was badly, if not treacherously, treated with respect to consignments of ammunition sent to her from Western Europe, which were deliberately side-tracked on Russian railways and there delayed by orders, civilian not military, from Petrograd.

It remains to be added that on September 4 Mr. Lloyd George (War Minister) wrote to Mr. Asquith a letter about the probability of Rumania being attacked, ending it thus :—

I therefore once more urge that the General Staff should carefully consider what action we could, in conjunction with France and Italy, take immediately to relieve the pressure on Rumania if a formidable attack is developed against her. There may be nothing in my fears, but no harm could be done by being prepared for contingencies.

I do not remember having any knowledge of this letter until it was published after the war in the *Atlantic Monthly*, nor do I understand why it was written. It implies that the question of assisting Rumania had been neglected, whereas it had been, as just described, under constant consideration for months past ; specific arrangements for giving assistance had been made ; and Mr. Lloyd George had been informed long before September 4 that we could do no more to help Rumania, as he had also been informed of the perilous position in which she had placed herself.

At the time when Rumania was being thrown back from Transylvania, General Joffre telegraphed to me that,

[1] General Alexeieff was a very easy colleague to work with as a rule, but in regard to Rumanian affairs he was apt to become a little impatient, and not without reason. He thought that politics played too prominent a part in them, both in Rumania itself and in Western Europe, and he once said in a message to me that the " diplomatists should cease interfering with military questions until the enemy is beaten. Then they may discuss politics."

with the object of affording her greater relief, the Salonika forces should be ordered to push forward into Bulgaria, and be no longer restricted to the mission of containing the enemy in their immediate front. When telling the War Committee of this on the following day, October 9, I again repeated that the only feasible method of giving help was by continuing the offensive in France, and, as far as remaining means would permit, in Macedonia also. Mr. Lloyd George did not agree. He contended that we ought to ask France and Italy to join with us in sending to Salonika a reinforcement of eight divisions and then advance on Sofia, quite ignoring the fact that some three months must elapse before the divisions could be got into the country and made ready to go on. For the moment, and at my request, no decision was taken.

As Mr. Lloyd George had on several previous occasions endeavoured to commit us more deeply in the Balkans than either the War Committee or the General Staff wished to go, I felt obliged to suggest to him, after the Committee meeting was over, that if he, the War Minister, opposed military plans submitted by me for the Committee's approval, and recommended the adoption of other plans in their stead, the conduct of the operations would become very difficult and confused, and must suffer accordingly. I added that if the Committee accepted his Balkan proposals the General Staff would have forced upon them a plan which they had frequently condemned as unsound, and therefore I should decline to be responsible for its execution.

Mr. Lloyd George replied that, as a Cabinet Minister, he had the right to put forward any plans, military or other, which he thought deserving of consideration, and that this implied no want of confidence in the General Staff, with whom he was anxious to work in close accord.

I cannot pretend to have been satisfied with this statement, for in effect it amounted to a claim on the part of a civilian Minister not only to disapprove of military plans prepared by military officials—which he had a perfect right to do—but to substitute plans of his own in their stead—which he was neither entitled nor competent to do. There were, however, many other questions demanding attention at the moment, and the matter was allowed to drop.

Before replying definitely to General Joffre's telegram I asked him to say how many additional divisions he estimated would be necessary in order to carry out the new mission which he had suggested. His answer was that the Salonika force ought to be instructed to co-operate " with the Russians in the decisive defeat of the Bulgarians," and that they should be reinforced or they would not be able to sustain their present efforts, and still less to increase them. If this were not done the enemy could withdraw troops for use against Rumania, the consequences of which might be serious. On the other hand, if two English and two Italian divisions were sent out, important results might be achieved. These arguments were not very impressive.

General Milne, the British commander, reported to me that not less than seven additional divisions would be needed to secure even a limited success, and that more would be required if anything of a decisive nature was to be accomplished. The British General Staff were of much the same opinion, and as no divisions could be spared from any of the other fronts, and the Italians were not able to produce more than one brigade, there was nothing to be done except to continue the pressure on approximately the same scale as before.

At the time the respective strengths of the contingents were as under:—

British	.	.	.	.	90,000
French	.	.	.	.	89,000
Serbian	.	.	.	.	85,000
Russian	.	.	.	.	19,000
Italian	.	.	.	.	14,000
Total	.	.	.	.	297,000

To ensure that the British contingent should take its full share of the operations I had already given orders for it to be reinforced by a yeomanry brigade and the equivalent of an infantry brigade from Egypt, by 23,000 drafts (of whom at least 10,000 had already arrived) from home, and had promised such additional heavy artillery as could be used. The majority of the War Committee would gladly have agreed with the General Staff not to send any further troops, but great pressure was put upon them by the French and Russian Governments, the Tsar, and the President of the French Republic, and after balancing the military and political pros and cons they decided to dispatch one additional division. This, with the reinforcements already ordered, amounted to much the same as the two divisions requested by General Joffre. Before finally deciding Ministers asked for my views, and I agreed that, having regard to the strong representations made to them, they could do no other than send the division, although it could not possibly serve any useful purpose beyond the sentimental one of showing our desire to help an ally in difficulty.

With the hostile occupation of Wallachia and the retreat of the Rumanians into Moldavia the operations of the Salonika army, considered as a relief offensive on Rumania's behalf, came to an end, and early in December

General Sarrail was instructed to revert to a defensive rôle, holding as much of the regained territory as possible. For the next few months proceedings within his command were governed more by the situation in Greece than by any action on the part of the enemy.

From the day that the Entente troops first began to disembark at Salonika the attitude of King Constantine and his pro-German adherents had been a perpetual source of annoyance and embarrassment, and during the summer of 1916 it became more tiresome than ever. On May 23 the Greek Government was told by the German Minister at Athens that Fort Rupel, an important place in the passes entering Eastern Macedonia, would shortly be occupied as a defensive measure, and two days later it was surrendered by the garrison to German and Bulgarian troops. This unfriendly act compelled the Entente Powers to take precautionary steps, for with mobilized Greek forces in being who might at any moment commence acts of hostility, the position at Salonika had become intolerable. An economic blockade of the Greek coast was instituted, and on June 21 the Entente Ministers presented a Note demanding the immediate demobilization of the Greek army, the formation of a new Ministry which should give guarantees for benevolent neutrality, and the dismissal of certain police officials who were believed to be connected with German propaganda. M. Zaimis again took office, on the basis of friendly neutrality, and demobilization was begun, but the demobilized men were organized into leagues of reservists pledged to further the King's pro-German policy.

In July and August the Bulgarians advanced into and occupied almost the whole of Eastern Macedonia, including the port of Kavalla, the garrison of which, amounting to 8,000 men, surrendered without firing a shot. Part of it was carried off to Germany as " guests " of the German Government, and the remainder made its way to Salonika to join the forces of the Entente ! The loss of so large a slice of Greek territory, and the refusal of the king to ally Greece with the Entente, played into the hands of the extreme elements of the Venizelists, and at the end of August a revolutionary movement was started at Salonika for the purpose of reinforcing the Entente with such troops as could be assembled to help in expelling the Bulgarians from Greek soil. General Sarrail had to interfere to prevent bloodshed, and the Greek troops quartered at Salonika either joined the movement or allowed themselves to be disarmed.

Finally, on September 24, M. Venizelos left Athens for Crete to head the revolutionary movement already in progress there. He organized a Provisional Government which took on all the functions of a sovereign administration in alliance with the Entente, raised a Greek " Army of National Defence," and a month later declared war against Germany and Bulgaria. From this time onwards Greece was practically divided into two hostile nations— one, pro-German, led by the king ; and one, pro-Entente, headed by M. Venizelos.

After the Venizelist *coup* at the end of August considerable bodies of Greek troops (royalists) assembled in Thessaly on General Sarrail's left rear, and the anxieties of which they were the cause during the operations already described materially restricted the free use of such reserves as he possessed. It was calculated that these troops might reach a total of some 80,000 men, and although they were not of great fighting value by themselves they might nevertheless prove troublesome should the enemy, having finished his task in Rumania, decide to employ his surplus divisions in Macedonia. This was not very probable because the brunt of the campaign in Wallachia had fallen on the Germans, whose casualties had been considerable, and the Eastern Front now to be held had, by Rumania's intervention, been lengthened by about 250 miles. Moreover, Germany's obligations on the main fronts seemed sufficient to prohibit another campaign in the Balkans. (She had, in fact, already begun to take steps for retiring to the [shorter] Hindenburg Line, though we did not know it at the time.)

The contingency of a hostile advance into Macedonia from the north could not, however, be entirely ignored, especially as the Greek royalists were daily becoming more arrogant as a result of Rumania's defeat. Matters were brought to a climax in the first week of December, when the demand for the delivery of certain war material to the Entente representatives at Athens produced an *émeute* in which the royalists and Entente troops came into collision, the Allied Legations were insulted, and many of the principal adherents of Venizelos were murdered.

The situation had now become quite impossible, and on December 7 the Entente announced a strict blockade of the Greek coasts, while on December 14 an ultimatum was delivered demanding the withdrawal of the entire Greek force from Thessaly and the transfer of a large proportion of the Greek army to the Peloponnesus. The ultimatum was accepted, but the Greek Government continued to quibble about its terms, and on December 30 a second Entente Note was delivered containing additional demands. This Note brought forth further evasive replies, and for all practical purposes matters continued as unsatisfactory as before. The king was in constant correspondence with Berlin, and still hoped that an offensive by the Central Powers would solve the problem for him by driving the Entente forces out of Salonika and into the sea.

Meanwhile the British and French General Staffs had been engaged in considering what further military measures were required. The French idea now was that General Sarrail should be reinforced by two British, two French, and three and a half Italian divisions, thus bringing up his strength to twenty-nine divisions in all. This seemed to be quite unnecessary, for even if an actual rupture took place the number of troops which Greece could put into the field would not seriously endanger the Entente position unless combined with an offensive from the north. Of this there was no sign, and even if it should materialize the Entente forces then at and under orders for Salonika would be capable of holding their own provided they were properly commanded and timely measures were taken to place them on a defensive front suitable to their strength. I therefore suggested to the French authorities that instead of employing more divisions a defensive line in rear of the present one should be selected and prepared ready for occupation, but that it need not be taken up nor any of the recently won ground, including Monastir, need be abandoned until the necessity for that step arose. The matter of immediate urgency was to draw the Greek teeth before the Central Powers could deliver their attack—assuming that they had any such intention—and it was fairly certain that the blockade, and the severance of her communications with the outside world, would bring Greece to her knees before the attack could be launched.

It occurred to me, too, that in proposing the dispatch of reinforcements French G.H.Q. were, as for some time past, unduly influenced by the desire to meet the wishes of their Government, with whom their relations were not too good. A few days later General Joffre was, in fact, superseded by General Nivelle, other changes in the staff were made, and the control of the Salonika campaign was taken away from G.H.Q. and once again vested in the War Ministry in Paris.

It was at this period, too, that Mr. Lloyd George took the place of Mr. Asquith as Prime Minister. The new War Cabinet endorsed the action proposed by the British General Staff, but the French Government did not, and in the last week of December two of its members, MM. Ribot and Thomas, came to London to urge that the reinforcements above-mentioned should be sent. French Ministers seemed convinced that General Sarrail would be attacked, and, unless reinforced, would be defeated ; that Monastir would fall, and the Serbians thereby be induced to make a separate peace. Further, these results would, it was feared, almost certainly involve the downfall of the French Ministry.

After a discussion lasting for three days the proposal to send reinforcements was given up, and it was formally agreed, in accordance with the advice of the British General Staff, that :—

" The Allies should continue to hold Monastir on the line at present occupied as long as this can be done without exposing the force to defeat. Meanwhile a shorter line should be prepared for occupation in case of need, which would enable the force to hold its own against any attack which may be made."

The French Government was not really satisfied with this policy, and within a week of its approval the question was again brought forward, this time at the conference held at Rome, to which Generals Sarrail and

Milne were summoned. Here the French case was presented by M. Briand with his customary eloquence, and as British Ministers had on previous occasions yielded to his persuasive powers though not approving of his views, I became anxious lest the same thing should happen again. One evening, while the matter was still unsettled, I wrote informally to Mr. Lloyd George expressing the hope that he would stand firmly by the London agreement, and he replied that he had every intention of doing so. Thanks to him, the extra divisions were not sent, and it was further decided that the operations should for the present be governed by a waiting policy—a sort of compromise between the French proposal to employ more troops, and the British desire to bring away all not needed for purely defensive purposes.

With regard to Greece, it was agreed to send her another and final ultimatum before proceeding to extreme measures. King Constantine was slow to perceive that he had exhausted the Entente patience, and that, as Germany had her hands too full in other theatres to admit of beginning a new campaign in the Balkans, he had no choice but to submit to such terms as the Entente might impose. Before the month of January expired the transfer of his troops to the Peloponnesus began, the Government made their formal apology to the Entente Ministers, the Entente flags were solemnly saluted by representative detachments of Greek soldiers and sailors, and the other demands made were fulfilled. For the moment the Greek situation was adjusted.

The Rome policy was reviewed at the historic Calais conference [1] held on February 26, as it was desirable that the armies on all fronts should be as active as possible while the projected operations in Champagne and Artois

[1] Described in Chapter XII.

under General Nivelle were in progress. It was decided, however, that the Salonika army could not go beyond its present mission and the conclusion recorded was to the following effect :—

As the co-operation of the Russo-Rumanian forces against Bulgaria is not yet possible, the Conference agrees to confirm the decision of the Rome Conference, and decides that for the present the decisive defeat of the Bulgarian army is not a practical objective, and that the mission of the Allied forces at Salonika is to keep on their front the enemy forces now there and to take advantage of striking the enemy if opportunity offers.

Another decision taken at the Rome conference was to strengthen General Sarrail's position as Allied Commander-in-Chief. It was laid down that the arrangement "should be based on the principles which governed the relations between the British Commander-in-Chief and the Commander of the French forces in the Gallipoli Expedition, that is to say, the Commander of each of the Allied Forces shall comply with the orders of the Commander-in-Chief as regards military operations subject to the right of direct communication with and reference to his own Government." The suggestion that had rather frequently been made before the conference to supersede General Sarrail thus terminated for the time being.

There was, as there always is when allied armies are operating in the same theatre, much to be said in favour of unifying the chief command, but there was also something to be said against it—more than Ministers at first realized. The disadvantages were particularly pronounced in the case of Salonika, for General Sarrail did not take the other commanders into his confidence to the extent usually practised in similar circumstances, and therefore the General Staff in London had no means of learning what his intentions were. The result was that the best arrangements could not be made by the War Office for carrying out the British share of his plans, and, secondly, members of the War Cabinet, who expected to be kept fully informed of all operations, past, present, and future, were constantly asking for information which could not be supplied. I could only tell them that there was none to give, and when, at the end of March, they found that their authority at Salonika was of no account, and complained to me of the " discreditable inactivity " which prevailed there, I reminded them that as the supreme command had been entrusted to General Sarrail the responsibility for the operations rested with him and not with the British commander or the British General Staff—both of whom were powerless in the matter.[1]

It was, of course, to be regretted that at a time when shipping was so valuable and men so short that France and ourselves should each have some 200,000 troops tied up in a distant theatre doing nothing. But that unsatisfactory feature had been characteristic of the Expedition from its inception, and the blame for it could not be attributed to General Sarrail or to any other local commander. The two Governments would agree neither to the troops being brought away nor to their being reduced to the requirements of passive defence—the only remedies of any use—and therefore the inactivity complained of had to continue.

The impotent position in which British Ministers found themselves was the more irritating because they were not at one with the French Government as to the best way of dealing with King Constantine. Unity of military command will always be more embarrassing than helpful if unattended by unity of policy, and this is what happened

[1] General Staff memorandum, April 2, 1917.

in the case of Greece. The French were continually pressing for drastic action and the invasion of Thessaly ; Sarrail was always eager to recommend that course, and seemed to devote at least as much attention to Greek politics as to the defeat of the Bulgarians on his front ; while the British and Italian Governments did not wish to resort to extreme measures unless they were obliged to do so. The Entente Powers were also at variance in their estimate of Venizelos. France supported him ; Britain admired him ; and Italy suspected him, as pursuing aims which might be detrimental to Italian ambitions.

The resulting moderate policy pursued in the handling of the Greek problem was criticized at the time as lacking in firmness, and therefore it is only right to say that the British General Staff were in favour of it and said so. In their opinion the more high-handed course advocated was unwise, since it was essential that we should not embroil ourselves in complicated matters unconnected with the main object in view, and therefore should not for choice enter upon a new campaign in Thessaly in addition to the one in which we were already engaged in Macedonia. It had to be remembered, too, that internal disturbances might be even more troublesome than a Greek declaration of war. Our diplomatic and military representatives on the spot were unanimous in reporting that the hostile invasion of Greek territory by Entente forces and the deposition of the king would inevitably lead to civil war, and thereby necessitate the occupation and subjugation of the whole country.

Following the cessation of operations in December, 1916, the situation on the battle-front remained unchanged until, in pursuance of the policy laid down at Calais at the end of February, 1917, General Sarrail made preparations for a general attack on the enemy's position in April. What he hoped to achieve I am unable to say, as the British General Staff were not told. The plan was that the French, Russian, Italian, and Serbian contingents should carry out the main attack east of Monastir, commencing on April 26, this to be preceded by a British attack on the 24th. The latter was intended to " contain " as many Bulgarian troops as possible, and thus prevent them from being used to reinforce the front east of Monastir. After the British attack had been launched General Milne discovered to his surprise that the French and Serbians were not yet ready, partly on account of the bad weather but mainly because insufficient time had been allowed for preparation. The attack was therefore a waste of effort and life.

On May 8 the British attacked a second time, the other contingents making the main attack on the following day. The measures taken by G.H.Q. for co-ordination were again inadequate ; friction occurred between the armies, some of whom accused others of failing to support them ; and by May 23 General Sarrail had no choice but to order the operations to be suspended and revert once more to the defensive. As in previous offensives, there was never the least prospect of achieving anything in the nature of a decisive success, for in addition to the defects just mentioned the forces possessed neither the resolution, cohesion, nor the numerical superiority required to dislodge the enemy from the naturally strong and well-entrenched positions in which he was established. So evident was this that before the operations commenced the British General Staff again pointed out to the War Cabinet the uselessness of attempting anything beyond a defensive rôle, and they repeated their recommendation that the strength of the British contingent should be reduced to that basis. The recommendation was not accepted.

For a variety of uncontrollable reasons, stationary forces have a habit of increasing the number of mouths to be fed out of all proportion to the number of men employed in the front line, and the Salonika armies were no exception to this. At the time their approximate ration strength was :—

British	.	.	.	240,000
French	.	.	.	210,000
Serbian	.	.	.	130,000
Italian	.	.	.	50,000
Russian	.	.	.	17,000
Venizelist	.	.	.	23,000
Total	.	.	.	670,000

Besides the futility of retaining these vast numbers for unprofitable offensives, the shipping position was becoming increasingly serious. It was not a matter merely of providing the tonnage required for the maintenance of the troops, but also of detailing naval escorts which were badly needed for use in Home waters and the Mediterranean, where the losses from the enemy submarines were becoming very heavy. The climate, too, was making serious inroads into our man-power resources. During the summer of 1916 no fewer than 90,000 men had been incapacitated by sickness, and of these 37,000 had to be sent out of the country.

The whole situation was re-examined at an Allied conference held at Paris early in May, after the failure of General Nivelle's operations in Champagne. The French and British naval staffs then agreed in stating that by the end of the year the Salonika forces would be in danger of starvation from want of ships unless a beginning was at once made to reduce them ; while the combined military staffs reported that no military object would be served by retaining the Expedition if it had to be reduced. (This was as far as the French General Staff would go with their British colleagues. It would have been equally true to say that no military object would be served if the Expedition were *not* reduced.) Moreover, in the not unlikely event of Russia falling entirely out of the war, we would, sooner or later, be compelled to cut down the forces in all secondary theatres, and therefore we might as well begin at once with Macedonia.

These opinions, although emphasized by the impaired morale of the French armies which had resulted from the disastrous operations in Champagne, seemed to fall on deaf ears so far as French Ministers were concerned. They were intent upon nourishing their own political aspirations in Greece, and therefore were opposed to any reduction of the Salonika forces. Their thrusting policy eventually led, in the month of June, to the dethronement of the king and the formation of a Venizelist Government, but this settlement of the Greek problem, welcome though it was, had little or no influence on prospective operations against Bulgaria. Recent events on the Western and Eastern fronts were much too strong for that, and were fast producing an effect on the general military position which could not be disregarded. The French Government felt obliged by the losses in Champagne to make it a definite policy to economize their dwindling man-power by avoiding battle ; the Italian Government began to press for the withdrawal of some of their troops for employment in Albania ; while the British General Staff renewed their efforts of the same kind.

Even the British Prime Minister, one of the earliest

and most persistent advocates of Balkan enterprises, now began to realize that no benefit, political or other, could be derived from them, and he accordingly ceased to take interest in them. But he was not prepared to use his influence in the Allied councils for the purpose of bringing divisions away if they were afterwards to be sent to the Western Front. His alternative to the threadbare Balkan project was an All-British campaign for the conquest of Palestine, and he told me quite frankly that if he consented to help the General Staff to extricate divisions from Salonika, he expected the General Staff to use the troops thus set free in furtherance of his Palestine plan. He seemed to regard this proposal as a perfectly fair and proper bargain, but, of course, it was a question not of bargaining but of doing the right thing. The right thing was to keep on strengthening the Western Front in proportion as the Russian defection became more pronounced.

As divisions were apparently not to be got away except on Mr. Lloyd George's terms, the General Staff could only acquiesce in their going to Palestine, where they would at any rate enjoy a better climate and be under British control. One division left in July and a second in September, these being the only reductions worth mentioning that I was able to effect during the remainder of my appointment as C.I.G.S. The French, on their side, were obliged by a general shortage of men to allow their divisions to run down so low that by the end of the year their strength was only 185,000 as against 175,000 British, although they had eight divisions in the country while we had but four.

In December, 1917, General Sarrail was relieved of his command by the new Clemenceau Ministry, General

Guillaumant being appointed Generalissimo in his stead. As C.I.G.S. I had been more than once unable to agree with General Sarrail's actions, and had complained to the War Cabinet of the unsatisfactory manner in which he supervised the operations. Hence it is only fair to add here that the complicated situation in Greece, the mixture of nationalities in his command, and the vacillating policy on which his plans had to be based, combined to make his task one of the most difficult that any commander has ever been called upon to perform.

Subsequent to the offensive which came to an end in May no further operations of much account were attempted during General Sarrail's tenure of office. This was owing partly to the reductions made in the strength of the forces to which reference has just been made, but chiefly to the fact that the heavy fighting in Flanders and Italy during the late summer and autumn, the complete collapse of Russia, and the entry of America into the war, combined to fix the final military trial of strength more and more in the Western theatre. Neither side was now disposed, or could afford, to press matters too closely in the Balkans, and before the end of the year the whole Macedonian front once more relapsed into a state of stagnation.

In the spring of 1918 about 25 per cent. of the British infantry and other reinforcements had to be taken away to fill up the gaps caused by the heavy fighting in France. Thenceforward, and for the first time since Mr. Lloyd George became Prime Minister, all efforts were concentrated on the object of prime importance—the defeat of the German main armies. Nothing more was attempted in Macedonia until the German resistance began to break down on the Western Front. Then, on September 14, 1918, was launched the attack which led with unexpected rapidity to the defeat of the Bulgarian armies. By the 21st the attack had become a pursuit ; on the 26th a Bulgarian staff officer arrived under a flag of truce at British head-quarters to ask for a suspension of hostilities ; and on the 29th Bulgarian delegates accepted the Allied terms.[1]

The British contingent and other Allied troops, all under the command of General Milne, were afterwards sent to operate against the Turkish forces in Europe and, on October 30, had just reached the environs of Adrianople when the general armistice with Turkey was signed at Mudros. In this way the Salonika Expedition came to an end.

The total number of British troops employed amounted to 414,207, the casualties in action being 26,750. The casualties due to sickness were exceedingly heavy, the admissions to hospital on account of malaria alone amounting to 160,381, of which 693 proved fatal. It is gratifying to be able to say that although the bad climate, the infrequency of leave, the deadly monotony of uncomfortable surroundings, and the consciousness that their labours would be unrewarded by any real

[1] At a meeting of the German Cabinet on October 3, German G.H.Q. are said to have represented that there was no possibility " of winning peace from our enemies by force of arms," owing to " the collapse of the Macedonia front, and of the weakening of our reserves in the West which this has necessitated." This was a very natural excuse for the authorities responsible for the conduct of the operations to make, and can only be regarded as such, for the collapse in Macedonia was expected by them long before that front was attacked, and as a result of what was taking place in the West. Referring to the course of events there in July and August, General Ludendorff has said : " The impression made on our allies by the failure on the Western Front was great. . . . Nothing was to be expected from Bulgaria. . . . It was quite obvious that Bulgaria was intent on peace."—" My War Memories, 1914–1918," pages 625 and 729.

success, all left their mark on the health and spirits of the troops, discipline at least remained sound and unimpaired. Opinions will probably always differ as to the incidence of responsibility for the lamentable waste of effort and health incurred, but everybody will agree that no praise can be too high for the resolute manner in which officers and men stuck to their thankless task during their three long years' employment in a "side-show" for which, as an effective means of bringing about the final overthrow of the enemy, few people had a good word to say. Commencing with the belated attempt to succour Serbia in October, 1915, the Expedition accomplished nothing really useful in a military sense, and it deprived the Allied armies in France of reinforcements which, had they been present, might have helped to turn partial success into decisive victory long before November, 1918.

CHAPTER XI

THE CAMPAIGN IN PALESTINE

Operations on Suez Canal, 1915—Considerations affecting the Defence
of Egypt—Proposals by Joint Naval and Military Staffs, October,
1915—Reorganization of Forces returned from Gallipoli and
their Dispatch to France—Troops remaining in Egypt for
Defence Purposes—Principle upon which Defensive Arrangements were based—Sinai Peninsula crossed, December, 1916—
Ministerial Proposals for sending an Expedition to Rabegh—
Difficulties experienced by General Staff in preventing the
Expedition—Mr. Lloyd George's wish to embark on Conquest
of Palestine—Objections to that Policy—The Policy postponed
until following Summer—First Battle of Gaza—Second Battle
of Gaza—Reversion to Defensive Policy—Murray succeeded
by Allenby—Prime Minister continues to press for Offensive
Policy—General Staff recommend Defensive Policy, which is
adopted—Instructions to Allenby—War Cabinet Project for
landing in Syria—General Foch's Plan for this Operation—
Mr. Lloyd George again urges General Staff to undertake an
Offensive Campaign in Palestine—They advise against it, owing to
serious Position developing on Western Front—Allenby's Advance
on and Occupation of Jerusalem—Renewed Demand to extend
Scope of Operations—General Staff again oppose it.

UNLIKE some of the other Eastern campaigns in
which British troops were employed during 1914–
18, the operations directed against the Turkish forces
based on Palestine were, in their early stages, both
appropriate and profitable, in that they helped to secure
an important link in the Imperial communications—the
Suez Canal. Later, they became objectionable, for they
absorbed troops which should have been sent to the

Western Front, where every available man was needed to assist in the great struggle then approaching its decisive phase.

Instigated by Germany, Turkey collected a medley of troops and Bedouins for threatening the Suez Canal soon after she entered the war. These forces, numbering between 12,000 and 15,000 men in all, laboriously wended their way across the Sinai Peninsula, some by El Arish in the north and others by Akaba in the south, and reached the vicinity of the canal in January, 1915. On February 3, after some aimless skirmishing, they made half-hearted attempts to establish a footing near Ismailia and at other places, which never had the least chance of succeeding and were easily beaten off. On the morning of February 4 the main body had disappeared, and in three or four days the whole were in full retreat back to the Palestine border whence they had come.

Subsequent to this fiasco hostile parties continued to hover about the Peninsula, occasionally endeavouring to damage the Canal and the shipping using it, but nothing of any consequence occurred until the autumn of 1915, when the alliance of Bulgaria and the conquest of Serbia gave the Central Powers direct access to Constantinople. This event enabled the enemy to menace Egypt and the Canal more effectively than before and so made more easy of attainment the object he had in view, namely, to draw British forces away from the main theatre of war. He was not, however, in a position to cause us any immediate anxiety and, while it was only to be expected that he should desire to entangle us in operations against non-German troops, it was equally a matter of common sense that we should not play into his hands.

Some difference of opinion at first prevailed as to the most suitable method of defence to be employed. Lord

Kitchener, as already explained, was in favour of indirect defence, his idea being that we should operate from Alexandretta, making use of the troops to be withdrawn from Gallipoli. A plan of this kind had already been examined by the Admiralty and War Office Staffs, who made out so strong a case against it that it was rejected. A landing farther to the south was also suggested, and as to this the view of the Admiralty Staff was that the naval

conditions are adverse to military operations on any scale larger than that involved in mere raids. There is no anchorage along the Syrian coast like Ayas Bay, where transports and warships can be secure both from bad weather and hostile submarines. . . . Under favourable conditions, military landings might no doubt succeed at various points . . . but the winter is coming on, and any one of these disembarkation operations might be interrupted at any moment. . . . The Admiralty War Staff consider that it would be very unwise to repeat the experience we have undergone, and are now suffering from (i.e. at Gallipoli) of trying to keep an army supplied with stores, and to undertake embarkations and landings of troops on a beach or at a port which can be shelled by the enemy from surrounding heights, and is open to submarine attack.[1]

The combined staffs therefore came to the conclusion that Egypt must be defended by direct and not indirect methods, and there can be no question that the conclusion was sound. No hostile force of the composition and efficiency required to constitute a serious menace could possibly reach the Canal except as the result of long and careful preparation, and therefore we could count upon having ample time in which to make dispositions for dealing with it. There was, moreover, no difficulty with respect to the provision of troops, for there were already far more in Egypt than were wanted. The

[1] Memorandum dated October 19, 1915.

pressing need was to organize, equip, and train them ; to transfer to other theatres those for whom no useful employment existed ; and to make the plan of defence much more active in character than it had hitherto been.

At the end of 1915 Egypt was the base of all operations in the Mediterranean, and there were in it, or would be when the troops in process of being withdrawn from Gallipoli had all arrived, twelve infantry divisions, three mounted divisions, two infantry and three dismounted yeomanry brigades, besides large reinforcements in the shape of partially trained personnel from Australia and New Zealand and other partially trained drafts for Salonika, the whole constituting an unwieldy mass of well over 300,000 men. The task of sorting out and refitting this chaotic jumble of units and personnel devolved upon Sir Archibald Murray, who had recently been sent to Egypt to command a portion of the troops in that country, Sir John Maxwell being in command of the remainder. This dual arrangement proving to be quite unworkable, Sir John Maxwell was brought home and Sir Archibald Murray took over command of all the troops.

By July, 1916, he had reorganized, re-equipped, and shipped off to other theatres, mainly France, nine divisions, three independent infantry brigades, nine batteries of heavy artillery, other combatant and administrative units, aggregating about 240,000 men. This fine achievement went far to rectify the faulty dispositions previously existing, and it greatly helped to frustrate the enemy's desire to see British troops locked up in the East when they ought to be in the West.

The force remaining available for the defence of the Eastern Front consisted of four territorial divisions, two independent brigades, and some garrison battalions (about 60,000 rifles in all), in addition to one mounted division and one brigade of yeomanry. The original plan of defence contemplated the establishment of a series of defensive positions along the whole front of the Canal, and the provision of certain mobile formations for use in advance of it. Murray rightly decided to make a change, and to aim at operating offensively along the road leading by the northern edge of the Peninsula to El Arish, about 20 miles inside the Egyptian frontier. The General Staff agreed, and as a first step the construction of a railway from Kantara to the Katia Oasis, 25 miles beyond the Canal, the laying down of a pipe-line to convey drinking-water, and other measures were taken in hand. It may be explained that the brackish water obtainable in the Peninsula, though tolerable to the Bedouin and even to the Turk, was injurious to European soldiers, and also to European animals if restricted to it alone.

In deciding to move the defensive dispositions farther towards the eastern frontier the fact was not overlooked that by keeping the Peninsula, an almost waterless desert of some 150 miles in width, between ourselves and the enemy we would be able to attack him on emerging from it, when weary, strung out, and at a great distance from his base. But it was considered that greater advantages could be derived from the alternative policy of going forward. The farther the defence was removed from the Canal the less would be the chances of unrest in Egypt in the event of attack. El Arish was the principal place on the only route across the Peninsula which was capable of supporting a force strong enough seriously to threaten the Canal, and at it water could be obtained for some 50,000 men even in the hot season. Consequently, by holding it we would block the only good road to Egypt, and would also be on the flank of any force that might attempt to use the two other routes available, and which were incapable of supporting more than comparatively small bodies. El Arish could, moreover, be held by fewer troops than would be required to hold the Canal, if the enemy were free to use the route passing through it. Finally, the movement for Arab independence, proclaimed by the Sherif of Mecca in the month of June, would be assisted by the presence of a British force at El Arish, which would threaten the Turkish communications between Syria and the Hedjaz, and serve to encourage the disaffected tribes of Syria to throw in their lot with the Sherif. With the approval of the War Committee, Murray was accordingly instructed on July 6 to make preparations for the occupation of El Arish, but whether that step would actually be taken was left over for final decision at a later date.

Shortly afterwards, enemy forces coming from El Arish, and commanded by the German Colonel Kress von Kressenstein, began to collect opposite the Katia front, and on the morning of August 4 the long-talked-of attack, which had been elaborately prepared, was delivered. It was of the nature of a forlorn hope, and before darkness fell the British troops, superior in number and better equipped, had won a substantial victory and the enemy was in full retreat. Out of a total of about 18,000 men Von Kressenstein lost half—4,000 in prisoners and 5,000 in killed and wounded. No further fighting took place for several months.

Meanwhile Murray continued to extend his advance eastwards in accordance with the instructions of July 6, and by the middle of December sufficient progress had been made to enable him to move on El Arish. That place was occupied without opposition on December 21, the enemy having abandoned his positions some forty-eight hours before. He retired towards the south-east, and ten days later some 1,600 infantry were surrounded at Magdhaba, about 20 miles from El Arish, the whole of them being either killed, wounded, or taken prisoners. On January 9 the same fate befell a detachment, 2,000 strong, at Rafa, a frontier post on the road leading from El Arish into Palestine. As a result of these actions Egyptian territory was effectively cleared of all formed bodies of Turkish troops, who fell back in the direction of Gaza–Beersheba.

Before dealing with the subsequent operations in this theatre mention may be made of a connected project for dispatching a force to Rabegh, a place on the Red Sea coast between Jeddah and Yambo. The project did not go beyond the proposal stage, and was intended to be of quite modest proportions, but it was the cause of more than a little controversy between the Ministers who advocated it and the General Staff who opposed it. When the Sherif of Mecca proclaimed Arab independence his levies at once laid siege to the Turkish garrisons of Jeddah, Mecca, and other places. We had previously promised to supply him with arms and ammunition, and the attack on Jeddah, which ended on June 15 with the surrender of 1,400 Turkish prisoners and 16 guns, was supported by the fire of two British cruisers then off the coast. These and other forms of assistance were arranged by the British authorities in Egypt, who received their instructions from the Foreign Office, not from the War Office, and an officer representing the Sirdar of the Egyptian Army was attached to the Sherif.

The revolt spread rapidly. Kumfidah, a Red Sea port 150 miles south of Mecca, and Yambo, the port of Medina, both fell to the Arabs before the end of July; Medina, the terminus of the Hedjaz railway, was closely hemmed in ; and Turkish reinforcements, some of whom had been destined for the invasion of Egypt, were hurried south from Syria to deal with the situation. Exaggerated reports regarding the enemy's strength and intentions immediately became current, and those Ministers who believed them maintained that unless more active steps were taken in sustaining the revolt it might collapse, with a corresponding loss of British prestige not only in Arabia but also in Egypt, Mesopotamia, and India.

At about the same time the High Commissioner in Egypt, acting apparently on the advice of the Sirdar's representative with the Sherif, recommended to the Foreign Office that a brigade of British infantry should be sent to Rabegh to give the Sherif that "moral support" of which he was thought to be in need. He was to be told that the brigade would not go beyond Rabegh, that it was the maximum that would be sent, and that it would be withdrawn as soon as the existing crisis had passed over. The Foreign Office laid the proposal before the War Committee, and it was then referred for the opinion of the General Staff, who were thus brought into contact with it for the first time.

The desirability of encouraging the revolt was obvious, but the method proposed for doing so was objectionable. The suggested condition of limited liability was especially fatuous, and one wonders how it came to be put forward so soon after the disasters we had experienced in other " side-shows." By this time, the autumn of 1916, everyone should have realized that although we might in the first instance send a brigade with the intention of not going inland, of not reinforcing it, and of withdrawing it when we thought fit, circumstances might later compel us, in order to avert a disaster, to employ more troops and so do the very thing that we wished to avoid. If the brigade got into difficulties—and seeing the instability of the Arabs no one could be sure that it would not—it could not be left to its fate.

Again, once we sent troops to assist the Sherif we would be bound to see him through to the end, for if we deserted him at a time when he was in special need of help the loss of prestige would be greater than if we had never attempted to assist him at all. Finally, and quite apart from the action of the enemy, it was uncertain what the effect of our intervention on the Arabs themselves might be. The Sherif's authority was as yet of the slenderest kind, and some good judges thought that the tribes might quite likely turn against him if British (Christian) troops were introduced into a dispute which concerned the guardianship of the Holy Places. The whole proposal bristled with tiresome uncertainties which made its adoption most undesirable.

There was, too, the question of wastage from sickness. A more atrocious climate for British troops than that of the Red Sea littoral could not be imagined ; the only shelter at Rabegh consisted of three small Arab villages of the usual wretched type ; and the water supply was impure and inadequate.

These views [1] were submitted to the War Committee, with the recommendation that no troops should be sent, and that we should continue to limit our assistance to such as the Navy could give, and to the provision of money, munitions, and supplies. The Admiralty undertook to have the stores at Rabegh placed where they could be commanded by the ships' guns, and in order to provide for future contingencies it was further recommended that the Sirdar should raise a force of Sudanese Moslems to be paid and equipped at Imperial expense.

[1] General Staff memorandum, September 20, 1916.

Lord Curzon, Mr. Austen Chamberlain, with one or two other Ministers, did not agree with these recommendations. They maintained that the officials in close touch with the situation, such as the High Commissioner, must know better than the General Staff in London what was the right thing to do. What the other members of the War Committee thought I cannot say, but it was settled that the views of the Viceroy of India and the Commanders-in-Chief in Egypt and Mesopotamia should be obtained before a decision was given.

To the Ministers who were instrumental in soliciting them, the answers received were disappointing. The Viceroy gave several reasons why the dispatch of troops would be objectionable, and said that the collapse of the revolt would be far less prejudicial to us both in India and Afghanistan than would military intervention in support of it. General Murray, while declining to prophesy what the effect of a collapse would be, thought that no troops, either British or native, were needed at present. General Maude, in Mesopotamia, believed that the tribes in his sphere were not sufficiently interested in the revolt to care whether it succeeded or failed.

When the replies came before the War Committee, and notwithstanding their adverse nature, Ministers in favour of the expedition still insisted that troops ought to be sent. The Prime Minister then asked me what I thought, and my answer was that I had nothing to add to what was recorded in the memorandum submitted a fortnight before. This created something like an *impasse*, and it was decided that no troops should be sent, except that a native mountain battery from the Sudan was to be prepared to go when two batteries being furnished by the French were ready, if the situation should then demand it. Later, some misunderstanding arose amongst

Ministers as to the exact meaning of this decision, and on October 17 it was more definitely laid down that no troops, British or Sudanese, were to be sent to " Rabegh," but the Sirdar was to have full discretion to send to the " Sherif," when he deemed necessary and desirable, a flight of aeroplanes previously approved by the Committee, and any material assistance which could be spared from Egypt, as well as the mountain battery already mentioned.

I hoped that no more would be heard of the project, but its supporters were not disposed to let it drop, and the receipt of information unfavourable to the Sherif served to keep it alive. One report was that Turkish forces had left Medina for Mecca via Rabegh, and were already within three days' march of the latter place. The General Staff did not believe the report and said so, but certain Ministers took a different view. They referred to what was then happening to Rumania and had happened a year before to Serbia, because we had been " too late," they said, in making up our minds to give assistance, and they drew a gloomy picture of the figure we would cut in the eyes of the world if another ally were allowed to perish for want of help.

Arguments of this kind put forward with much adroitness and resource by practised debaters were not easy to meet on the spur of the moment. The only safe course was rigidly to adhere to the conclusions previously reached, conditions having meanwhile undergone no material change. The possible occupation of Rabegh by the Turks had never been a matter of much importance, and whether it took place or not made no difference to the General Staff's contention that to start a brand-new expedition in the Arabian Peninsula would be unwise. The War Committee, however, disliked the idea of doing nothing to meet the " urgency of the situation disclosed " by the new information, and as the General Staff remained obdurate it was decided to do the best with the Navy and send such assistance as could be provided by the Sirdar. The instructions of October 17 were accordingly amplified on November 2 as follows :—

The Naval Commander-in-Chief, East Indies Station, was to give all the naval protection to Rabegh which he could, concentrating there whatever ships and monitors he deemed necessary, and he was authorized to land a naval detachment if he considered it desirable. If, with this help, the Arabs were not able to hold the place, the Sirdar was to send whatever British or Sudanese military assistance might be immediately available. The French Government were to be informed of this action, and asked to send whatever troops they had available in East Africa, whether Christian or Mohammedan.

For the moment, therefore, we appeared to be hastening towards a miniature repetition of our previous mistakes in the war, and the instructions themselves were such as to give rise to misunderstandings and confusion. Not only did they contain nothing definite regarding the object to be attained, but no one was placed in charge of the operations. This important question was apparently left to be adjusted by the naval Commander-in-Chief and the Sirdar, neither of whom could appropriately take command. Liability to trouble was the greater because the arrangements were controlled through the Foreign Office, whose officials had not the requisite experience to foresee the technical complications that might arise, or to guide the local naval and military authorities in carrying out the wishes of the War Committee, whatever they might be.

Fortunately the instructions remained more or less a

dead letter, for on November 7 the Sirdar reported that he had discussed the situation with the naval Commander-in-Chief, and had come to the conclusion that, in order to hold Rabegh against a strong attack, and after making allowance for naval assistance, *at least* one brigade of regular troops, with a due proportion of artillery, or, in the alternative, a trained Arab force of 5,000 men, with artillery, would be required. Thus, as anticipated by the General Staff when they originally objected to the proposal, the requirements were fast mounting up, as they usually do in all such cases. At first, one brigade, with no artillery, was regarded as the *maximum*, and its duty was to afford " moral support." Now, one brigade, with artillery, was to be the *minimum*, and its task was to defend the place against a " strong attack." As it had been decided on November 2 that no troops were to be sent, the Sirdar proposed to dispatch the aeroplanes, guns and machine guns for which approval had been given ; to arrange for the dispatch of the French artillery; and to take steps to organize a force of Arabs.

About the same time the French Government repre-sented to the Foreign Office, quite erroneously and with-out having any means of knowing what the situation was, that the Turks in front of Murray on the Sinai border had recently been much reduced in numbers, and there-fore that he could well spare a brigade to go to the assistance of the Sherif. They deprecated sending French artillery and machine guns without infantry sup-port, and in order to facilitate the withdrawal of troops from Murray they offered to send him from Jibouti two Senegalese battalions who were not suitable for employ-ment at Rabegh.

The majority of the War Committee were by this time heartily tired of the whole question, and they decided to refer it to a committee composed of the Foreign Secretary (Sir Edward Grey), the Secretary of State for India (Mr. Austen Chamberlain), and Lord Curzon. Sir Edward Grey, as usual with him, was averse to overriding military opinion on military matters. The two other Ministers, however, had invariably been foremost in urging that an expedition of some sort should be sent. The committee met at the Foreign Office on November 10, and I then repeated the objections previously submitted, but without avail, Lord Curzon and Mr. Chamberlain both suggesting that the General Staff were making a great fuss about a small matter—one infantry brigade. But much more than one brigade might be involved. Other units might have to follow, and drafts would constantly be needed to fill up the gaps caused by excessive sickness.

The two Ministers also maintained that the question was mainly political, and that political as well as military considerations should be taken into account. That was so, of course, and I recalled that it had already been admitted in my memorandum of September 20, where the statement was made that :—

In war there is no real difference between political and military considerations. It is a commonplace that policy and strategy must be in harmony. Strategy is bad if it aims at results which are politically undesirable, and the converse is equally true. In a war of this magnitude neither policy nor strategy should be local in their aims ; every proposal, whether political or strategical, must be examined as regards its effect upon the war as a whole.

My only contention was, and I did not presume to advance any other, that the proposed expedition was thoroughly bad from a military standpoint.

After a long and rather unpleasant discussion the three Ministers decided that it was of the " highest importance " Rabegh should not fall into the enemy's hands, and they requested me to report to the War Committee what force was required to hold it against such an attack as it might have to withstand. In undertaking to make this report I expressed the hope that the Committee would not alter its decision of October 17, as I could never bring myself to issue an order for British troops to be employed in the manner contemplated and under the bad climatic conditions which prevailed.

The report was duly laid before the War Committee on November 13, and in it I stated that if, as Ministers said, it was of the " highest importance " to us to keep the Turks out of Rabegh, it was obviously of the " highest importance " to them to get in, and consequently we must assume that they would not send a boy on a man's errand. The Sirdar had put our minimum requirements at one brigade of infantry, with artillery, but we had already had more than sufficient experience of the folly of undertaking operations with minimum forces. It was necessary we should be strong enough to meet the maximum, and not the minimum, number which the enemy could employ. He was said to have had at Medina about 15,000 men and several batteries of artillery, and to deal with these we required at least two brigades of infantry, two of artillery, and two companies of camel corps. As there was no shelter and no good water supply a strong detachment of engineers would be needed, which, with Army Service Corps, Army Medical Corps, and other auxiliary services, would bring the Force up to a total strength of about 16,000 men.

With the exception of those under training at home we had no reserves available from which this force could be found, and Gallipoli and Loos had shown the waste of life incurred by sending newly raised troops straight into action. In France the troops had been fighting hard on the Somme since July, and needed a rest rather than to be transferred to the deserts of Arabia. From Salonika no troops could be obtained, for we had only just sent reinforcements there ; nor could they be had from Mesopotamia, for preparations were there being made, by order of the War Committee, for the capture of Baghdad. They could only be got from the force in the Sinai Peninsula, and even there, again by order of the War Committee, preparations were being made to occupy El Arish in about six weeks' time. If troops were withdrawn the operations would have to be suspended, whereas if they were continued they would, by threatening the enemy's communications with the Hedjaz, and by encouraging the discontented elements in Palestine and Syria to rise against him, so increase his difficulties as altogether to stop any attempted advance on Mecca. Summed up, we had no troops readily available to send and if we had there was no need to send them, since Murray's operations from the Sinai Peninsula would be far more effective than anything that could be achieved by starting a new expedition based on the Red Sea.

It was, moreover, improbable that the reported advance from Medina on Rabegh and Mecca was being attempted, and, if attempted, that it would succeed. The distance from Medina to Mecca was 300 miles, Rabegh being about midway between the two places ; water was very scarce ; the country was seething with revolt, and local food supplies would not be forthcoming. In many ways the difficulties to be overcome would be enormous, even for the Turks who were accustomed to desert warfare, and whose medical, supply, and other administrative methods were of the crudest kind. In submitting these observations the opinion was maintained that the expedition ought not to be sent.

THE CAMPAIGN IN PALESTINE

The Prime Minister (Mr. Asquith) and most (not all) of the members agreed ; pressing political questions connected with the change of Government which occurred three weeks later began to claim attention ; and the subject of Rabegh accordingly fell into the background, and there it remained. Although intended to be a small affair, the expedition might, had it materialized, have become almost as notorious as some of the other ill-starred enterprises attempted during the war.

The report that the Turks were within three marches of Rabegh proved to be quite untrue, and may have been circulated by them for the express purpose of misleading us. The levies of Emir Faisal soon discovered, under the inspiration of Colonel Lawrence, that their proper rôle was to avoid coming into contact with the better-equipped and better-disciplined Turkish troops, and to turn their energies to the destruction of the communications linking Medina with the north. So well did they carry out this task that within a few weeks the Turks were compelled to relinquish all idea of retaking Mecca and to confine themselves to the defence of Medina and the protection of the railway in rear of it.

Up to December, 1916, the operations beyond the Suez Canal, though offensive in character, had been essentially defensive in principle, the Government and General Staff alike being consistently of opinion that the extension of our activities eastward must be determined by the requirements of security and not by motives of aggression. One no less than the other realized the predominating importance of the struggle then taking place on the Somme, and the consequent necessity of ensuring, as a primary measure, that the armies engaged there should receive the utmost possible support.

Unfortunately, as already indicated, the same unanimity between Ministers and soldiers did not obtain after the Premiership had changed hands. The General Staff wished, as always, to keep the operations in secondary theatres subordinate to the demands of the main fronts, while the new Prime Minister, Mr. Lloyd George, had no belief in the efficacy of offensive action on those fronts, and asserted more strongly than ever that the principal enemy could easiest be brought down by attacking the allies who supported him. This fundamental difference of opinion was particularly obtrusive in the case of Palestine, and it was the more prejudicial because the situation underwent some unexpected changes which were difficult to meet effectively, and with the necessary promptitude, when the Prime Minister was constantly pulling one way and the General Staff another.

Impatient to present the country with a dazzling success, the new War Cabinet had been in existence only a few days when it directed the General Staff to examine the possibility of extending the operations into Palestine during the current winter, the capture of Jerusalem being assigned as the chief objective. The request showed that, in spite of our unhappy experiences during 1914–15, Ministers were still without any proper conception of the time required for changing over from one plan to another, or for starting a new one. No doubt there was something to be said in favour of the policy they proposed, just as there had been in the case of Gallipoli and Mesopotamia. The conquest of Palestine would help to raise British prestige ; would stimulate the Arab revolt ; would draw Turkish troops away from Armenia, and so indirectly assist the Russians ; would have a similar effect on our own operations in Mesopotamia ; and would contribute towards the expulsion of Turkish rule from Middle

Eastern countries in general. These advantages were not to be ignored, but there were other considerations to be taken into account—time and space for example.

The invasion of Palestine, if attempted at all, must proceed by way of the Sinai Peninsula, which, as everybody knew, contained practically no food for man or beast and but little water, while Palestine itself had been denuded by the Turks of such few supplies as it normally produced, and the inhabitants were literally starving. The invading army must therefore be supplied from Egypt, and this entailed the extension of the Sinai railway to some place near the line Gaza–Beersheba, and the establishment there of a base capable of meeting the needs of the troops operating in front of it. But the railway was still 37 miles short of Rafa on the Palestine border, and in the most favourable circumstances could not reach it before the end of February, 1917. Another two months would elapse before it could be extended to Gaza or Beersheba, and therefore the winter season would be over before the proposed campaign could begin.

Lack of troops made the plan equally impracticable during the summer. The enemy was thought to have between 40,000 and 50,000 men at his disposal, while Murray had four and a half divisions, seven mounted brigades, and ten camel-corps companies. Of these a considerable portion would be wanted for the local defence of the Canal and for guarding the communications, thus reducing the number actually available for the front to about 50,000 combatants. Murray accordingly reported that if he was expected to act offensively beyond the frontier he would require two additional divisions and also more mounted troops. The General Staff put his requirements at three additional divisions, and these could only be obtained from the armies on the Western

Front, where we had already agreed to co-operate in full strength with the French early in 1917.

Finally, the employment of more troops in a distant theatre meant the absorption of more shipping, and as to this the General Staff had to say that :—

At the present time we are faced with a situation which amounts practically to a break-down in our shipping arrangements, and which has completely upset our programme for the dispatch of artillery and drafts. We have, in fact, reached a stage where the available shipping is inadequate to meet requirements. The situation may seriously affect our plans for future operations, and any measure which tends to aggravate it is to be avoided. . . . We may presumably expect an even more ruthless submarine campaign in the spring, and to place an additional strain on our shipping at such a moment could not but prove a grave source of embarrassment, and would certainly injure our prospects of success in France.[1]

Having regard to these circumstances there was clearly nothing to be done but to set the project aside, at any rate for the present, and meanwhile make such preparations for an offensive at a later date as were feasible. The campaign in East Africa was believed to be drawing to a close, and would set free some troops as well as a certain amount of shipping. Several new battalions in process of being raised in India would also become available, while some of the Indian battalions already in Egypt

[1] General Staff memorandum, December 29, 1916. No one was more nervous about the shipping position at this period than the Prime Minister, and yet he paid little or no attention to the fact that its critical state was largely due to those operations in distant theatres which he was desirous to see extended. Mr. Winston Churchill does not greatly exaggerate, though he uses the argument to support a different case, where he says in his book that the " maintenance of these three great expeditions (Salonika, Palestine, and Mesopotamia) over large distances of sea threw a strain upon the maritime resources of Great Britain which, combined with the unlimited U-boat warfare, came near to compassing our complete ruin in the spring of 1917."— " The World Crisis, 1915," page 510.

were being duplicated. By these and other means the General Staff hoped to liberate British battalions for service in France and, within the limits imposed by shipping, simultaneously build up in Egypt a force ready for use in the autumn if required—a matter that would depend upon the situation at the time, and more particularly upon what had happened on the main fronts.

These conclusions were disappointing to Ministers who wished to see Palestine occupied at once, but they could not be refuted, and on January 11 Murray was informed that his primary mission for the present would be the defence of Egypt. Subject to these instructions, and after sending one of his divisions to France, he was, by aggressive action, to hold as many enemy troops on his front as possible so as to prevent them from being used elsewhere.

A month had barely elapsed when the War Cabinet asked me to report what progress was being made in preparing for the autumn campaign, and therefore I had to point out that if the campaign, fully examined a short time before, and not due for execution for several months to come, was to be frequently discussed in written reports passing through the hands of numerous secretaries (official and private), typists, and other subordinates of the War Cabinet, all chance of keeping it from the knowledge of the enemy would soon disappear. Moreover, as Ministers were assuming that the campaign would in any event take place, I thought it desirable to remind them that no one could possibly say whether it would prove to be practicable or not until the time came, some eight or nine months later in the year. The final decision must await the developments of the summer.

Early in March, Murray, in pursuance of the instructions sent on January 11, made preparations to attack the enemy's position 15 miles to the north of Rafa, but before the troops could reach it the defenders fell back to other positions on the line Gaza–Beersheba. To prevent a repetition of these tactics, as well as to cover the construction of the railway beyond Rafa and, if possible, to capture Gaza itself, Murray determined to strike again as soon as arrangements could be made. The enemy was brought to battle on March 26 and the extension of the railway was assured, but the delay caused by fog in the morning combined with the waterless nature of the country to rob the troops of the greater results which would have been achieved had Gaza and its garrison fallen into their hands. Murray reported that the operation had been " most successful " and just fell short of complete disaster to the enemy only because of these two unavoidable hindrances.[1]

Meanwhile important events had occurred in other Middle Eastern theatres which, taken in conjunction with the engagement just mentioned, made it necessary to consider whether the defensive policy ought not to be modified. The Turkish army defending Kut had been decisively defeated by Maude, and had practically ceased to exist as a fighting body, while the subsequent occupation of Baghdad had deprived the enemy of his best base of operations both in Mesopotamia and Persia. The Arabs had acted energetically and successfully against the Turks in the Hedjaz. The Russian forces in Persia were making good progress, and the Grand Duke Nicholas had promised to undertake at an early date a vigorous offensive in the direction of Mosul. Further, all intelligence went to show that the people of Turkey were thoroughly tired of the war, and that food was every-

[1] Telegram dated April 1.

where scarce, both for the troops and the civil population. Desertions in the army were rife, and much friction was said to prevail between the various Turkish head-quarters.

Murray, as already explained, had been deprived of one of his divisions, and had not yet received all the reinforcements which it had been agreed he would want for operations beyond the frontier. On the other hand, he was believed to be superior to the enemy, not only in general efficiency but also in numbers, and there was a prospect of bringing to Egypt very soon one British division from Mesopotamia, as well as more native battalions from India. After balancing these and other considerations, the War Cabinet decided on March 30 that Murray's mission should now be the defeat of the enemy's forces south of Jerusalem and the occupation of that city. I cannot quote the exact words used in the instructions sent to him, as no copy of them is in my possession. Several telegrams on the subject passed between him and the General Staff during the next few days, the salient points of which are given in the following extract from one of his dispatches [1] :—

I replied [to the telegram of March 30] drawing attention once more to my never-varying estimate of the troops required (five divisions), that a rapid advance could not be expected unless I were fortunate enough to inflict a severe blow on the enemy, and that heavy fighting with considerable losses would have to be expected if the Turks held, as I anticipated, a series of strong positions between the Gaza–Beersheba and the Jerusalem–Jaffa lines. After consideration of this reply by the War Cabinet, I was informed (on April 2) that the War Cabinet relied on me to pursue the enemy with all the rapidity compatible

---

[1] Dated June 28, 1917, and published in the *London Gazette* of November 20, 1917. The extract here given and other statements explanatory of policy were omitted in the *Gazette*.

with the necessary progress of my communications, and was anxious that I should push my operations with all energy, though at the same time no additional troops were to be sent to me, since it was considered that, in view of the military situation of the enemy, my present force would suffice. At that time, as always, I had fully appreciated the importance of offensive operations in this theatre, and, having failed to take Gaza by a *coup de main*, I was anxious to take it, if possible, by more deliberate operations before the enemy was further reinforced, chiefly on account of its water supply. I was therefore ready, as I stated at the time, to attack with my present force before the end of April, and had good hopes, provided the enemy was not heavily reinforced, of capturing that town.

The second battle of Gaza was fought between April 17 and 20. The enemy, well entrenched, was found to have been reinforced up to a strength about double that of the first battle, and after our troops had suffered considerable loss the attack had to be broken off. On the 22nd Murray reported that he was pushing on his preparations for a resumption of the attack, but he also said that he did not think he had sufficient troops to ensure more than a local success. For the effective continuance of the offensive he repeated that he required five fully equipped and complete divisions, whereas he had only the three depleted by the recent fighting, one just formed and indifferently trained, and half the infantry needed for the fifth. As it was not convenient at the time to provide these reinforcements, owing to the unsatisfactory situation on the Western Front and elsewhere, a further modification of policy was necessary, and there was another reason why a change had to be made.

The Russian revolution was beginning to exert its baneful influence on the Asiatic as on the European front, and General Alexeieff had recently informed me that he could now hold out no hope of his Caucasus armies taking the offensive, and none in Mesopotamia unless we could supply his troops. This entirely altered the outlook in Palestine, quite apart from the check at Gaza, since it left the Turks free to send reinforcements both to Mesopotamia and Syria, whereas we had been led to believe that the Russians would not merely hold the large number of Turks there opposed to them, but would deal them heavy and destructive blows. Exactly what reinforcements could be sent would depend upon the number the Turks could supply, but it was calculated that in Syria a maximum of 200,000 might be employed, of whom about 60,000 could be maintained south of Jerusalem. The balance would, of course, be available to replace wastage, and generally to make resistance more effective.

While, therefore, the fighting superiority of our forces over those of the enemy entitled us to count upon gaining a certain amount of success, full adherence to the instructions of March 30 was no longer possible. Murray was accordingly informed on April 25 that he should take every favourable opportunity of defeating the forces opposed to him, and follow up with all means at his disposal any success gained, the object being to drive the Turks out of Palestine as and when that became feasible. This direction left the General all the latitude possible as to the action he might take, and throughout the month of May he gave special attention to the improvement of his communications and to such other matters as would enable him to assume the offensive as soon as sufficient troops became available.

Having referred to the impatience shown by Ministers early in the year to push forward into Palestine, it is right to say here that the instructions of March 30 were issued on the initiative and by the advice of the General Staff. I knew, of course, that the change from the defensive to the offensive would be welcomed by the War Cabinet, but that had no influence on the advice I gave. It was governed by three other factors : the confident tone of Murray's reports on the first battle of Gaza, the necessity for co-operating with the Russians, and the wish to draw towards Palestine from Aleppo, where a hostile concentration was in progress, enemy troops which might otherwise be sent to Mesopotamia. In my opinion the instructions were both justifiable and essential, and if Murray was induced by them to attempt more at the second battle of Gaza than he believed his troops were capable of doing, the fault lay not so much in the decision to change the policy as in the defective drafting or wrong interpretation of the instructions designed to put the change into practice. The alterations of policy ordered doubtless increased the difficulty of Murray's task, but that could not be avoided. The operations in Palestine were merely a part—and a comparatively minor part—of the total Entente effort against the Central Powers. They had, therefore, of necessity to be made subsidiary to the operations on the main fronts and be kept in conformity with them. They could not be determined solely, or even chiefly, by the situation in Palestine.

At the end of June Murray was succeeded in the chief command by General Allenby, who was directed by the War Cabinet to report on the situation as soon as possible after arrival in the country so that the question of policy might be reviewed afresh. Previous to leaving England he had a conversation with the Prime Minister in which future plans were discussed, and from the account which he gave me of what was said I gathered that the Prime Minister told him to demand to the full everything that he considered requisite for the prosecution of an offensive designed to achieve the conquest of southern Palestine up to and including Jerusalem. He was given to understand that if the War Cabinet decided that his demands were to be met, then he, on his part, would be expected to produce successful results. If, on the other hand, his demands could not be met, then he would merely be held responsible for doing his best with what was allotted to him. After having had the case put to him in this manner by the head of the Government, he would have been more than human had he erred on the side of moderation in submitting his demands, and as will be seen presently he did not so err.

His estimates were received in the second week of July, and included a request to be supplied with heavy artillery on the same scale as on the Western Front (where he had been serving since the commencement of the war) ; the doubling of the railway to Rafa ; a reinforcement of two divisions in addition to the five already in the country ; more might perhaps be needed when the Jaffa–Jerusalem line was reached ; and more would certainly be wanted for an advance beyond that line.

Meanwhile the defection of Russia, which at first we had hoped would be temporary and local, had become more widespread and pronounced, and we now had to reckon with the possibility of her dropping out of the war altogether and leaving the whole Turkish forces in Asia on our hands. On the Western Front, too, it was clear that we would have to carry a greatly increased burden for several months to come, owing to the heavy losses and impaired morale recently suffered by the French armies in Champagne.

The shipping situation had also become worse, and in this connexion it was necessary that sufficient tonnage should be available not only to convey the reinforcements wanted in the first instance, and to maintain the total forces asked for, but there must also be a liberal surplus to meet possible additional requirements for holding the Jaffa–Jerusalem line. Otherwise, if shipping became short, we might find ourselves in the course of a few months hanging on to our line, wherever it might be, unable either to retire or to advance, and so be immobilized for an indefinite period.

The whole problem was very different from what it had been early in the year, and while the General Staff were anxious to meet the Prime Minister's wishes they were compelled to pronounce the offensive policy which he favoured to be impracticable. They could do no more at present than suggest that steps should be taken to double the railway to Rafa and to bring the force up to strength in all possible respects, and in the meantime continue to press the enemy so as to assist Maude in Mesopotamia and the Arabs in the Hedjaz. They believed, and said, that Allenby would be able to do considerably more in this way than his estimate indicated, once his existing divisions were given their proper strength.

The War Cabinet were, as before, dissatisfied with this advice, but there was no way of evading it, and, with their reluctant consent, I instructed Allenby on August 10, as follows :—

During the coming autumn and winter it is necessary to strike the Turk as hard a blow as possible, since a good success achieved against him will tend to strengthen the staying power and morale of this country during the season when important successes may not be possible in Europe, and on the other hand it will increase the general dissatisfaction and war-weariness of the Turks with their German masters. In view of the situation in Russia, the Turks may shortly be free to concentrate the greater part of their forces against Maude and you, and under these circumstances it is not possible now to assign any geographical objective to you, and therefore it will be your object to defeat the Turks opposed to you and follow up your success as the situation allows. It is important you should press the Turks opposed to you to the fullest extent of your resources available as early in September as possible, so as to relieve pressure upon Maude by forcing the enemy to divert troops to Palestine and to take advantage of the Arab situation.

I also made it clear that while deficiencies in men and material would be completed as far as possible, there was at present no prospect of being able to send the additional reinforcements asked for in the telegram received in the second week of July.

Matters remained more or less in this position until the last week of September, when the War Cabinet instructed me to re-examine the old project for landing a force in Ayas Bay (Alexandretta) with the object of interrupting the Turkish communications. The idea was that the requisite troops could be spared from the Western Front during the coming winter, after the close of the operations in Flanders, and could complete their task in Asia in time to be back in France for the opening of active work in the spring. Rejected as unsound in 1914 and again in 1915, the plan was still more impracticable in the autumn of 1917. The Mediterranean was then more infested with hostile submarines ; Russia was rapidly falling out of the war ; and the additional Turkish troops thus set free placed the enemy in a superior position for opposing us. At least six divisions would be wanted for the new project, and there were no grounds for supposing that even then anything useful could be achieved.

There was, too, as always, the question of sea-transport, which Ministers always seemed to forget when putting forward plans involving the movement of troops. For the conveyance of six divisions something like a million tons of shipping would be necessary, and no examination was needed to show that they could not be provided. Already our Allies were constantly asking for more shipping ; we required more for ourselves, the depleted state of food supplies being the cause of great anxiety ; while tens of thousands of American troops were unable to cross the Atlantic because no shipping was available to convey them.

From the standpoint of time the project was childish. After making allowance for collecting the requisite ships from different parts of the world, for railing the troops, horses, guns, vehicles, stores, etc., from Flanders to Mediterranean ports, for embarking them, for the inevitable delays in landing them on a beach with improvised piers, it was obvious that, quite apart from any question of fighting, the leading divisions would have to begin re-embarking at Alexandretta before the rear divisions had even arrived there, otherwise they would be too late for their appointed work in France in the spring. Instead of being dispatched on such an errand it was imperative, after their strenuous exertions during the past year, which were not yet concluded, that the armies should be given opportunities for refitment, training, and rest, so as to be in good fighting condition when the contest was resumed in the spring. There was not, in fact, a good word to be said for the project, and the naval and military staffs combined in condemning it in the strongest possible terms.

A few days later it was again brought forward, this time at an Anglo-French conference held at Boulogne, and General Foch, who was then acting in a capacity similar to my own, was requested by the Ministers present to prepare a plan. Like the British General

Staff, General Foch expressed the opinion that an isolated operation in Syria would soon be opposed by large numbers and consequently would require a large force, say eight to ten divisions. He considered that no such enterprise ought to be contemplated, though he suggested that a small force of two or three divisions acting against the Turkish communications might give good results if launched at a moment when the Turkish forces in Mesopotamia and Palestine had already been defeated and were in retreat. He mentioned certain preliminary measures that might be undertaken, at once, but as the date of the operation depended upon the progress made in Palestine and Mesopotamia and could not be forecast, the bulk of the troops required were not to be assembled until actually wanted, so that their services should not meanwhile be lost on the fronts where they were then employed.

In other words, his plan was to be put into execution only when a favourable situation arose similar to that of the autumn of 1918. He specified four places where a landing might be attempted, and concluded by saying that the feasibility of the whole project depended upon whether sea-transport could be provided—a matter which the British authorities alone could decide, as they would have to provide it. The opinion of the Admiralty was that the necessary transports, escorts, small craft, lighters, etc., could not be found without seriously dislocating important services on which they were then employed, and that three of the four proposed landing-places were unsuitable from a naval point of view. No more was heard of this or any other project for landing on the Syrian coast.

While these Syrian schemes were being investigated,

the question of taking stronger action in Palestine was again raised. The Prime Minister, still intent upon " knocking down the props," maintained that Turkey's general condition, regarding which all reports certainly gave a dismal account, was such that a severe defeat, coupled with the occupation of the Jaffa–Jerusalem line and including both those places, might, if followed by suitable diplomatic measures, induce her to break with her allies and so definitely eliminate her from the war. The General Staff were again requested to report on the subject, and to ask Allenby what further reinforcements he would require.

Since the campaign was last under review in July–August, Allenby's forces had been strengthened by two divisions withdrawn from Salonika and a considerable amount of heavy artillery, and other improvements in fighting efficiency had been effected. But the enemy had not been idle. A series of strong works extended from Gaza to Beersheba—a distance of 30 miles—and Gaza itself had been converted into a modern fortress, heavily entrenched and wired, and offering every facility for protracted defence. Between this line and the Jaffa–Jerusalem line it was known that a number of other defended positions had been prepared, which meant that we might have to fight at least three battles before Jerusalem would be captured. As to the strength of the hostile forces there were believed to be 52,000 men south of Jerusalem ; two divisions to the north of it within call ; farther north in Syria, there might be as many as 200,000 men available ; and two German divisions from Europe were said to be *en route* to Aleppo.

If the enemy stood to fight on the Gaza–Beersheba line and was dealt a severe blow, he might collapse in the same way as he had at Kut, and Allenby's fine body of mounted troops might be able to follow him up and prevent him rallying to the south of Jerusalem. But this was altogether too problematical to be relied upon in preparing a plan of campaign, and the conclusion of the General Staff was that, although Allenby might be able with his existing forces to seize the Jaffa–Jerusalem line, he would, in order to hold it and have the requisite troops for relief purposes, need a reinforcement of five divisions. My report to the War Cabinet contained the following passages [1] :—

If it is eventually decided that, in order to win the war, it is essential, in the first instance, to get Turkey out of the war by a combination of military and diplomatic action, Turkish territory will become, for an indefinite period, the decisive theatre and the Western Front must meanwhile be relegated to secondary importance. This is so because we have not sufficient resources to seek a decision in two theatres at the same time. No country ever has had, or probably ever will have. The first rule in all wars is to concentrate in the main theatre all forces that can be made available. Any departure from this rule has invariably proved to be disastrous.

It is quite impossible to say how long it may take to eliminate Turkey, or how many troops we may eventually require for the purpose. If it is to our interest to get Turkey out of the war it is equally to Germany's interest to keep her in—that is, to help her. Any policy based on the assumption that Turkey can be got out by diplomatic means, coupled with a military defeat of a certain severity less than the decisive defeat of her main armies, or by a given number of men or in a given time, will be of the nature of a gamble, and a gamble at this stage of the war would be even more dangerous than usual. The consequences of our adopted policy, whatever that policy may be, must be clearly faced, and we must determine to carry it through although possibly at considerable cost to other operations and interests.

Further, it must be recognized that any troops sent this winter from France cannot be relied upon for fighting in France next summer. Communications alone are against this possibility, to say nothing of the necessity for training and the limitations of physical powers, and

---

[1] General Staff memorandum, October 9, 1917.

I must once more remind the War Cabinet that we are at an enormous disadvantage in moving troops as compared with the Germans. They can move at least ten divisions a month from the Eastern to the Western Front, or vice versa. It has recently taken a month to move one of our divisions from Salonika to Egypt, although several weeks' warning of the move was given previous to the commencement of embarkation. For the movement of divisions from Marseilles to Egypt the Admiralty Transport Department states that a commencement cannot be made before November 15, and then divisions can be moved only at the rate of somewhat less than two a month. To refit a division for service in Palestine and rail it to the front three weeks are required after its arrival at Alexandria.

It must also be remembered that by increasing our forces in Palestine we put a further permanent strain upon shipping. The Shipping Controller can advise as to this and the Admiralty as to naval escorts. All I need say is that we must look well ahead, and bear in mind the necessity of supplying our Allies and helping to bring over and maintain the large armies which America can produce.

As to the moral effect upon Turkey of our occupation of the Jaffa–Jerusalem line, I do not claim to speak with more authority than anyone else, but the military effect would be of no value to us. On the contrary, considerably more troops would be required to hold it and the additional communications than would be required for the Gaza–Beersheba line, and this increased commitment would, as I have already said, be for an indefinite period. . . .

Unquestionably, it is very desirable to reduce the number of our enemies, and I can assure the Cabinet that I and my Staff have given the question most careful and frequent attention during the last few months. But since Russia collapsed and we have been faced with the proposition of dealing with the whole Turkish army, reinforced probably by German troops, and having regard to the military situation as a whole, we have never been able to regard an extensive offensive campaign in Palestine as a sound military measure.

During the past week I have again reviewed the situation and I can come to no other conclusion than that the right military course to pursue is to act on the defensive in Palestine and the East generally, and continue to seek a decision in the West. I believe that this would give us the best chance of final victory. It entails, of course, that all resources should be sent to the Western Front other than those which are absolutely required for the defence of our Eastern possessions, and for the moment we have ample for this purpose. With the troops we already have in Palestine, combined with the Arab activities which have been arranged, we may hope to obtain good local successes and to keep up strong pressure on the Turks. Shipping is being assembled for the transport to the East of reinforcements from France in the event of any being needed. Until they are needed they should not be sent. Early in the spring we should withdraw as many troops and guns as can be spared from the East and send them to France.

This is my advice and I can only leave the matter in the hands of the War Cabinet. I need hardly say that success in the West, or indeed anywhere, requires that the War Cabinet should feel able to support in practice the policy of which they approve in principle, whatever that policy may be. Once the decisive theatre has been selected it must be regarded as such, and all other theatres must be ruthlessly treated as secondary and made to do the best they can with what is given them.

The day after the above memorandum was submitted the estimate which the War Cabinet had directed me to obtain from Allenby was received. He put his requirements at seven additional divisions for use at the front, plus six others to be concentrated on the Suez Canal for the purpose of replacing worn-out divisions. His demands thus amounted to thirteen divisions, as compared with the General Staff estimate of five. The figure came as a great disappointment to the Prime Minister, and he complained to me that it had been caused by the way in which the General Staff had drafted the telegram sent to Allenby asking for his estimate. The passage in the telegram to which he took exception read thus :

Beyond the arrival of one Turkish regiment we have no information of enemy concentration towards Mesopotamia east of Aleppo, and therefore are still in doubt whether enemy's reported contemplated offensive will be in that theatre or in Palestine. You should also remember that two German divisions are reported to be preparing for the East, and German facilities for increasing this force should be borne in mind.

181

The Prime Minister maintained that there was no necessity to make this allusion to the enemy's intentions, and that it was a direct inducement to Allenby to put forward extravagant demands. I tried to explain that not a word more was said in the telegram than Allenby would expect to be told, or than ought to be said in order to help him to reach a right conclusion. To him the statements would merely appear as items of information to be taken into account, and nothing more than that. Moreover, Allenby and I had been fellow-students at the Staff College some twenty years before, and subsequently had been brought together at manœuvres and on many other occasions. There was a complete understanding between us, and not the least probability that he would read into the telegram more than it was intended to convey.

As there was no possible way of providing the thirteen additional divisions demanded, Allenby's mission had to remain unchanged : he was to defend Egypt, and, by such offensive action as he deemed feasible, compel the enemy to divert to Palestine troops that might otherwise be used against Maude in Mesopotamia. The wisdom of being content with this policy was demonstrated a week or two later when five British and five French divisions had to be withdrawn from the Western Front to assist the Italians after their reverse at Caporetto.

In his final dispatch [1] on the campaign Allenby stated :—

I desire to express my indebtedness to my predecessor, Lieut.-General Sir A. J. Murray, who by his bridging of the desert between Egypt and Palestine laid the foundations for the subsequent advances of the Egyptian Expeditionary Force. I reaped the fruits of his fore-

---

[1] Dated June 28, 1919.

sight and strategical imagination which brought the waters of the Nile to the borders of Palestine, planned the skilful military operations by which the Turks were driven from strong positions in the desert over the frontier of Egypt, and carried a standard-gauge railway to the gates of Gaza. The organization he created, both in Sinai and in Egypt, stood all tests and formed the corner-stone of my success.

This tribute was as well deserved as it was generously given, and the valuable spade-work accomplished by Murray, together with the arrival of considerable reinforcements, placed in Allenby's hands a far more powerful weapon than that which existed when offensive operations were suspended after the second battle of Gaza.

There were at Allenby's disposal three mounted and seven infantry divisions, or about 110,000 rifles, with a fair complement of heavy artillery, and although this force was not strong enough to warrant the assumption that it could march through southern Palestine without experiencing any serious check, it could be relied upon to secure good results in the execution of the more restricted rôle assigned to it. Much would depend upon transport, water supply, and extension of the communications, all which presented difficulties no less formidable than the resistance to be expected from the enemy's troops. These, as already stated, were estimated by the General Staff to be 52,000 strong, with two other divisions within a few days' call of the front.

Allenby put his force in movement towards the end of October, and met with a greater measure of success than had been expected. On the 31st, thanks to skilful leadership and fine endurance on the part of the troops, Beersheba, " a very strong position "[1] on the extreme left of the enemy's line, was taken with slight loss. This achievement laid open the flank of the main Turkish

[1] Allenby's dispatch, dated December 16, 1917.

position for a decisive blow, and by November 9 the
" operations had reached the stage of a direct pursuit
by as many troops as could be supplied so far in front
railhead." [1] The enemy's defences on the Jaffa–Jerusalem
line fell into our possession in the second week of December, and the operations were then brought to a close
for the time being. The enemy had suffered the loss
of probably not less than half his strength, including
12,000 prisoners and about 100 guns. Several units
known to have been in northern Syria previous to the
advance were discovered to have come south in order
to assist in stemming it. The main purpose for which
the operations had been undertaken—the disarrangement
of the enemy's concentration about Aleppo preparatory
to an offensive campaign in Mesopotamia for the recapture of Baghdad—was thus fully achieved, and the
possibility of any such offensive being again attempted
was effectively destroyed.

The War Cabinet afterwards complained to me that
as Allenby had accomplished with his seven divisions
a task for which he had said that twenty were necessary
his Intelligence service could not be very efficient, otherwise a more accurate forecast would have been made of
the opposition likely to be encountered. It was no
business of mine to defend Allenby's requisition for
twenty divisions, more especially as it was eight divisions
in excess of my own estimate, but as the allegation seemed
unfair to him and his troops, and also had a bearing on
future plans, it could not be allowed to remain in the
War Cabinet's records unanswered. I therefore pointed
out that the forecast made by the General Staff as to
enemy numbers had, in fact, proved to be substantially
correct, namely 52,000 men immediately in front of

[1] Allenby's dispatch, dated December 16, 1917.

Allenby, plus two divisions, or 15,000 men, within call, or a total of 67,000 men as against the 58,000 reported to be actually present at the first engagement fought on the Gaza–Beersheba line. No one could predict to what extent the enemy would draw upon the divisions which he had in northern Syria, since that would depend upon the rate of Allenby's advance and other conditions of which we could have little or no previous knowledge. The advance had progressed so rapidly that the enemy was given little time in which to bring up reinforcements, and it would have been much slower had not the wells of Beersheba been found undamaged and with sufficient water in them to enable the troops to continue going on. As it was, the margin was so slight that some of the men on this flank had to live for forty-eight hours on a single water-bottle apiece. No General dare base his plans on chances of this kind, and if, owing to lack of water or other cause, the turning movement by Beersheba had failed—and no one could guarantee that it would succeed—the whole character of the operations would have been changed, and a slow, deliberate advance against a series of defensive positions would have become necessary. In that case Allenby might not have reached Jerusalem before the end of January, and the Turks would then have had ample time to bring forward from Syria fresh divisions to replace and reinforce exhausted troops at the front. To meet this contingency Allenby, in his turn, needed divisions in reserve upon which he could call.

It occurred to me, too, though I refrained from suggesting it, that he was not likely to have forgotten his conversation with the Prime Minister before leaving England, when he was told to ask for everything he wanted and then, if given it, he would be expected not to fail. The War Cabinet would probably have had less cause for complaint had they permitted the General Staff to do its own work, and to arrange with Allenby direct the strength of force required. They would not allow this, but preferred to have from him a report for themselves, which, when received, they neither liked nor understood.

While the operations were in progress, and when the fall of Beersheba and Gaza foreshadowed the successes that were to follow, Ministers again became eager to push on farther and more rapidly than the General Staff deemed to be right. " Cannot you give us Jerusalem as a Christmas Box for the people, so as to cheer them up ? " was a remark made to me at the time. There was much to be said, politically, for giving it, but the place had no military value, and I was afraid that, in the hope of getting Turkey out of the war, Ministers would not be content with the possession of Jerusalem, but would wish for the operations to be still further extended. This was not desirable, and I said so in a fresh review of the situation, dated November 15, for which the War Cabinet had called. Turkish man-power was no doubt seriously diminishing, and the Turkish people were becoming tired of the war, but exactly the same could be said of any other belligerent country. For many reasons the prospect of Turkey consenting to conclude a separate peace seemed much too remote to justify an increase of military effort in Palestine, while the situation on the two main fronts was such as utterly to condemn it.

The campaign was also referred to in a General Staff memorandum, dated November 19, in which it was repeated that we could not afford to lock up troops in Palestine, but must give first consideration to the needs of the Western Front.

Three weeks later the occupation of Jerusalem led, as I had anticipated, to a further demand for developing the operations. Allenby made his formal entry into the city on December 11, and next day, on the initiative of the Prime Minister, I was directed to send him the following telegram :—

In view of the change in position created by your recent victory over the Turks, and by revised information as to enemy's strength and break-down in his transport, War Cabinet would like to have your opinion by telegram as soon as possible as to manner in which, and extent to which, it is possible to exploit your success in Palestine with forces now under your command, plus the division under orders from Mesopotamia.

The day after this telegram was dispatched, and without waiting for a reply to it, the War Cabinet requested me to consider a project for carrying out the following alternative policies :—

(a) Complete the conquest of the whole of Palestine, and hold the country for the remainder of the war.

(b) Continue the advance through Palestine and Syria to the vicinity of Aleppo, so as permanently to interrupt railway communication with Mesopotamia.

Allenby's answer to the telegram of the 12th was received on the 14th. It read :—

I consider it essential, at present season, with rains imminent, and after recent experience of effect of comparatively small rainfall, that any advance northward during next two months can only be made step by step ; owing to badness of roads I must depend on the progress of my railway. After January weather will keep on improving and in this part of Palestine summer weather is more suitable for campaigning than winter. I accordingly propose first, as essential, to advance to the line of the Wadi Auja flowing east, and the Wadi el Jib—Wadi Abu Lejja—Nahr Auja flowing west, and to consolidate on that line. Secondly, I hope to operate against Hedjaz railway during wet season, and while waiting for my railway to overtake me, as there are still 20,000 Turks south of Amman. If found practicable this seems to offer best prospect of exploiting success already gained. Thirdly, if circumstances are favourable, I may gradually push forward my left towards Tul Keram, covering railway construction and perfecting preparations for offensive with naval co-operation. Either as a reinforcement on this front, or in the improbable event of trouble arising in Western Desert, the division from Mesopotamia will be very valuable.

The question to which this telegram was an answer having become absorbed in the more ambitious policies (*a*) and (*b*), I next asked Allenby for his views on the later proposals, especially in regard to the time they might take to carry out in each case, for I knew that the War Cabinet entertained much too sanguine an opinion on that point. He replied on December 20 as follows :—

(*a*) I calculate I might be able by June or July to place force of my present strength north of Nazareth–Haifa line, assuming enemy cannot oppose me with more than about 60,000 fighting strength and provided there are no special difficulties met with in railway construction.

(*b*) To advance farther towards Aleppo would mean to move against Damascus and Beirut. On that front enemy is served by broad-gauge railway with good lateral communications and apparently ideal ground for defence. Broad-gauge railway would put him on level with me as regards numbers that could be maintained. I should require 16 or 18 divisions besides my mounted corps to ensure success against Damascus–Beirut line if strongly held, but this is probably more than my railway could support even when doubled and when allowance is made for sea-transport. My estimate is made on the supposition enemy will make use of his broad-gauge railway to its full capacity. I would point out that Aleppo is 350 miles distant and my single-line railway advances about half-mile a day. Rail-end of my double line is at Bir-el-Mazar, but the doubling of railway has had to be stopped during my present advance. For my immediate plans see my telegram of 14th December, and I think it advisable before advancing much farther north to clear Turkish forces on Medina railway.

With these estimates the General Staff were broadly in agreement, and in a memorandum dated December 26, in which the position was once more reviewed, the proposed policy of conquest was again shown to be objectionable and dangerous.[1] The War Cabinet thereupon referred the question to the " technical advisers " of the Supreme War Council, who recommended that a " decisive offensive " should be undertaken. On February 6, a few days after this recommendation had eventually been accepted by the Council, Mr. Lloyd George, who now seemed to have decided to act quite independently of the General Staff, sent General Smuts, a member of the War Cabinet, to Palestine to arrange with Allenby for carrying out the new policy. Having made such arrangements as were feasible, the General returned to London on March 1, and on March 7 Allenby was formally instructed to proceed. A fortnight later, when the long-expected German attack in the West was launched, the orders of March 7 had to be cancelled, the " decisive offensive " had to be abandoned, and all troops not required in Palestine for purely defensive purposes were hurriedly dispatched to France to assist in staving off the disaster with which the British armies there were threatened.

In September, when German resistance in the West was beginning to break down, Allenby, having meanwhile reconstructed his depleted army, commenced the advance which, within a few weeks, resulted in the final overthrow of Turkey's military power in Asia and the occupation of her territory up to and including Aleppo.

The maximum number of troops employed in the Palestine campaign at one time amounted to 432,857, and the battle casualties to about 58,000. This figure, however, has little relation to the gross wastage, for the total numbers employed in the campaign up to October, 1918, amounted in all ranks to 1,192,511.

[1] See page 272 *et seq.*, where the whole question is discussed in connexion with the general preparations for 1918.

CHAPTER XII

THE WESTERN FRONT, 1917

Joffre-Haig Plan for 1917—Mr. Lloyd George's Plan for a Campaign against Austria—War Cabinet approves of Plan proposed by Nivelle, the Austrian Plan being temporarily dropped—War Cabinet decides to place British Army under Nivelle—The Calais Conference, February, 1917—Friction between Nivelle and Haig —New French Government has no confidence in Nivelle's Plan —The Plan fails—Effect of Failure on French Government, French Army, and General Military Position—Situation made worse by increasing Defection of Russia and enemy Submarine Activity—Governments agree to necessity of continuing the Offensive in France—Mr. Lloyd George again proposes that Main Effort should be made against Austria—Offensive in France receives Cabinet approval, and Austrian Plan again falls into Abeyance—Mr. Lloyd George revives it on several subsequent Occasions—Having become impracticable it is finally dropped in September—Disappointing Results of Operations on Western Front.

IT now remains to deal with the operations on the main front subsequent to the battle of the Somme, and in following them due regard should be had to the influence exercised by the policy adopted on the secondary fronts, an account of which has been given in the previous chapters. Every one of the campaigns in which we had become engaged reacted to a greater or less extent upon every other, and only by remembering this can the momentous events of the closing years of the war be placed in their right perspective and their complexities be properly understood.

During 1915 our military resources, seen to be so woefully deficient in 1914, had rapidly increased, though they still proved to be too small for our commitments, which had grown with equal rapidity. Four considerable campaigns had been started in the East in addition to the major one in the West, and statesmen, soldiers, and sailors alike had erred in expecting from them greater results than, speaking after the event, they could reasonably hope to achieve. By the autumn of 1916 the prospect of victory had been brought much nearer; and although all the Allies, France in particular, had suffered heavy losses in the process, the resources of the British Empire, both in men and material, had been expanded to a degree undreamt of before the war, and even yet had not reached the limit of their possible development. How would the British Government use them in their endeavour to bring to a satisfactory termination the world-wide conflict that was being waged?

On November 15, 1916, a conference of the Entente military representatives assembled at French G.H.Q. at Chantilly to decide upon a plan of campaign for the coming year.[1] The exhausted condition of the German armies on the Western Front, due to the protracted struggle at Verdun and on the Somme, was not then so well known to us as it has since become, but we knew sufficient about it to appreciate the importance of keeping up the pressure during the winter, and of resuming the attack as early as possible in the spring, so that the enemy might not have an opportunity either for strengthening his defences or for giving to his tired troops the rest of which they stood in need.

A plan designed to meet this situation was agreed upon, and, in the language used at the time, it was intended

[1] Britain was represented by Sir Douglas Haig and myself.

to be of a " decisive character." It comprised a series of offensives on all fronts, so timed as to assist each other by depriving the enemy of the power of weakening any one of his fronts for the purpose of reinforcing another. A further conclusion reached was that, in order to meet as far as possible any new situation that might arise, all the armies must be ready to begin operations, with the full resources at their disposal, by the middle of February. As regards the Western Front in particular, the view was held that : " Since the Anglo-French front contains the main forces of the enemy Coalition, and since it may be the theatre of operations in which decisive results can be reached most rapidly, we should consider it as the principal front, and declare that the part of our forces allotted to it should not be touched. These should, in our opinion, be the paramount premises on which every plan of operations for the Coalition should be based." At a subsequent conference of the Entente Governments these various conclusions were ratified *ad referendum* to a conference about to assemble in Russia.

An understanding was also arrived at between Joffre and Haig as to the rôles which their respective armies were to play in the general plan. The chief principles settled were that pressure was to be continuously exerted throughout the winter, and that the British armies would take a larger, and the French armies a correspondingly smaller, share of the main offensive in the spring than had hitherto been the custom. In the first instance, as soon as all the Allied armies were ready to commence, the battle of the Somme would be resumed—the British armies directing their efforts against the front Bapaume –Vimy, while the French northern group of armies would attack between the Somme and the Oise. Later, the French central group would attack on the Aisne front.

Photo : Mеiеy.

Au général et à Madame Robertson
Cordial souvenir !
J. Joffre   24 - 9 - 19

As soon as the British attack had secured certain local objectives, the main offensive was to be transferred to the Flanders front, and there continued during the summer so far as available forces would permit. This action was designed to comply with instructions which Haig had received from the General Staff in November, 1916, saying that there was no measure to which the War Committee attached greater importance than the expulsion of the enemy from the Belgian coast, and that arrangements should be made to include a plan of that nature in the operations of the following year.

If these intentions had been carried out, and assuming that all available resources had been utilized, decisive success or something closely approaching it might have been achieved before the year had expired.[1] Unfortunately, two events occurred to interfere with them: the Chantilly plan was so altered as to cause serious delay in preparation and thereby much of the advantage gained on the Somme was lost, while the revolution in Russia, beginning in the month of March, made a simultaneous offensive on all fronts impossible. We are concerned here mainly with the first of these events.

Soon after becoming Prime Minister, Mr. Lloyd George made it clear that, notwithstanding the Government acceptance of the Chantilly recommendations, an offensive policy on the Western Front was as distasteful to him as ever. He manifested anew his distrust of British leadership; criticized the Somme operations, as having entailed losses out of all proportion to the

---

[1] According to M. Painlevé this was also the opinion of General Foch, who wished to resume the Somme operations with the least possible delay, and with the full resources of the French armies.— " Comment j'ai nommé Foch et Pétain," pages 7 and 9.

results achieved ; and refused to believe that these results were nearly as great as the General Staff estimated them to be.[1] It therefore became necessary, as at the end of 1915, to ask that a definite ruling on the question of policy might be given.

This request was made in a General Staff memorandum of January 2. The policy laid down by the Government on December 28, 1915,[2] and which in its main lines still held good, was recalled, and it was pointed out that, with the approval of the Government, the recent Chantilly agreement formed the basis of our preparations for the spring campaign. If, therefore, it was desired to substitute another policy—a course which the General Staff did not recommend—the War Office and Commanders-in-Chief ought to be informed at once so that the preparations might be revised. The change must also be notified to the Allied Powers, with whose armies we were under a promise to co-operate.

After all that had been said and written during the past

---

[1] Statements since published by certain German commanders show that the condition of the German armies was more and not less critical than the British authorities had supposed. " There is no doubt that the relative strength of our own forces had changed still more to our disadvantage at the end of 1916 than had been the case at the beginning of the year " (Hindenburg). " We were completely exhausted on the Western Front. . . . We now urgently needed a rest. The Army had been fought to a standstill, and was utterly worn out. . . . G.H.Q. had to bear in mind that the enemy's superiority in men and material would be even more painfully felt in 1917 than in 1916. They had to face the danger that ' Somme fighting ' would soon break out at various points on our front, and that even our troops would not be able to withstand such attacks indefinitely, especially if the enemy gave us no time for rest and for the accumulation of material " (Ludendorff). " G.H.Q. doubted seriously whether we could hold out for another year " (Tirpitz).

[2] *Vide* Vol. I, page 254.

year, examples of which have been quoted in preceding
chapters, there could be no doubt in the minds of the
War Cabinet as to the policy through which, in the
opinion of the General Staff, victory should be sought.
The memorandum now submitted gave to Ministers the
opportunity to decide whether they did or did not approve
of that policy, and if they did not, to alter it and to consider the desirability of selecting another head of the
General Staff who would be more in sympathy with the
new course which they wished to follow.

No direct answer was returned to the memorandum
so far as I recollect, but one was indirectly supplied at the
conference held in Rome during the first week of January.
There the Prime Minister surprised all present by producing a plan for a combined French-British-Italian
offensive through the Julian Alps to Laibach and Vienna,
the object being to put Austria out of the war. The
Italians were delighted with the plan, since it promised
to make their front more secure ; the French, whose
front was to be weakened, were not delighted with it ;
and neither Italian nor French Ministers were accustomed to accept at short notice important military plans
drawn up by Ministers, as this one had been, without
any reference to the responsible military chiefs. Hence,
although it was recorded in the conference proceedings
that Ministers were " impressed " by the new proposal,
they decided to refer it to the military advisers of the
Governments concerned for opinion before taking
further action, General Cadorna in the first instance to
work the plan out in detail.

Who actually drew up the document containing the
plan, or whether it was the work of the Prime Minister
himself, I am unable to say. The British General Staff
had previously heard nothing about it, and none of the

other Entente staffs had any knowledge of it. The
incident was not a good omen for the future, since it
was not only another proof of Mr. Lloyd George's
indifference to military opinion on military matters, but
it disclosed the intention to make use of his position in
the Allied councils to secure approval to military plans
of his own conception, and to which his own General
Staff were unlikely to agree. It was also calculated to
lower the General Staff in the eyes of the High Commands
of other countries, and that at a time when British
interests required that British control of the war should
be increased.

On the way home from the conference the British
and French delegates were met at a railway station near
Paris by General Nivelle, who had just succeeded General
Joffre as French Commander-in-Chief. He came to
solicit the co-operation of the British Government in
another plan—the one which he proposed to substitute
for the previously arranged Chantilly plan, and he had
probably been summoned by his Ministers so as to
ask for what he wanted before the Laibach plan was
allowed to go too far. After some desultory conversation, in rather inconvenient conditions, he was invited
to come to London, and at a conference held there on
January 15–16 he explained his plan to the War Cabinet.
The essence of it was that the French armies should do
more, and the British armies less, than had been arranged
by Joffre and Haig, and that the main operation should be
short, sharp, and decisive, thus avoiding a repetition of
the long-drawn-out fighting on the Somme and its heavy
losses. The plan was described by the General as
being divided into three phases :—

(1) Attacks by both British and French forces on the
Arras front and to the south, with the primary object of

drawing in and exhausting the enemy's reserves. This phase was expected to occupy anything between a week and a fortnight.

(2) When it had produced the necessary effect large French forces would deliver the main attack, as a surprise, on the Aisne front, the object being to break completely through the enemy's positions. A period of twenty-four to forty-eight hours was allowed.

(3) If at the end of this time the rupture made was considered by Nivelle to be sufficiently large it would at once be exploited laterally and in depth by an overwhelming rush of armies, which would roll up the whole of the hostile forces and deal a paralysing blow at their communications. If, on the other hand, the rupture did not admit of being exploited the battle would at once be broken off. Again, if the plan succeeded the Belgian coast would automatically fall into our hands, and the projected Flanders offensive would be unnecessary ; while if the plan did not succeed, measures for clearing the coast could still be undertaken as previously intended. Hence, according to this argument, the substitution of the plan would not be to the detriment of the Flanders operations which the British Government wished to see undertaken.

The plan strongly appealed both to French and British Ministers, though for different reasons. The former liked it because it assigned the chief rôle in the offensive to the French armies and not, as the Chantilly plan had done, to the British armies. The French Government naturally desired that the glory of delivering the final blow should fall to France, and they believed her to be still capable of delivering it provided a commander could be found who would break away from the costly tactics hitherto employed, and devise some method by which the war could be won quickly and at a more reasonable expenditure of men and material. The British Government, as represented by Mr. Lloyd George, welcomed the new plan because in addition to offering a shorter cut to victory than any yet suggested, it promised, so Ministers thought, by the subsidiary part allotted to the British armies, to avoid a repetition of the heavy losses suffered in 1916.

But just because the plan was so attractive it required to be the more carefully scrutinized, so as to make sure that the advantages claimed for it were real and not merely theoretical, and that they did not obscure latent dangers which might be difficult to surmount once the plan was put into execution. To Haig and myself the plan seemed to have in it many fallacies. For instance, a breach in the enemy's defences on the scale contemplated could not possibly be effected within a space of forty-eight hours, but only after severe fighting lasting over a period the length of which neither Nivelle nor anyone else could calculate. Nor was it to be supposed that the battle could be broken off as and when he might wish, for the feasibility of doing that would depend, as always, upon circumstances which could not be foreseen, and not least upon the will of the enemy. Therefore, the so-called subsidiary part to be taken by the British armies in no way justified Ministers in assuming that our losses would be less than under the original plan. In fact, Nivelle's own words were that these armies were to make " a violent attack on a wide front " to be " carried through with determination—as all attacks should be— and with the intention of breaking the enemy's front." Naturally the British armies would be expected to make the greatest effort of which they were capable, and for as long a period as the question of success or failure continued to hang in the balance. As to the subsequent offensive in Flanders, resources as well as time had to be taken into account, and these would be governed by the expenditure incurred in men and material during the fighting which had previously to be done. Hence it was necessary to realize that the Flanders project, upon which the Government and the Admiralty had laid so much stress, was in fact being relegated to second place, and would no longer constitute, as under the original plan, the main operation of the year.

These and other objections raised at the London conference failed to convince British Ministers that the plan was different from what they believed it to be. They decided to accept it, and promised to support it to the full extent of their power. They went farther, and the day after the conference directed me to send to Haig a " special instruction " recording the importance which they attached to the agreement being carried out " both in the letter and in the spirit," and to the British armies taking their share of " the operation at the date laid down, or even before that date, with the forces available at the moment, if the weather and other conditions make the operations possible and advisable. . . . On no account must the French have to wait for us owing to our arrangements not being complete. Further, it was to be borne in mind that as the Germans might attack us before we do, we, by making every effort to advance our arrangements, should be assisting to nullify any effort of theirs."

It may be explained here how the question of date was so materially affected by the change of plan. The Chantilly plan contemplated a renewal of the attack on the Somme front with the British armies in the same positions as in 1916, but by Nivelle's plan the British were to take over an additional section of front so as to make more troops available for the French attack, and the British attack was to be made not on the Somme front but on the Arras front. In order to extend his front, Haig required six more divisions, which were coming from Egypt and home, the last of which could not arrive until the end of February. Nivelle's plan therefore involved a drastic recasting of previous arrangements, and while they were being made the German retreat to the Hindenburg line took place, which still further delayed preparations. Had the original plan stood the Germans might have been brought to battle before their measures for retreat were completed.[1]

In order that the position might be correctly understood, the General Staff laid before the War Cabinet a memorandum[2] summarizing what had been said at the London conference, and in it the question of date was referred to thus :—

For quite obvious and elementary reasons, political, economic, military and naval, it is eminently desirable to resume the offensive at the earliest possible date. Everyone will agree as to this. On the other hand, it is equally obvious and elementary that no plan is of use unless it succeeds. This is especially true in the present case because if we are not successful the effect on our Allies in general and the French in particular may be highly unpleasant—to say nothing of the effect on the enemy and neutrals. France has suffered very heavy losses already, and it is not inconceivable that the absence of a good success next time may leave her disinclined, and perhaps unable, to

---

[1] In November, 1917, Mr. Lloyd George informed the House of Commons that " the whole campaign of the year has been the result of the advice of soldiers." (" Hansard," November 19, page 903.) The account here given clearly shows that it was not upon the advice of British soldiers that the Nivelle plan of campaign was accepted, and that Ministers, well aware of the dislike which Haig and I entertained for the plan, were afraid that we might place fictitious difficulties in the way of its execution. Hence the issue to Haig of the " special instruction " mentioned.

[2] Dated February 24, 1917.

attempt further offensive operations.[1] Disappointment would not be wholly absent in our own country, and accordingly war-weariness and pacifism may greatly embarrass His Majesty's Government. In short, the next great battle on the Western Front may govern the final decision of the war, and therefore we should strain every nerve in order to make sure not only of succeeding but of succeeding well. This I understood to be General Nivelle's view also, and if it is the right view all our preparatory arrangements connected with the battle become of vital importance. If we begin so early that Italy and Russia are unable to co-operate effectively and before we ourselves can make our maximum effort we shall to that extent be playing the enemy's game—a game which his interior position and excellent communications enable him to play with the greatest advantage. The ideal arrangement would be for Italy and Russia to begin first, so as to pin the enemy down, and then for the decisive thrust to be made in the West. This, however, might mean waiting longer than could be justified by reasons other than military. But there is no doubt that the chances of success will be reduced and perhaps seriously so unless there is co-ordinated effort on all fronts. . . . If therefore, Russia and Italy cannot commence before the date which they have intimated, we on our side ought not to commence on our own choice before the latest date mentioned in the Nivelle Agreement.[2]

Another matter to which attention was drawn was the amount of publicity which had been given to the plan. The second phase, or main attack, which was to break through the German defences, admittedly depended for success upon the element of surprise, but practically all hope of surprise had already been destroyed. When Nivelle first sent his plan to Haig in December he forwarded a copy of it to his Government, who in their turn transmitted a copy to the British Foreign Office, where further copies were made and, to my knowledge, were distributed to no fewer than ten different people in London. The plan had, too, again to my own know-

---

[1] This, it will be seen later, proved to be not an inaccurate forecast.
[2] To the best of my recollection this date was the first week of April.

ledge, been openly discussed by General Nivelle himself across a luncheon table in London in the presence of several persons of both sexes.

About ten days after the London conference the Prime Minister received from the Italian Government the plan which Cadorna had been directed to prepare for the campaign against Austria. The General asked to be reinforced alternatively by 300 Anglo-French medium and heavy guns, or for a more ambitious scheme by eight divisions in addition. The question therefore arose what was to be done seeing that the French and British Governments were now committed to Nivelle's plan. I could only suggest that the Italian Government should be informed of the fact, and told that in the circumstances neither guns nor troops could be spared. Whether this reply was ever sent I cannot say.

Mr. Lloyd George realized, of course, that the Austrian plan must be given up, temporarily at any rate, but he nevertheless asked the General Staff to make arrangements for its execution as soon as Nivelle's offensive on the Western Front came to an end. To this I was obliged to demur. During the six weeks that had elapsed since the new Government came into office three different plans of campaign had been under consideration—the Chantilly, Mr. Lloyd George's, and Nivelle's—and it was imperative that undivided attention should now be given to the one into which it had been decided that full efforts should be put. We could not as a matter of fact properly consider future operations in Italy without consulting French G.H.Q. and there we were already suspected of having no confidence in Nivelle's plan. Suspicion would naturally be increased if further doubts were cast upon its success by suggesting the examination of a project which might have to follow it. There was, in addition, the Flanders offensive to be remembered, regarding which the instructions of the Government still held good, and while two plans of so far-reaching a nature were in being no useful study of a third one could be made. A General Staff paper elaborating these arguments was laid before the War Cabinet, and for the moment the subject was allowed to drop.

Mr. Lloyd George's initiation of the Austrian scheme and the favourable reception which he gave to the Nivelle plan proved that he had no intention of being in any way guided by the advice of the British military authorities unless it coincided with his own ideas. For two years past he had repeatedly shown that he regarded British methods of making war as commonplace, costly, and ineffective, and within a fortnight of the time when he became Prime Minister I was led to remark in a letter to Haig that " there is a very dangerous tendency becoming apparent for the War Cabinet to direct military operations." It so happened that the same tendency prevailed in France, where a group of politicians were loud in their criticism of the French High Command. They asserted that the operations of the past year had been mismanaged ; resented the powers exercised by Joffre as being too autocratic ; and were apparently determined to take advantage of his removal to bring his successor more strictly under ministerial control.

To make matters worse, Ministers of both countries were practically compelled to intervene in military questions owing to the lack of agreement between the two Commanders-in-Chief, and on this point something may now be said. Nivelle's requested extension of the British front in relief of French troops was a special source of trouble. The General was too exacting both as to the amount and date of extension, while Haig had to remember that his troops needed opportunities for rest and training preparatory to the coming campaign. Nivelle, not being able to obtain from Haig all that he wanted, appealed to his Government, who in their turn communicated with the British Government, and the question then became the subject of ministerial discussion and correspondence. Inadequate facilities for railway transportation within the British area were another cause of disagreement, and as the necessary improvement was not made Haig appealed to *his* Government for assistance. In this way purely military questions which ought to have been adjusted by the two commanders were referred for ministerial arbitration, and with the reference necessarily went a greater share in the control of the operations than Ministers were competent to exercise.

When the transportation difficulty was first brought to the notice of the War Office I hoped that the two commanders would settle it between themselves, and in writing to Haig on February 14 I said :—

In the circumstances I think you were quite right to send the telegram asking for a conference, but I also think that I am right in having got the War Cabinet to ask you to see Nivelle first. This seems to be our only chance of getting back to the lines upon which you used to work before Nivelle came on the scene. So long as Ministers take part in the discussion of plans of operations we shall always have trouble of the worst kind, I am sure. Soldiers understand each other, and I still hope that Nivelle will see you, and that the two of you will come to a satisfactory agreement. The problem seems perfectly simple. The railways have broken down, and until we can get them right we ought not to go off. The sooner we get them right and the sooner we can get off the better, in my opinion, subject to the other Allies also getting off at the same time, more or less. This is our old idea and it is the right one. But we will never get an agreement of this kind with Ministers. They have so many axes to grind, whereas if you and Nivelle can come to some sort of a settlement the two Governments will have to agree. If you do not come to a settlement they will have to intervene, I suppose.

The conference eventually appointed to deal with the dispute assembled at Calais on Monday, February 26. France was represented by M. Briand, General Lyautey (War Minister), and General Nivelle; Britain by Mr. Lloyd George, Haig and myself. On the previous Saturday the Secretary of the War Cabinet, acting presumably on the Prime Minister's instructions, had telephoned to me to say that unless I had any special question to bring forward I need not attend the Cabinet meeting that day—a very unusual occurrence. Having none, I did not attend, and had no reason to suppose that any question connected with the coming conference would be considered. On going to Calais, therefore, transportation was, so far as I knew, the only subject to be discussed, and in the course of a long conversation on the way the Prime Minister said nothing to indicate the contrary.

The conference commenced business in the evening, and the proceedings in regard to transportation occupied a very short time. They seemed to have no attraction for either M. Briand or Mr. Lloyd George. The British case was that sufficient rolling-stock was not being provided; the French, who controlled the railways, maintained that we were asking for more than was necessary; and, following the usual course of such discussions, the matter was at last referred to a committee of French and British officers and railway experts for investigation and report.

About 10 p.m. the conversation turned to the forthcoming offensive, and on being asked by Mr. Lloyd George whether anything further could be done to render British co-operation more effective, General Nivelle produced a typed document embodying the well-known scheme for placing the British armies in France under his command. He proposed that—

Par délégation du Comité de Guerre Britannique, avec l'assentiment du Comité de Guerre Français, et dans le but d'assurer l'unité du commandement sur le front occidental le Général en Chef Français aura à partir du 1er Mars, 1917, autorité sur les forces britanniques opérant sur ce front, pour tout ce qui concerne la conduite des opérations, et notamment :

Le plan et l'exécution des actions offensives et defensives ;
Le groupement des forces en armées et groupes d'armées ;
Les limites entre ces grandes unités ;
La répartition des moyens matériels et resources de toute nature entre les armées.

At French G.H.Q. was to be a British Chief of the General Staff, who would communicate direct with the War Cabinet, issue Nivelle's instructions to the British Commander-in-Chief, and have under him a suitable body of General Staff officers and also a Quartermaster-General. Personnel and discipline were to be dealt with by the War Office. Finally, " *Au cas où le Commandant-en-Chef Français disparaîtrait, ses attributions passeraient au nouveau Commandant-en-Chef Français à moins de décision nouvelle des deux Comités de Guerre.*"

Thus the great New Armies, to the raising of which so much patriotism and labour had been devoted by all classes in the Empire, and which had just attained their maximum strength and proficiency, were, with the disposal of vast stocks of war material, to be handed over, within forty-eight hours and for an indefinite period, to a foreign General having no experience in the duties of High Command, and whose optimistic views of the coming campaign were shared by no responsible soldier in the British Army and by few or none in the French. The authority of the British Commander-in-Chief and of the War Office were both to be eliminated, except in regard to personnel and discipline, and for legal reasons these had necessarily to be left in British hands.

The proposal took Haig and myself completely by surprise, and our amazement was increased when Mr. Lloyd George expressed his agreement with it, though its details must, he said, be considered by his military advisers before he could accept them. After some desultory talk the conference adjourned till the following day, the representatives of the two countries withdrawing to consult between themselves. Haig and I then heard from Mr. Lloyd George, again to our astonishment, that on the previous Saturday the question had been specially considered by the War Cabinet, who had then decided, in principle, to place the British armies under Nivelle, whose orders were to be obeyed by Haig "in exactly the same way as by the commander of a group of French armies." Mr. Lloyd George proceeded to tell us that Nivelle's scheme went farther than he approved, and he asked us to prepare an alternative one which the three of us could talk over at breakfast next morning previous to laying it before the French delegates for acceptance. We were again enjoined to remember that it was intended the British commander should come definitely under the orders of Nivelle, and be liable to move his troops as and where that General might direct. After consulting together until near midnight we came to the conclusion that the change proposed was far too serious a matter to admit of being rushed through in the course of a few hours ; that the method proposed for giving effect to the change was in itself bad ; and that we could not properly consider and prepare an alternative scheme by the time requested.

Not being able to understand why Nivelle had put

forward his scheme without having first mentioned it to me, and wishing to find out before meeting the Prime Minister, I sent an aide-de-camp to the General early next morning to inquire whether I could see him. He at once accompanied the aide-de-camp to my room (we were all quartered in the same hotel), and it was evident from his manner that he suspected trouble of some kind had arisen. Coming straight to the point, I expressed surprise at the action he had taken, and suggested that unless we adhered to the custom followed when Joffre was in command, and talked over important questions before submitting them to Ministers for approval, confusion and waste of time must result. He quite agreed and replied : " But the idea of placing the British armies under my command did not originate with me. It was the subject of communication between the two Governments before we came here, and I was instructed to work out the details of the scheme and lay them before the conference for consideration, the understanding being that it would receive the support of your Prime Minister. Naturally, therefore, I assumed that you knew as much about it as I did." My answer was that I knew nothing about it until he proposed it—a statement which the General seemed quite unable to believe—and that in my opinion there were many objections to it. These were discussed in a perfectly friendly spirit, and before we parted the General several times expressed his regret that he had, unwittingly, been the cause of the misunderstanding of which I had complained.

I have since learned from the published papers of General Nivelle [1] that amongst them was a report from Major Bertier de Savigny, a French officer attached to

[1] Rapport Bérenger, Archives de la Commission sénatoriale de l'Armée. Reproduced in " L'Offensive de 1917," page 40.

my staff, dated February 16, 1917, saying that he had had on the previous day a conversation with Mr. Lloyd George and Lieutenant-Colonel Hankey [1] in which the former had expressed his entire confidence in General Nivelle and felt quite certain that he alone was capable of bringing the operations of the year to a successful conclusion. But for that, Mr. Lloyd George was reported to have said, it was necessary that General Nivelle should be able to dispose in the last resort of all the troops operating on the French front, of ours as well as of the French armies. The prestige which Haig enjoyed with the British public and the British Army would probably not allow of his being put directly under the French Commander-in-Chief, but if the War Cabinet thought that such a measure was indispensable they would not hesitate to give secret orders to Haig to that effect. General Nivelle never imagined that a proposal of this kind, communicated to him a fortnight before the conference took place by an officer attached to my staff, would be put forward by the Prime Minister not only without consulting me, but entirely without my knowledge.

Wishing for a little more time in which to consider the position, and never being attracted by invitations to breakfast, I sent a message to Mr. Lloyd George after my talk with General Nivelle asking him to see me later. Sir Douglas Haig also asked to be excused, his attitude being that the selection of an Allied Commander-in-Chief was not a question upon which he could appropriately advise. He gave me, however, a note, which I afterwards showed to the Prime Minister, saying that in the short time available he had considered the War Cabinet's decision, as conveyed to him overnight, and

[1] Secretary, War Cabinet.

had come to the conclusion that only two courses were open :—

1. To leave matters as they were, and
2. To place the British armies entirely under the French Commander-in-Chief.

The second of these meant the disappearance of the British Commander-in-Chief and G.H.Q., and so drastic a change at a moment when active operations on a large scale had already commenced as a result of the enemy's withdrawal on the Ancre would, he said, " be fraught with the gravest danger." Having placed these opinions on record he desired to stand aside and await the War Cabinet's instructions.

Further discussion with the Prime Minister was thus left to me alone, and after hearing what Nivelle had just said it was rather difficult to know what was the right thing to do. Nothing could be of greater military importance than the change of command proposed, and I could not understand why the War Cabinet—or Mr. Lloyd George, whichever it was—should have deliberately kept me in ignorance of their intentions and of their communications with the French Government. It was equally impossible to judge, from Mr. Lloyd George's account, what had really happened at the Saturday meeting to which the secretary had said that it was unnecessary for me to go. If it had then been definitely settled to make the change, irrespective of what responsible British military opinion might be, there was clearly nothing for me to say, and the War Cabinet must be left to pursue its own course. If, on the other hand, it had merely been agreed in a general way that the Prime Minister should ascertain at the conference that the arrangements for co-operation were satisfactory, the case would be different. Being in this state of uncertainty as to what the position really was, it seemed more desirable than ever to adhere to the overnight conclusion and, until better informed, decline to put forward any proposals for carrying out the decision which I had had no proper opportunity to consider, and which so far as I had considered it at all appeared to be unsound.

I told the Prime Minister this, and suggested that co-operation between the two armies was already secured, so far as circumstances would permit, by the Government instructions which had been issued to Haig when he assumed command in December, 1915, reinforced by those of January 17, and that even if this were not so it would be extremely unwise to entrust the command of our armies to a foreign General about whose qualifications so very little was known. I reminded him that officers and men preferred to fight under their own commanders; that the Dominion Governments might object to having their troops placed under a foreigner; and that in point of fact no British soldier could constitutionally be put under the *orders* of anyone not holding His Majesty's Commission.

He was not impressed with these arguments, and, repeating that he had no intention of accepting the French scheme as drafted, he produced an alternative one of his own, drafted, apparently, after we had parted the previous evening. It was less objectionable than the French version in that its duration was limited to the coming operations, but it might nevertheless prove to be the thin end of the wedge for bringing the British armies completely and permanently under French control, an arrangement which certain French Ministers had for long hoped to achieve. To that principle all British military opinion had been opposed from the day that war was declared, and finding that his draft was regarded almost as unfavourably as the original scheme the Prime Minister lost his temper. He said that he had come to Calais by the request of the War Cabinet to arrange for placing Nivelle in supreme charge of the operations, and that the arrangement must be made. If the soldiers (meaning Haig and myself) assumed an attitude obstructive to it, he would break up the conference, return to London, and the Cabinet would then have to act.

My first instinct was to allow this situation to arise, as being more simple and straightforward than to compromise on a matter of principle. But although tempting it was not a course to be lightly adopted, and after the Prime Minister had agreed to certain alterations being made in his draft I took it to Haig to ascertain if he thought it would prove workable. We made a further alteration in the direction of retaining the armies under British command, but this the Prime Minister would not accept, for, as he rightly said, it would neutralize the whole effect of what he wished to be done. He agreed, however, to the same instruction being inserted in the draft as had been given by the French Government to General Gouraud when that officer was acting under British command in the Gallipoli Expedition. In this its final shape the draft prescribed that the British Commander-in-Chief would " conform to the orders " of General Nivelle, subject to a right of appeal to the War Cabinet should he receive in tactical matters such directions as would in his opinion unduly imperil the safety of his troops.

The insertion of this proviso, regarded by Mr. Lloyd George as a concession, was in fact obligatory, since responsibility for the safety of British troops must necessarily rest with a British officer and could not be entrusted to a foreigner. The proviso was, moreover, both unfair and impracticable ; unfair because while the power of the British Commander-in-Chief over his troops was reduced, his responsibility for their security remained as before ; and impracticable because differences of opinion between the two commanders in regard to tactics could not possibly be decided by a body of Ministers or anyone else located in London. Time alone, to say nothing of knowledge, was an effective bar to any such arrangement. These defects were fundamental and no amount of goodwill on the part of the two commanders would suffice to overcome them.

The proposal to establish a British General Staff and Quartermaster-General's department at French G.H.Q. was negatived, but to the British Mission already there a more senior General was to be appointed as Chief, and an officer of the Quartermaster-General's department was to be added. The Prime Minister asked me if the final draft compelled Haig to obey Nivelle's order like a French commander. I said " Yes," and he replied that was what the Cabinet wished. During the day the agreement was signed by the delegates of both countries, including Haig and myself.

It may be conceded that the War Cabinet had a perfect right to set up any system of military command that they might choose, but they were undoubtedly at fault in the methods they employed for setting it up. Everyone having experience in the handling of men knows that while there must be no question as to who is master and who is man, the master will not go far or fast on the road he wishes to travel unless he carries his men with him, and especially those who are nearest to him. The War Cabinet deliberately excluded their two nearest subordinates from their counsels, purposely withheld from them all knowledge of their intentions, and then expected to secure their acquiescence in carrying out a system which was repugnant to both and which required to be introduced with the utmost circumspection. They knew that the General Staff, following the lead given by Lord Kitchener, would never lightly consent to the command of the British armies passing into French hands. They might also have known, if they did not—there was no scarcity of evidence—that Haig would never believe that French G.H.Q. was in any way superior to his own. They were also expecting much of human nature to suppose that he, a Field-Marshal, who had held the post of Commander-in-Chief for more than a year, would suddenly see the justice of being placed under the orders of a junior and comparatively unknown General of another nation. In short, the way in which the matter was handled completely destroyed all prospect of the new system being successfully applied, and in addition it created an atmosphere of distrust between Ministers and the military chiefs which never afterwards disappeared.

In order that all members of the War Cabinet might be accurately informed of what had taken place at Calais, I furnished a report to them on my return to London giving an account of the proceedings and explaining that my signature to the agreement did not mean that I approved of the principle of placing the armies under Nivelle, but only that I concurred in the procedure proposed for carrying it out. Ministers had, I understood from Mr. Lloyd George, decided on the principle before the conference was held, and without asking for my advice, and therefore with them would rest responsibility for the consequences. Not being a member of the War Cabinet, it was not for me either to approve or disapprove of what they had done. My first intention had been not to sign the agreement, but from what the Prime Minister had said the conference would be broken up unless the War Cabinet decision was accepted. As that might have caused serious embarrassment to the Government, at a rather critical stage of the war, I felt it must be avoided. Finally, I submitted that the decision to change the command ought not to have been taken without first hearing responsible military opinion, and while giving an assurance that Haig and myself would do our best to carry it out, the task would " be very difficult and causes me grave anxiety as to our final success in the war."

As a result of these representations, which were to have been discussed by the War Cabinet but had to give way to other business, some Ministers would have been glad to see the agreement modified, or cancelled altogether. " Milner," I wrote to Haig on March 6, " has just returned and he certainly does not like the idea of what has been done, while Curzon also is not easy in his mind. The whole difficulty has arisen because the Cabinet took the decision without first obtaining military opinion, and then the proposal was sprung upon you and me at ten o'clock at night. We have not heard the last of it yet by any means."

The agreement had in it, moreover, much of the personal element, and should not be attributed, as it sometimes is, solely to a desire on the part of Mr. Lloyd George to unify the command. It was due in no small measure to his mistrust of Haig's qualifications for the post of Commander-in-Chief, and he probably derived quite as much satisfaction from seeing Haig's powers cut down as he did from seeing Nivelle's increased. More than once during 1917, when affairs on the Western Front were being discussed, he said to me that his chief complaint was that I would persist in always supporting what Haig did, and there is no doubt in my mind that a recommendation from me, as C.I.G.S., to appoint a new Commander-in-Chief would have met with his instant approval. Without such a recommendation, which could if necessary be publicly quoted in justification of the appointment, Mr. Lloyd George was not prepared to act and therefore no change was made. This personal aspect of the matter is recalled because, unless it is borne in mind, neither the Calais agreement nor the treatment of other questions connected with the Western Front during 1917 can be properly understood.

Within a week of the signing of the agreement serious friction between French and British head-quarters began to arise, and the mutually helpful relations which had invariably subsisted throughout Joffre's term of office became acutely strained. The agreement itself was interpreted in different ways, and there was a difference of opinion regarding the situation created by the retirement of the enemy from his positions on the Ancre. The result was that ministerial intervention was again brought into requisition, and important questions which ought to have been settled within the precincts of military head-quarters once more became the subject of correspondence passing through the Foreign Offices and Embassies of London and Paris, and liable to be read by many inquisitive persons who had no concern with the operations and ought to have known nothing whatever about them.

On the same day as the Calais conference dispersed, February 27, Nivelle addressed a letter to Haig in which he confirmed the plan of operations previously arranged, designated Cambrai as the first British objective, fixed

April 8 as the date of the British infantry attack, asked to be supplied with the orders that had been issued to the British armies, referred to the question of transportation, and requested that the British Mission at French G.H.Q. should, as proposed at the conference, be at once enlarged, with General Sir Henry Wilson as its chief.

Haig replied, on March 4, that he had been engaged during the last few days in studying the possibilities arising out of the enemy's retirement, and that he had purposely delayed sending an answer until he had completed the study. He thought that the retirement might indicate the commencement of a more extensive withdrawal to the Hindenburg line (about the preparation of which much had recently been heard), the object being to shorten the line held defensively so as to set free divisions for offensive action elsewhere. The British Second Army front between Lille and the sea presented many attractions as a possible objective, and Haig therefore thought it desirable to make arrangements at once for rapidly reinforcing that flank by troops from the Fifth Army on the Ancre front, if and when the situation required it. Already the Fifth Army was opposed only by rear-guards, and to continue offensive operations on a large scale in that area would merely be to play the enemy's game. Pending the receipt of Nivelle's views on the point, Haig would proceed with preparations on his First and Third Army fronts, but was doubtful whether, under the altered conditions, the selected objective, Cambrai, would be feasible. For reasons beyond his control, he also held out little hope that his preparations would be completed by the date fixed. He added that he had forwarded to me, for the consideration of the War Cabinet, a memorandum reviewing the whole position, and he enclosed a copy of it for Nivelle's information. As to transportation, he expressed regret that the French could not meet his requirements, while in regard to the composition of the Mission he stated that he was submitting the names of certain officers for War Office approval, but suggested that before the appointments were actually made the duties of the Mission should be further discussed and then clearly defined, in writing.

In the letter sent to me covering the transmission of the memorandum, which was dated March 2, he pointed out that, as a result of the Calais agreement, he might not find himself free to deal adequately with an attack on his left flank, should it be attempted, and therefore he felt it necessary to report, under the provisions of the agreement and for the information of the Government, what steps he proposed to take to minimize the danger. In the memorandum itself he stated that the safety of his armies might be gravely compromised if they were committed beyond recall to an operation which would prevent him meeting possible eventualities, and he maintained that sufficient reserves for meeting them ought for the present to be retained in his own hands.

Both documents were laid before the War Cabinet on March 6, and it was agreed for the moment that no ministerial action need be taken. The two commanders were still considering the situation, and only if they failed to reach an understanding would it be necessary for Ministers to intervene.

On the same day Nivelle replied to Haig's letter of March 4, and enclosed a " directive " explaining his views and the manner in which he desired the British armies to co-operate. He quite properly declined to discuss Haig's memorandum, on the grounds that it was not addressed to him, but since it had been sent to the War Cabinet he had felt obliged to send a copy of it to the French Government.

To this correspondence Haig replied on March 9, and enclosed some observations on certain points referred to in the directive. He stated that he regarded the instructions given in the directive as unsatisfactory because they contained orders beyond the scope of the agreement. There was, however, to my mind, less difference of opinion between the two commanders than the length of the correspondence indicated. Both agreed that the original plan must be modified in order to meet the new conditions caused by the enemy's retirement, and they parted company chiefly because Haig was desirous of giving primary attention to measures for securing his left flank, whereas Nivelle argued, quite fairly, that other sections of the front were also liable to attack, and that there was as yet no definite evidence that an attack would be made anywhere. He therefore wished to push on with the preparations for carrying out the original plan, subject only to such modifications of it as were necessary.

As to the composition of the Mission Nivelle " insisted " that Sir Henry Wilson should be appointed, while Haig objected that so senior an officer was not wanted. This objection could not be upheld, for as I reminded Haig in an unofficial letter of March 6 : " It was agreed at the conference that a more senior officer should be appointed and you did not demur. I think that if you say, as you would be quite justified in saying if you so desire, that Wilson would not be suitable, your wishes would not be opposed [by the War Cabinet], and at any rate you would have a clear-cut case which we here could support. I have talked it over with Derby

[Secretary of State for War] and we both agree that it is impossible to support your objection on the question of rank."

In referring to same subject two days later I wrote :—

" I earnestly suggest to you that you raise no difficulties about the Wilson Mission affair. Assuming that you get the right man there you can leave the rest to time. It will please the Cabinet if you would agree to Wilson going."

Meanwhile, on March 7, a long communication had been received from M. Briand through the French Ambassador in London complaining that Haig had delayed for six days sending a reply to Nivelle's letter of February 27 ; that even then the questions asked by Nivelle had not been properly answered ; and that Haig's memorandum of March 2 disclosed an inclination not to accept the decision of the Calais conference, and a tendency, continually repeated, to reopen the consideration of plans of operations which the two Governments had definitely accepted. The French Government therefore requested that Haig should be ordered to conform without delay to the decisions of the conference and to the instructions sent him by Nivelle, and that the Mission should at once be strengthened as had been verbally agreed upon. Unless steps were taken to remedy these inconveniences the French Commander-in-Chief could not possibly ensure that unity of the operations which both Governments desired to see established.

The letter was considered by the War Cabinet on the day it was received, with the result shown in the following extract from a letter sent by me to Haig on March 8 :—

The War Cabinet were much disturbed yesterday by the receipt of the communication from the French Government. I proposed that the matter should be left to be settled between the Generals, and that I should go over and attend the discussions and represent their views [1] and get the thing straightened out. Certain members of the Cabinet would not agree to this. They think that the situation as portrayed in your appreciation [2] is so serious that Ministers must again intervene. (I wish to goodness the Calais conference had never been held. I always dreaded it.) After a long discussion the only thing I could get settled was their consent to a preliminary discussion on the part of the Generals, the Ministers to follow next day. There was much excitement yesterday and the usual amount of suspicion, but by to-day the atmosphere had cleared a good deal.

The chief bone of contention was, as just suggested, the interpretation of the agreement itself, and not the plan of operations for the furtherance of which the agreement was meant to provide. Very difficult of application from the first, the agreement had during its ten days' existence been applied in such a way as to render friction inevitable. French Ministers were bent upon so using it as to acquire the greatest possible amount of control over the British armies—at least so the British military authorities thought—while the tone of Nivelle's communications addressed to Haig was rough and dictatorial when it should have been conciliatory. It might have been fitting enough if employed towards one of his own Divisional commanders, but it was not appropriate in the case of a foreign officer holding higher rank than himself and commanding incomparably the largest British Army that had ever taken the field. Ignoring the sacrifices of national sentiment involved by the new procedure, Nivelle forgot that bare orders, though legitimate, might nevertheless be highly inexpedient, and that they were less likely to produce satisfactory results than friendly consultation and cordial personal co-operation.

Haig, on his side, clung to the procedure in force

[1] The War Cabinet's.   [2] Memorandum of March 2.

before the agreement was made. Now, as then, he was ready to do his best to meet the wishes of the French Commander-in-Chief with respect to the plan of operations, but he claimed the right to meet them in his own way and expected to be treated as an ally and not as a subordinate. These were also my views, broadly speaking, and I supported them whenever the question came before the Cabinet, as it had done practically every day since the agreement was signed.

The members of the War Cabinet, with one exception, also resented Nivelle's peremptory attitude, and were in favour of making things easier for Haig so far as that could be done consistent with the maintenance of the agreement in some form or another. The exception was the Prime Minister, to whose initiative the curtailment of Haig's powers had been mainly due, and who now suspected him of seeking to regain them by the creation of difficulties where none existed. Undoubtedly Haig's aim was to secure a degree of control proportionate to his responsibilities, but it was not the fact that he deliberately raised difficulties in order that the agreement might break down. They were real and fundamental, and were bound to present themselves whatever the action of Haig might be.

On the suggestion of Mr. Lloyd George another conference was assembled in London on March 12, General Lyautey (French War Minister) and myself, as representing the two Governments, and the two Commanders-in-Chief being brought together to unravel the tangle into which affairs had drifted. This was the method of solution for which I had from the first contended, and it had the support of General Lyautey, who was equally insistent that military questions ought to be settled by military people.

The chief obstacle round which a way out had to be discovered was the system of communication between the two Commanders-in-Chief. Both French Generals now realized that *orders* could not be given to Haig as if he were a subordinate commander in the French Army, and that, as a matter of custom, they could not be issued to him by the Chief of the French Staff, or the Chief of the British Mission. It was also realized that members of the War Cabinet were for the most part no longer prepared to sanction that system. Consequently some other authoritative means of establishing French control had to be found, and General Lyautey was in favour of the British Mission being located at the French War Office, where he himself would ensure that co-ordination was adequately and smoothly preserved. Nivelle, on the other hand, wanted to keep the Mission himself and through it deal with me, who, as C.I.G.S., would issue to Haig the orders which he, Nivelle, wished to have carried out. Neither of these proposals could, I felt, be accepted, since timely and effective co-operation could only be obtained by close and direct intercourse between the two commanders and their staffs.[1] Further, I could not consent to act as intermediary between Haig and anyone, if only because my hands were much too full already with other duties, including the supervision of four other considerable campaigns. Thanks to the

---

[1] On page 198 in " La Guerre vue d'en bas et d'en haut," by Abel Ferry, I am credited with having written to General Nivelle on March 13, " *avec bon sens, ces paroles qui sont comme l'épitaphe de l'unité de commandement tant recherchée : ' Depuis quelque temps nous avons examiné et établi bien des conventions, mais la chose la plus essentielle de toutes est que nous travaillions ensemble avec cordialité et que nous ayons les uns dans les autres une entière confiance.' "* I have no record of the correspondence, but it certainly represents what often passed through the minds of myself and others at the time.

goodwill of both parties a settlement of a different character was reached, which, if not conceding everything that had been hoped for, at least put an end to the dangerous friction that had recently grown up, while it enabled both Ministers and soldiers to turn their attention to more profitable matters.

The first section of the " Agreement between Field-Marshal Sir Douglas Haig and General Nivelle, on the application of the Calais Convention of the 27th February, 1917," laid down :—

1. The French Commander-in-Chief will only communicate with the authorities of the British Army through an intermediary of the British Commander-in-Chief. This arrangement does not apply to the relations between neighbouring Groups of Armies, nor to the carrying out of the duties of the French Mission such as they are at the present time.

2. The French Commander-in-Chief receives from the British Commander-in-Chief information as to his operation orders as well as all information respecting their execution. The operation orders of subordinate units are communicated to one another by neighbouring units in conformity with the usual custom, as required by the necessities of war.

3. All the British troops stationed in France remain in all circumstances under the orders of their own chiefs and of the British Commander-in-Chief. If the development of the operations should cause the French Commander-in-Chief to ask the British Commander-in-Chief to use a part of his forces for an action independent of the rest of the British Army, the British Commander-in-Chief will do his utmost to satisfy this demand. The Commander of the Force thus detached may receive, as long as his independent position lasts, direct orders respecting operations from the French High Command.

Section II defined the duties of the British Mission which was to be attached to French G.H.Q., and placed under the charge of Sir Henry Wilson. General Nivelle was empowered to utilize members of the Mission in studying and drawing up the instructions afterwards to be sent to Haig, and General Wilson was held responsible for transmitting them. But, in principle, all instructions and communications so sent were to be signed by Nivelle himself, though he might in case of absence or in an emergency delegate the duty to the Chief of his Staff or to the Chief of the Mission. The latter was further responsible for keeping Haig informed of Nivelle's intentions; of the situation of the French armies and the development of their operations; and of the resources of every kind which the French High Command could place at the disposal of the British armies. Similarly he was to keep Nivelle informed of Haig's intentions and the general situation of the British armies; of the orders given to them for the preparation and execution of the plans of operations, as well as of the way in which the operations were developing; and of the material situation in every respect.

The agreement was dated London, March 13, 1917, and was signed by both Nivelle and Haig, the latter adding the note :—

I agree with the above on the understanding that, while I am fully determined to carry out the Calais agreement in spirit and letter, the British Army and its Commander-in-Chief will be regarded by General Nivelle as allies and not as subordinates, except during the particular operations which he explained at the Calais conference.

Further, while I also accept the agreement respecting the functions of the British Mission at French head-quarters, it should be understood that these functions may be subject to modifications as experience shows to be necessary.

Unfortunately, the position as between the two Generals was no sooner clarified than a change of Government in France created a fresh batch of troubles. In the third week of March M. Briand's Ministry fell, M. Ribot became Premier, and General Lyautey was succeeded by M. Painlevé, who immediately let it be known that the whole plan of campaign was distasteful to him. He was alarmed at the depleted condition of French man-power, and wished to avoid further heavy losses ; and he had no faith either in the tactics of Nivelle or in his chances of success. Confirmation of these doubts was not difficult to obtain, for, as already recalled, most of the French Generals were equally disinclined to believe that the anticipated results would be attained.

The unhappy difference of opinion which thus arose between the General and his Government is not an appropriate subject for discussion here, but it is necessary to observe that considerable anxiety was created in the minds of the British authorities as to what the outcome of the disagreement would be. For three months past M. Briand and his colleagues had insisted that the right policy to follow was an offensive of the most vigorous kind, and they had been supremely confident of its success or at any rate of keeping it within such bounds as they might desire. They had even gone so far as to accuse Haig of trying to evade it, and in order to reassure them the War Cabinet had time after time impressed upon him and upon me the necessity of complying as far as possible with everything they asked us to do. Mr. Lloyd George's repeated injunction was that the greatest care should be taken to prevent the French Government from being able to say, should the results prove to be less favourable than expected, that Britain had in any way failed to fulfil her obligations. But the new French Government, holding views entirely opposite to those of their predecessors, would have been glad to see the proposed offensive abandoned, and a

waiting, temporizing policy substituted in its stead. [1]As
late as April 6—that is after the British artillery bom-
bardment had commenced, and only three days before
the infantry attack was due to begin—the leading French
Generals were summoned to Compiègne to meet the
President of the Republic and certain members of the
Government in order that the plan might again be
examined and discussed.

The reluctance shown by our Ally at this period, and
for the first time in the war, to engage in operations of
an offensive character, was the more disquieting because
of the defection of Russia. An Anglo-French mission
sent there by the two Governments at the beginning of
the year had returned without bringing back any warning of the revolution that was so soon to break out, and
when it occurred in the second week of March the
British Government, for some incomprehensible reason,
welcomed and praised it as being of advantage to the
Entente cause. The British General Staff took quite a
different view of the position. They thought that

while there are many incalculable factors in the situation, it is evident
that we cannot depend on the restoration of a stable government in
Russia, and that the policy of that country is largely in the hands of
a Socialist caucus animated by pacifist and revolutionary ideals. This
situation has already gravely impaired the efficiency of the army and
navy, and has greatly reduced, if not entirely destroyed, Russia's
value as an Ally. Previous to the revolution our plans were based
on the assumption that Russia could at least take such offensive action
as would tend to contain a large number of German and Austrian
divisions in the Eastern theatre, and that she would undertake an offensive in Armenia, and also effectively co-operate with our force in
Mesopotamia. So far as we can now foresee, not only is there no pros-

---

[1] It is only right to recall that the Russian revolution and the probable
entry of America into the war were new factors that could be regarded
as favouring a less aggressive policy for the time being.

pect of the Russians undertaking an offensive on the Eastern Front, but there is a great probability of their being unable to hold anything like the number of enemy divisions at present on that front. As regards Asiatic Turkey, Alexeieff has definitely informed us that, owing to supply and transport difficulties, of which he has only just been made aware, he can hold out no prospect of offensive action on the part of the Caucasus armies, and none in Mesopotamia unless we can feed his troops. We must consequently expect the enemy to transfer more forces from the Russian Front to the West, while the Turks will be able to transfer divisions from the Caucasus to Mesopotamia and Syria.[1]

These considerations, coupled with the declining strength of the French military forces and the hesitating attitude of the French Government, made it imperative that the British authorities should re-assume control over their own armies on the Western Front as soon as possible, and in a General Staff memorandum sent to the War Cabinet on April 17 a recommendation to that effect was made. During the past fourteen months the advisability of acquiring a greater share both in the diplomatic and military management of the war had repeatedly been suggested by the General Staff, but so far we had gone in the opposite direction and handed over the greater part of our armies to a French commander in whom not even the French Government itself had appropriate confidence. This subordinate rôle had been accepted by us, or rather voluntarily assumed, in spite of the fact that we had become the principal opponent of the Central Powers, and the financial, naval, and, to a great extent, the military mainstay of the Entente. The General Staff had no desire to dwell upon the reasons which had induced the Government to place the armies under an untried foreign commander, nor did they suggest that any change should be made while active operations were in progress, as that might do more

[1] General Staff summary for the week ending April 19, 1917.

harm than good. The object of the memorandum was to give the War Cabinet time in which to consider the matter and so be ready to make the change at the earliest opportunity. The attitude shown by Mr. Lloyd George at a conference held in Paris early in May, to which reference will presently be made, was an indication that the advice was not without effect.

The battle of Arras was opened by the British on the date arranged, April 9, and the French main offensive on the Aisne was launched on April 16. As the latter did not produce that decisive breach in the enemy's defences for which Nivelle had hoped, the question arose should the offensive be continued with some other object or should it be altogether abandoned? There was only one answer, but it had to be strongly pressed before the French Government would assent to it. Writing to Haig on April 26, I said :—

We have heard several rumours here recently that the French are becoming rather lukewarm in the execution of the much-talked-of Nivelle plan, but as I did not hear anything from you I paid no attention to the rumours. However, there must be something in them or you would not have been asked to go to Paris.[1] We have reached a critical stage of the war. You and I have always agreed that the Western Front is the main front, and therefore to us everything that happens there is of main importance and consequently we need to do the right thing there. It seems to me that at present the right thing to do is to continue fighting. . . . I shall be glad if you will kindly keep me informed, either by private or official letters, of your views in order that I may represent them whenever the question comes before the War Cabinet, which it is apt to do any day. It is only natural that the War Cabinet should be anxious. The situation at sea is very serious indeed. It has never been so bad as at present. . . . There may soon be a serious shortage of food in this country, and this has

---

[1] By the request of M. Ribot, Sir Douglas Haig went to Paris on April 26 to be consulted about the situation.

to be taken into consideration in regard to all theatres of war. For us to stop fighting now would seem to be a confession of failure, and would allow the enemy to do as he likes. Moreover we are undoubtedly winning and should do well provided the French play their part.

The views held by the General Staff regarding the attitude of the French were confirmed by the following note I received from Sir Henry Wilson, always a friend of France, on April 30 :—

> The French at the present moment are in an uncertain frame of mind. They have no man of really commanding presence and outstanding ability either in the Government or the country or the army. They are disappointed and sore at the failures of Nivelle's attacks as compared with the hopes they had entertained, and this soreness is accentuated by our greater successes. They are—for the first time in this war— dreading further losses, and yet they are as determined as we are to win the war but depressed because they don't see how to do it. The Government are therefore frightened to face the Chamber, and are determined to stop heavy losses. . . . The moment is favourable for our Government and our military chiefs to take an increasing responsibility and power in the superior direction of the war, bearing always in mind that . . . it is essential that we handle them (the French) with care and treat them with consideration.

The French Government favoured a defensive policy chiefly for three reasons. They thought that the loss of life would be less, and therefore a prolongation of the war would be less unpopular (not a very convincing argument) ; that Germany might be starved into submission (a possibility, but by no means a certainty, especially as she already had Rumania to draw upon and might later have Russia) ; and that further offensive measures ought to be deferred until American assistance became available (an impracticable proposition because of the long delay involved). America certainly had vast man-power resources, and in the course of manufacturing for the Allies had acquired much experience in, and provided enlarged facilities for, the production of war material. On the other hand, her regular forces were small, and not well adapted either to rapid employment in the field or to expansion. The authorities had carefully followed the events of the war, but until recently had not acted as though they would be closely affected by it. They had taken no steps to establish the elaborate machinery which the formation and maintenance of modern armies require, and—so it appeared to the British General Staff—they were amazed at the magnitude and complexity of that machinery as disclosed to them by their Allies. It was improbable, therefore, that American troops to the number of, say, a quarter of a million men would be ready for use in France before the spring of 1918.[1] By then, moreover, shipping might not be available to convey and maintain them there, for it might not even be sufficient to meet the needs of the Allies in Europe.

Again, assuming that the French and British peoples would stand the strain of a year's inactivity while enduring constantly increasing privations—not a light assumption to make—other nations of the Entente might find it difficult to hold on if the Central Powers were free to attack them as and where they wished. Already Russia was an easy prey, and what would be the attitude of her new Government if the Franco-British armies idly looked on while she was being overwhelmed? It might be said that could not be avoided, as she had ceased to count. But she had made great sacrifices on our behalf in 1914–15, and so long as her Government continued

[1] In April, 1918, there were in France only five combatant American divisions—say 180,000 men. M. Painlevé says that in June, 1917, General Pershing promised to have a million men in France by July, 1918.—" Comment j'ai nommé Foch et Pétain," page 206. The General never spoke to me in that sense.

to adhere to the Entente she was entitled to receive all the consideration and help that could be given. Indeed, as just mentioned, the British War Cabinet seemed to think that she would be a more, not less, valuable ally after the revolution than before it. Italy, too, would have reason to complain if the enemy forces on the Western Front were not kept employed, and already the necessity of having to assist her with reinforcements had been recognized.

In general, and having regard to the increasing violence of the submarine campaign and to the fact that the enemy still retained possession of large tracts of Entente territory, there seemed to be a real danger—as the situation presented itself at the time—that the adoption of a passive defence might so discourage some of the Allies as to precipitate peace movements of a serious character, and once defection set in there was no telling where it would stop. As General Smuts, a member of the War Cabinet, said : " No doubt the weight of America would be felt in 1918, but the danger is that we may not get there unless active operations are prosecuted, and a continuance of military success buoys up the spirit of the nations to fight on till America can come in as a decisive factor."

Finally, it was necessary to remember that the enemy was feeling the strain quite as much as the Entente, and in a General Staff memorandum of April 30, in which the situation was reviewed and the foregoing considerations were set forth, it was pointed out that, for the first time in the war, Germany was confronted with serious labour troubles, and that her plan was to act defensively in the West and hold us up there until her submarine campaign had time to take effect.

She is hopeful that this will happen before next harvest, for in the interval between this and then the privations of her people will be severe. If we can add anxiety regarding the military situation to anxiety as to food, we may bring her to terms. We are making her fight against her wishes, and that of itself justifies continued prosecution of the offensive. On the other hand, if we, by our inaction, leave her free to win easy successes on fronts other than the Western, and allow her to proclaim to the world that we have failed, she will certainly keep both her people and her allies together. With these advantages and a harvest, the yield of which will be increased by the Rumanian crops, she will in 1918 be in such a position as will enable her to regard with indifference the arrival of a dozen or so American divisions on the Western Front, even if shipping be available to bring them over.

The same opinion was expressed in the General Staff summary for the week ending May 3 :—

The French offensive, although it has achieved important results, has not met with the success expected from it. This is principally due to the fact that the French plans aimed at attaining objectives which were in fact unattainable in the present conditions of warfare on the Western Front. In spite of this, however, the results of the British and French offensives are such that the German Army has suffered the heaviest blow it has yet incurred ; the enemy's plans have been completely upset ; and there is abundant evidence that the general situation is causing him acute anxiety, and that there is increasing unrest in Germany. In these circumstances, it is important that offensive operations should be continued throughout the next few months with all the forces at the disposal of the British and French armies.

Steady perseverance with an offensive policy was, in fact, imperative, and the General Staff accordingly urged that steps should be taken to induce the French Government to accept that view. If they rejected it, or gave only a half-hearted assent, we should as a *pis aller* insist upon the French armies taking over part of the front held by the British so that the latter could complete their preparations for carrying out the offensive in Flanders to which the Government had drawn Sir Douglas Haig's attention six months before. Whether that operation would eventually prove practicable and likely to lead to the desired result of clearing the Belgian coast, would depend upon the amount of assistance, direct and indirect, which the French might supply; upon the enemy reinforcements which might arrive from the Russian front; and upon various other contingencies that could not yet be determined. The important thing at the moment was to press on with the preparations so that the project could quickly be put into execution if and when a suitable opportunity was afforded.

The War Cabinet unanimously agreed with the General Staff that a defensive policy could not be entertained, and that the time had arrived to have a frank discussion with the French Government on the whole question, so as to ascertain exactly what their intentions were. A conference accordingly assembled in Paris on May 4, France being represented by M. Ribot, M. Painlevé, Admiral Lacaze, with Generals Nivelle and Pétain, and Britain by Mr. Lloyd George, Lord Robert Cecil (Minister of Blockade), Admiral Jellicoe, with Haig and myself. General Pétain was present as Chief of the General Staff at the War Ministry in Paris, an appointment that had been revived a few days before, while General Nivelle had so lost the confidence of the French Government that his supersession as Commander-in-Chief was expected to take place at any moment.

The proceedings commenced with a meeting of the military and naval representatives only, who were asked to examine the situation and advise how to meet it. It fell to me to preside, and at a later meeting, when all the delegates were present, to report to Ministers the conclusions reached. As the latter formed the basis of the Western Front campaign during the remainder of the year, and not having in all cases been accurately described in the accounts hitherto published, they are reproduced here in full as I gave them :—

I conferred this morning with Generals Pétain and Nivelle and Field-Marshal Sir Douglas Haig. We reviewed the whole situation, including the situation in Russia and Italy and the entry of America into the war, and we arrived at the unanimous opinion that it is essential to continue offensive operations on the Western Front. A large proportion of the enemy's reserves have already been exhausted by the French and British attacks. If the enemy is given time to recover, the fruits of this success will be lost. He will be free to attack either Russia or Italy, neither of whom are at present in a condition to resist an attack in great force. His present object is certainly to encourage his people to hold out until the submarine warfare has taken effect, and if he is left free to gain easy successes where he can, and allowed to proclaim to the world that he has defeated his two principal enemies, he will attain this object. This might be fatal to our chances of winning the war. We are, however, unanimously of opinion that the situation has changed since the plan for the offensive, begun in April, was agreed upon by the two Governments, and that this plan is no longer operative. It is no longer a question of aiming at breaking through the enemy's front and aiming at distant objectives. It is now a question of wearing down and exhausting the enemy's resistance, and if and when this is achieved to exploit it to the fullest extent possible. In order to wear him down we are agreed that it is absolutely necessary to fight with all our available forces, with the object of destroying the enemy's divisions. We are unanimously of opinion that there is no half-way between this course and fighting defensively, which, at this stage of the war, would be tantamount to acknowledging defeat. We are all of opinion that our object can be obtained by relentlessly attacking with limited objectives, while making the fullest use of our artillery. By this means we hope to gain our ends with the minimum loss possible.

Having unanimously agreed to the above principles, we consider that the methods to be adopted to put them into practice, and the time and place of the various attacks, are matters which must be left to the responsible Generals, and that they should at once be examined and settled by them.

Discussion of these recommendations was, to the best of my recollection, opened by Mr. Lloyd George, who described them as excellent and announced his readiness to accept them. He admitted that they would entail losses, but since we were at war losses could not, unfortunately, be avoided. He deprecated taking a gloomy view of the situation, and pointed out that although the operations planned by General Nivelle had not given all the results hoped for, they had cost the enemy 45,000 prisoners, 450 guns, and 800 machine guns. What would the public in Britain and France have thought, he asked, had the position been reversed? Hinting at the prevailing rumours of undue interference by French Ministers with the conduct of the operations, he suggested that Commanders-in-Chief should not be expected to explain and justify their plans in every detail, but should be left to carry them out in their own way, and he dwelt with special emphasis on the importance of having a clear understanding as to what the recommendations of the Generals really meant. The phrase " limited offensive " should not be interpreted as implying merely the employment of small forces of, say, two or three divisions. Much more than that was needed. There must be a genuine intention on the part of both Governments to combine in maintaining throughout the summer the most aggressive action of which their armies were capable, and as Haig was planning to use his full strength, with the object of dealing the enemy a heavy blow, if nothing more, equally energetic action would be required from the French Commander-in-Chief. Mr. Lloyd George desired to know, for the information of the British Government, whether that action would be forthcoming. In fact, he did everything that a Minister could do to put matters on a proper footing ; to dispel the state of depression into which his French colleagues had fallen ; and to induce them to accept the recommendations which the Generals had made.

The French Ministers replied to the effect that, subject to Government control over questions of policy, they quite agreed that the execution of approved plans ought to be left in the hands of the military commanders ; that the French Government had never contemplated reverting to a purely passive defence ; and that Mr. Lloyd George need have no doubt as to the French share of the campaign being continued with the utmost energy possible.

The recommendations were eventually approved, both Governments undertaking " to continue the offensive on the Western Front in accordance with the principles agreed to by Generals Pétain, Nivelle, Robertson, and Field-Marshal Haig . . . and to devote the whole of their forces to this purpose."

The conference served to clear the air considerably, and to restore to the British military authorities that power of control over the British armies of which they had been deprived at Calais two months before. But the prospect of imparting to the campaign during 1917 that " decisive character " aimed at by the Chantilly conference of November, 1916, had meanwhile been greatly reduced by the revolution in Russia, and the failure of the operations in France.[1] " There is no doubt," I wrote

[1] Referring to the situation on the Western Front in 1917, Ludendorff says that " had the Russians attacked in April and May, and met with even minor successes, we should then, as in the autumn of 1916, have had a desperate struggle. . . . In spite of our Aisne–Champagne victory, it was the Russian revolution alone that saved us from serious trouble " (" My War Memories," pages 426–7). This admission shows the straits to which the enemy had been reduced by the punishment he had suffered in the Verdun and Somme fighting of the previous year.

to Haig on May 17, " that at the back of the French mind
there is a strong desire to avoid casualties, and after all
that is another way of saying that they are reluctant to
take offensive action. The War Cabinet are quite consistent in the desire to support our views as to the necessity
for continuing a real offensive, but at the same time they
are equally desirous of the French doing their share,
because if they do not it is quite clear that you will have
on the top of you all the German divisions which can
be scraped together. . . . The news from Russia becomes worse every day. The various Committees pass
resolutions calling upon the people to do the fighting,
but as a matter of fact the whole country seems upside
down and, as you know, it is impossible for any army to
fight, even if it wants to, unless it is disciplined and
efficiently administered. Both these essentials are lacking."

Matters were made still worse towards the end
of May by the series of mutinies which occurred in the
French armies, owing to the incompetence and disregard for the lives of their men, which, rightly or
wrongly, the troops thought that the superior authorities
had displayed during the early stages of the campaign
just finished. Indiscipline and impaired morale were,
moreover, not confined to the army. They were spread
throughout the country by the soldiers on leave from
the front, and strikes, disorders, defeatism, were reported
from many quarters. "*Presque chaque jour, depuis la fin
de mai, les télégrammes du préfet annonçaient les pires cat-
astrophes et réclamaient des tirailleurs sénégalais et de la
cavalerie. Bref, il faillait faire face, à la fois, sur tous
les fronts, à tous ces périls.*" [1]

In these circumstances, General Pétain—who had

[1] " Comment j'ai nommé Foch et Pétain," page 160.

succeeded Nivelle in the chief command—naturally wished for the British armies to be as aggressive as possible, so that his own troops might be given time and opportunity to recover from the condition into which, for no fault of their own, they had unfortunately fallen. There was also the necessity of not leaving the enemy free to give his undivided attention to the destruction of Russia, or to an attack on Italy. On the other hand, the means available for keeping him occupied would, until such time as the French armies had been nursed back to a proper state of health, be greatly weakened, and consequently it was very difficult for the British authorities to know what to do for the best. One thing they could not do—remain inactive—and therefore they decided to adopt such a plan as would enable them to press the enemy in a direction most favourable to themselves, and exploit any success that might be gained, while at the same time it would permit of the operations being modified as the situation might demand. Haig accordingly continued his preparations for the Flanders campaign, and arranged with Pétain to extend the French front so as to liberate for Flanders as many additional British troops as possible. The battle of Messines followed on June 7, and measures for the main offensive to the east and north of Ypres were then taken in hand.

This offensive policy, so vigorously advocated by the Prime Minister at the Paris conference a few weeks before, soon ceased to enjoy his approval, and in its stead he proposed to go back to the plan which he had advocated in January at Rome for combining with Italy in an attack on Austria. He justified his change of mind on the grounds that the French armies had not as yet taken that share in the operations which had been promised, and which, as all parties at the Paris conference had agreed, was necessary if good results were to be achieved. He argued, too, that if we were successful on the Isonzo front, and if Trieste were captured, a separate peace with Austria could be made ; that Bulgaria and Turkey would automatically have to go out of the war ; that the forces in Salonika, Egypt, and Mesopotamia would be released ; that Italy could be bound by a previous arrangement to support the French and ourselves in attacking the Germans ; and that, in general, victory would be assured. He considered this plan preferable to the Flanders project because, amongst other advantages, the distance over which the armies would have to fight to Trieste was less than the distance to be covered before reaching Ostend.

These views were not such as could be agreed to by the British General Staff, who still insisted upon the primary importance of the Western Front, and the whole question of British strategy was therefore once more thrown into the melting-pot and entrusted for decision to the " Cabinet Committee on War Policy." This body, a section of the Imperial War Cabinet and formed on June 8, consisted of the Prime Minister, Lords Curzon and Milner, and General Smuts. On appearing before it on June 20, I stated that although, owing to increased disaffection, French military assistance had certainly not come up to promise, General Pétain was reported to be satisfied that he now had the trouble well in hand, that his troops were already taking over a portion of the British front, and that others were to be employed offensively either in Flanders or elsewhere. Moreover, French disaffection, whether great or small, was not a good reason for sending British troops to another theatre, since Germany might counter that move by attacking the French in our absence, and under the assumption that

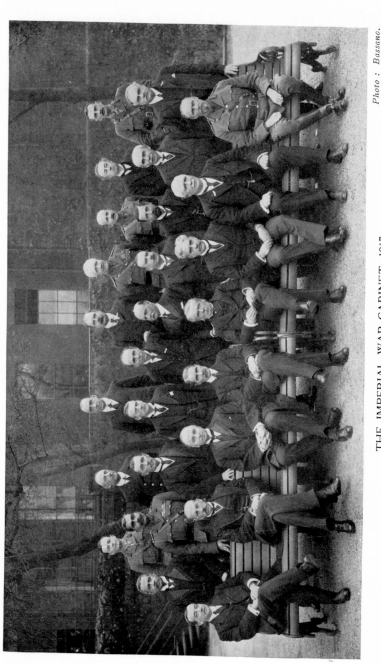

Photo : Bassano.

THE IMPERIAL WAR CABINET, 1917.

In the front row, from left to right, are seated : Mr. Arthur Henderson, Lord Milner, Lord Curzon, Mr. Bonar Law, Mr. Lloyd George, Sir Robert Borden, Mr. W. F. Massey, and General Smuts. In the middle row are : Sir S. P. Sinha, the Maharajah of Bikanir, Sir James Meston, Mr. Austen Chamberlain, Lord Robert Cecil, Mr. Walter Long, Sir Joseph Ward (Finance Minister, New Zealand), Mr. George Perley (Minister of Canadian Overseas Forces), Mr. Robert Rogers (Canadian Minister of Public Works), and Mr. J. D. Hazen (Canadian Minister of Marine). In the back row are : Capt. L. S. Amery, M.P., Admiral Jellicoe, Sir Edward Carson, Lord Derby, Major-General F. B. Maurice, Lieut.-Col. Sir M. Hankey (Secretary to Committee of Imperial Defence), Mr. Henry Lambert (Secretary to the Imperial Conference), and Major Storr (Assistant Secretary).

the latter were either unfitted or unwilling to fight the consequences might be serious. I further explained, in considerable detail and not for the first time, that Germany could always beat us in concentrating superior force on the Italian front if she so desired, and that before the Russian revolution General Cadorna had estimated that Germany and Austria together could bring against him ninety divisions and a powerful artillery. They might soon be able to do much more than that, and as Germany was doubtless quite as anxious to keep Austria in the war as we were to get her out of it, she might be trusted to supply all the help that was needed.

In general, my conclusions were that the

chances of obtaining good results are certainly no greater in Italy than they are in the north, while the risks involved are much greater in the former case than in the latter. I deprecate as strongly as anyone our incurring heavy casualties without a corresponding return, but the plan as outlined by the Field-Marshal [Haig] should secure us against this mistake. I have shown, and I understand the War Cabinet agree, that we must continue to be aggressive somewhere on our front, and we ought of course to do this in the most promising direction. The plan provides for this, and will enable us to derive a real advantage should the enemy show signs of weakening, while at the same time it permits of our easing off if the situation demands. No doubt the enemy will fight as hard as he possibly can, and will use as many troops and guns as he possibly can ; but he will also do these things on the Italian front rather than see Austria decisively defeated. I do not for one moment think that Germany is as yet near the end of her resources either in men or material. I think she may yet take a great deal of beating, and that it is necessary that France should be aggressive as well as ourselves. On the other hand, Germany may be much nearer exhaustion, both on the main fronts and at home, than we imagine, and there are many indications of this. Doubtful situations such as the present one have always arisen in war, and great mistakes have been made by endeavouring to find a way round as soon as the strain begins to be felt. We should be on our guard against this mistake. I am therefore in favour of continuing our present plan on the chance of getting a success in the north, not only because of the military situation but also because of the necessity of trying to improve the air and sea situation, and I am consequently averse from diverting any of our resources to Italy.[1]

The Prime Minister remained unconvinced, and at a meeting of the Committee held on June 21 he charged the General Staff with going back on the attitude they had taken up at Paris, where they had said that operations aiming at distant objectives ought not to be attempted unless a fair proportion of the German reserves were held fast on the French front. He also alleged that throughout the war every offensive undertaken had been accompanied by " sure predictions of success," and said that experience had made him sceptical of General Staff opinions.[2] Why should a greater success be anticipated on this occasion, the distance to be covered being 25 miles, than in the battle of the Somme when we succeeded in making a dent of only 5 or 6 miles? The fatal error committed in the present war had always been to attack where the enemy was strongest instead of at the point where he was weakest. Mr. Lloyd George concluded by asking me to consider the following plans :—

(*a*) The adoption of the Pétain tactics.

(*b*) The dispatch of reinforcements to Italy with the object of dealing Austria such a blow, including the

[1] Statement made to the War Cabinet on June 20, 1917. Post-war information has shown that Germany was, as here suggested, in a much more exhausted condition that could be proved when the statement was written.

[2] The procedure followed by this Committee was, I think, unique in the annals of military history, and it reminded one more of the Law Courts than a Council Chamber. Instead of being received as a military chief, the accuracy of whose views, so far as they were military, were not in dispute, I was made to feel like a witness for the defence under cross-examination, the Prime Minister appearing in the dual capacity of counsel for the prosecution and judge.

capture of Trieste, as would make her sue for peace, and to suggest any other alternative deemed suitable and practicable.

In reply[1] I stated in the first place that, apart from the military advantages to be gained by adhering to the plan already agreed upon, the naval authorities were continually urging that the Belgian coast should be cleared, as directed by the Government in November, 1916. In 1914–16 our main problem had been the provision of men and munitions. In 1917 it was how to preserve our mastery of the sea, which seemed to be in danger of failing us just at the most critical stage of the war. By speeding up the shipbuilding programme and introducing the convoy system and other new measures we were beginning to get on terms with the danger, but it was still sufficiently serious to constitute one of the two main factors in Germany's favour—the complete collapse of Russia being the other. This was not merely the opinion of the General Staff, but of the highest naval authorities. Only a few days before the First Sea Lord had placed on record that the facts were " conclusive in pointing to the absolute necessity of turning the Germans out of northern Belgium at the earliest possible moment. It must be done this summer. Every day that we wait the threat both from the sea and the air becomes greater. The operation cannot be carried out by the Navy alone, but it can be carried out as a joint business."

There was, too, the undesirability of Germany being found in occupation of the coast when peace came. " Such a situation," said the same naval authority, " would be a menace to the existence of Great Britain. Our Navy Estimates would in the future be of necessity of unparalleled magnitude. We should not only have

[1] General Staff memorandum, June 23, 1917.

to increase our naval forces to an unheard-of extent, but we would also have to construct harbours in which to station those forces ; those harbours must be on the south-east coast of Great Britain. Future generations of our countrymen would be heavily burdened because of our failure to realize the correct strategy to adopt at the present time. As to the correct steps to be taken there can be no possible dispute, and they should be taken at once."

The " sure predictions of success " of which the Prime Minister complained were denied. The General Staff had never made any such predictions if by the term was meant the defeat of the main German armies, or even breaking through the German line and reaching points many miles beyond. They certainly had not made them in regard to the Somme in 1916, while in 1917 they had told the War Cabinet quite plainly that Nivelle's anticipations were absurd. Nor did they predict success in the present case. The ultimate object was admittedly the Belgian coast, but the General Staff did not advocate spending our last man and last round of ammunition in an attempt to reach it if the opposition encountered showed that the attempt would entail disproportionate loss.

With respect to the alleged error of always attacking where the enemy was strongest, I could not refrain from saying " that the greatest of all errors was that of not providing before the war an army adequate to enforce the policy adopted. To our absurdly weak pre-war army can be attributed practically all the difficulties which now face us. Until this year we have not had the means to attack with the hope of getting a decision, and therefore we have had no choice in the point of attack."

Putting this governing factor aside, the General Staff

claimed that the defeat of the strongest enemy was the best object to aim at, since it brought with it the defeat of the weaker, though they agreed that if there was no reasonable prospect of success against the strongest, the next best course would be to defeat the weaker, if that were possible. To do this, however, it was necessary to hold the front against the strong enemy so as to prevent him sending troops to reinforce the weak one, otherwise the attempt to fight the weak would merely lead to fighting the strong in another place, and that after all the dislocation involved by a change of plan.

With regard to the so-called Pétain tactics, it was pointed out that there was no peculiarity about them except that they were not the Nivelle tactics, which the General Staff had been the first to condemn. The Pétain tactics were to attack on a wide front with limited objectives, and so to wear down the enemy. That was exactly what the General Staff desired to do.[1]

As to the argument that it would be easier to reach Trieste than Ostend because the distance was less, I pointed out that, in comparing the two operations, consideration should be given not merely to distance but also to ground, fighting value of the opposing armies, and the number of guns and amount of ammunition available. In all these respects Sir Douglas Haig had reported that the conditions in Flanders were in his favour.

---

[1] It is interesting to note that at the same time as Mr. Lloyd George was recommending the Pétain tactics to us, M. Painlevé was recommending the British tactics to the French. On June 14 he said in the Chamber of the future methods of the French Army : " Those methods are the same which you have seen applied in masterly fashion in the latest British battles, the results of which you know. They have been won at a cost in casualties so low as to appear almost incredible."—Painlevé : " Comment j'ai nommé Foch et Pétain," page 196.

There was also the question of Cadorna's qualifications for conducting the campaign. He had not shown any marked ability in the war as yet, and to transfer the main effort to Italy, and so entrust the fate of the war to him, was as serious a step as placing the British armies under the command of Nivelle, which Ministers now so keenly regretted.

Finally, and apart from all other objections, it could not be taken for granted that a decisive attack on the Isonzo would be allowed to materialize, for the geographical conditions were such that a counter-attack across the Trentino front, such as the Austrians had in fact made in 1916, would instantly bring the Isonzo attack to a standstill. Even if this did not happen, and if Trieste were captured, there was no certainty that Austria would ask for peace, for not until the Entente armies had gone half-way to Vienna would they constitute a serious military threat.

The memorandum concluded with the statement that

the war has now reached a stage when it becomes a matter of staying power and a determination not to be discouraged because opposition begins to harden, and in connexion with staying power is the submarine and air menace. The alternatives therefore seem to be :—

(a) Can we rely upon defeating Austria and getting her out of the war, and if so is it justifiable to run the undoubted risks of transferring a large part of our forces to Italy and of placing the decision of the war in the hands of a foreign General ?

(b) If the answer to the above is in the negative, or is uncertain, ought we not to continue with the plan at present approved, and, even if for nothing more, hope to improve the air and naval situations and so increase our staying power ? [1]

---

[1] Air-raids on England were particularly violent about this period, and were the cause of much anxiety to the Government—*vide* end of Chapter VIII. Hence, the necessity for breaking up the hostile air bases in Belgium.

In my opinion (*b*) is the right selection, and I can suggest no alternative other than those considered above. It is a source of deep regret to me that I cannot advise the adoption of the policy so greatly desired by the Prime Minister, for I fully recognize the responsibility which he has to carry. My own responsibility, I may add, is not small in urging the continuance of a plan regarding which he has " grave misgivings," but I can do no other than say that to abandon it and to attempt to seek a decision in Italy seems to me to be unsound.

General Foch, French Chief of the General Staff at the time, was equally opposed to the dispatch of infantry to Italy, though he was in favour of giving assistance with artillery if the Italians would undertake a serious offensive, but not to such an extent as would unduly weaken the British offensive in Flanders.

The War Policy Committee continued their investigations for several weeks after hearing the views of the General Staff, and summoned before them Sir Douglas Haig and various departmental authorities in London whose opinion on the different aspects of the war they desired to obtain. Haig was tentatively given permission, fairly early in the proceedings, to go on with his preparations, but nothing more definite was settled until the third week of July. This vexatious delay, which was a great inconvenience to those concerned with making the preparations, is explained in the following extracts from letters written by me to Haig at the time :—

6th July. He [the Prime Minister] is more keen than ever on the Italian plan, but I think it will right itself in time, because before long you will be on the point of going off [with the Flanders project] and I cannot conceive that the French will listen to any such proposal as the transfer of the major operations to Italy and the practical stoppage of operations on the West Front. . . . I gather that while the Prime Minister is keen on Italy, Smuts wants to land 150,000 men at Alexandretta (I do not know where he proposes to get them or the ships from),

Milner is rather inclined to think that the Balkans would be a good place, while Curzon sticks to our plan. It is pretty difficult doing business under these conditions.

18th July. You will remember that when you left here the Cabinet had not definitely approved of your plans, but said that you were to go on with your preparations. The War Policy Committee of the Cabinet, whom you met, have been continuing their discussions ever since, when Mesopotamia has allowed them to do so, but up to the present no official approval of your plans has been given. . . . Apparently the Prime Minister is the only one who is sticking out against them, and who continues to be in favour of the Italian venture. I have twice reminded him that time is running short, and that your preparations will soon be completed. . . . The Prime Minister had the War Cabinet members to dinner on Monday night, when there was a long discussion, and apparently while all the members except the Prime Minister were in favour of accepting our advice they all expressed, so I am told, at different times the fear that you might endeavour to push on farther than you were justified pending further artillery preparation, because they have all got on their mind, and correctly so, that the greatest losses sometimes occur in trying to take and hold positions too far in advance. I had a talk with one of the Cabinet on this subject yesterday, and impressed upon him that I thought they need have no fear as it is well understood that the extent of the advance must, roughly speaking, be limited by the assistance of the guns until such time as a real break-through occurs. He replied that so long as this step by step system of advance was adhered to he would back your plan for all it was worth. I understand that the Prime Minister asked one of the Cabinet when your operations ought to be stopped, if they did not seem likely to achieve complete success —that is how many losses we ought to incur before stopping. The Cabinet Minister gave a good answer. He said that he could not answer the question merely with reference to losses, and that the time to stop would be when it appeared that our resources were not sufficient to justify continuance of the effort.

21st July. I am sending you to-day a copy of the draft conclusions recently reached by the War Cabinet. We had a rough and tumble meeting yesterday. The fact is that the Prime Minister is still very averse from your offensive and talks as though he is hoping to switch off to Italy within a day or two after you begin. I told him that unless there were great miscalculations on your part, and unless the first stage proved to be more or less a disastrous failure—which I certainly did not expect it would be—I did not think it would be possible to pronounce a verdict on the success of your operations for several weeks. He seemed to have in mind what the French said last spring when Nivelle told them that he would be able to say in one or two days whether his operations had been successful or not.

He is very keen on capturing Jerusalem and this of course I also had to fight, and intend continuing to do so. Altogether I had one of the worst afternoons I have ever had, but find that, after all, I usually get more or less what I want. But it is very disturbing all the same to have these hankerings after other plans and mistrust of present ones.

Exactly what the terms of the " draft conclusions " were, or whether they ever went beyond the draft stage, I am unable to say, not having the necessary documents for reference. I have, however, a record of informing Haig, officially, that his operations had the War Cabinet's " whole-hearted support." The telegram conveying this information was dispatched during an Allied conference at Paris in the third week of July, and on the same day as it was sent, and notwithstanding the " whole-hearted support " promised for Flanders, the Prime Minister again revived the proposal for reinforcing the Italians with the object of " knocking out Austria."

Before going to Paris I had been requested by the War Cabinet to arrange with Generals Foch and Cadorna for the dispatch of assistance to Italy should the enemy reinforce that front, but that Mr. Lloyd George intended to raise afresh the larger question I had no knowledge. Foch, Cadorna, and I, on being directed to advise upon it, maintained that existing plans could not then be changed, and that the provision of Anglo-French troops for the Austrian plan could not be considered until after the Flanders operations had been completed and their results seen.

We were, moreover, somewhat anxious at the time because of the collapse of Russia, and it was agreed between us that, judging from the rate at which the American armies would probably arrive in France, the danger period for the Entente in 1918 would be between March and August,[1] and consequently that every effort should be made to strengthen the Western Front during those months. As to the reinforcement of the Italian Front in the event of attack, it was further agreed that complete plans for the dispatch, concentration, and maintenance of French and British divisions should at once be worked out by the respective General Staffs in combination with the Italians. These measures were duly completed in every detail by the middle of September—that is some six weeks before the need for the troops arose as a result of the battle of Caporetto.

The following week another conference was held in London when the Austrian plan was again brought forward, Mr. Lloyd George apparently hoping that, with French and Italian support, its adoption would be secured. What happened is described in a letter I sent to Haig on August 9 :—

Foch and I were told off to say what amount of heavy artillery could be sent from the West Front in time for operations on the Italian Front on the 15th September, and it was suggested by Thomas, Sonnino, and Lloyd George that it would perhaps be a good thing to postpone the contemplated Italian offensive, due to begin in a week's time, till the 15th September. The Italian General here pointed out the impossibility of doing this, and Foch and I later weighed in with the opinion that we could send no more heavy artillery to Italy in time for September 15. This was very distasteful to Mr. Lloyd George and his colleagues. I may say here that Baron Sonnino, and for that matter Cadorna, are both anxious to get heavy artillery out of us, and even divisions, and urged that they could then dispose of Austria.

---

[1] This proved to be the case.

This also is Mr. Lloyd George's plan for winning the war, with the result that there was a further long discussion on the subject yesterday. I expressed my opinion pretty freely in the morning, and said, amongst other things, that I was surprised to receive the impression I had from what Ministers had said, which showed that they attached no importance to the great and serious operations now taking place or about to take place on the West Front and in Italy. I said that I hoped that these operations would work a great change in the situation for the better. I added that I had already said that after the summer operations I would consider with Foch and Cadorna the possibility and opportunity of striking a blow at Austria in the spring, but that the question could not possibly be considered now, as it is impossible to say what can be done in eight or nine months' time.

Unfortunately, Lloyd George has got the French with him as well as the Italians. . . . I enclose some notes Foch gave me for my personal information, but which as a matter of fact he gave almost verbatim at the conference yesterday when called upon by Lloyd George to state his views as to what should be done in the event of Russia not being in a better position to help us later than she now is. Foch . . . seems to have made up his mind that it is hopeless looking for good results on the West Front. This will make my task much harder.

The result of the conference was that the British, French, and Italian staffs have to consider a plan of operations against the Austrians, and produce the result of their meditations at a conference which is to take place about the middle of September. For my part I shall produce no more than I have already produced. . . .

There is no doubt that had Mr. Lloyd George's wishes prevailed at this period the main British effort would have been transferred from France to Italy, just as in January, 1915, he wished to transfer it to the Balkans. Receiving no sufficient support from other members of the War Cabinet he allowed the soldiers' plan to go forward, and although more than once during its execution he assured Sir Douglas Haig of his confidence, he always disliked the plan intensely, and impatiently tried, first in one way and then in another, to get it superseded.

The Flanders campaign, beginning on July 31, had not been in progress a month when Mr. Lloyd George returned to the question of reinforcing the Italians, who a few days before had started an attack on the Isonzo front which they at first thought held out hopes of good success. Eventually, in order to meet his wishes, arrangements were made with Haig and Pétain to supply a strong force of artillery, but before it arrived Cadorna had decided to revert to the defensive so as to economize his resources for meeting the German-Austrian attack which might be launched against him should more enemy divisions be set free on the Russian front. In a letter of September 21, addressed to me and General Foch, the General stated that hostile reinforcements had already arrived ; that, including sick, his casualties had amounted to 720,000 men since the previous May ; and he gave other reasons for deciding that a defensive policy was necessary.

Considering that an eventual unsuccessful offensive might have most serious consequences for the Allied cause, and that such a failure would inevitably occur should the enemy's attack come upon us at a critical moment as regards drafts and ammunition, the Italian Comando Supremo has had, to its great regret, to decide to suspend the preparations for the proposed resumption of the offensive, and to provide, instead, for a reorganization of its forces, and to arrange for a stout defensive *à outrance* on the whole front, so that nothing arising out of the changed situation in Russia shall find us unprepared, either now or in the spring of 1918.

Looking back, it may be said that if, as desired by the Prime Minister, Anglo-French troops had been sent to the Italian Front in prosecution of a campaign against Austria, the Italian defeat at Caporetto would at any rate not have occurred even if the offensive itself had achieved nothing of importance. This would have depended, however, upon whether the troops sent were at the right place at the right time. The Italian defeat was caused by hostile troops breaking through on a comparatively narrow front and turning the Italian lines in the mountains which had no great depth, thus necessitating a retreat on a wide front. If the troops sent had not been on that section of the front where the attack was made, they would merely have become involved in the Italian retreat, as did the British artillery which had previously been sent. There was also the fact, from which there was no escape, that to withdraw troops from the Western Front in sufficient strength to achieve the desired object in Austria, would have so depleted the Western armies as to expose them to an attack beyond their powers to meet.

The detachment of Austria from the Central Powers would, of course, have been an invaluable counter-weight to the ever-increasing defection of Russia, and this consideration doubtless influenced the Prime Minister in pressing for action against her. But ways and means could not be left out of account. The conduct of war invariably involves taking risks, but the risk entailed by transferring the main effort from the Western to the Italian Front in the summer of 1917 was too great to be justified.

Circumstances making the Austrian project impracticable, the plan ordered to be prepared at the London conference was not produced, and the Prime Minister now turned his attention more particularly to a plan for taking decisive measures against Turkey. In a letter from me to Haig on September 24 this appears :—

The Prime Minister has been away during the last fortnight and his mind has consequently been very active. I have had to knock out a scheme for operating in the Aden hinterland involving the employment of not less than a division. I have also had to destroy one for landing ten divisions at Alexandretta, all of which would have had to come from you. Further, I have had to fight against sending more divisions to Mesopotamia. Generally, all round, I have been quite successful, although the expenditure of energy which ought to have been otherwise employed has been a little greater than usual. The whole Cabinet are anxious to give the Turk as hard a knock as possible this winter ; they have heard that he is sick of the whole business ; and they think if we gave him a hard knock and at the same time treated him liberally . . . it might be possible to arrange matters. Another thing that has been under consideration is Germany's intentions in Asia generally. Falkenhayn went there some months ago, and there is no doubt that he has been given orders to do what he can to make things unpleasant for us in that part of the world. . . . Further, there is no doubt that Germany is getting one or two divisions ready for use in Asia,[1] and we know for certain that she has sent a considerable stiffening in the way of experts, machine guns, and artillery. India is also somewhat excited because Persia is in trouble, and we have drained India nearly dry lately. It is thought that the Turks and Germans combined may make things very unpleasant in Persia and possibly for Maude, who has not got a very large force and certainly not a particularly good one, as to a great extent it consists of new units raised in India. Of course we shall not win the war merely by holding on to Baghdad . . . but the situation in the East requires careful watching during the winter months. After then it will become safer. . . . You will be interested to hear that as Cadorna has said he must go on the defensive the Cabinet are annoyed with him and I think also with themselves. I do not anticipate that we shall hear any more about your sending divisions to the Italian Front.

Concurrently with the Italian reversion to the defensive the Russian collapse became more pronounced, and in a letter to Haig of September 27 I stated that :—

Certain people here think it would be exceedingly difficult to bring about a decision on the West Front if the German troops there are materially reinforced (from the Russian front), and therefore they are incessantly looking about for means of detaching some of the hostile Powers. To detach them they maintain that more punishment is first required, and that naturally takes away from our concentration in the West.

---

[1] They were never sent, and perhaps were never made ready.

My views are known to you. They have always been " defensive " in all theatres but the West. But the difficulty is to *prove* the wisdom of this now that Russia is out. I confess I stick to it more because I see nothing better, and because my instinct prompts me to stick to it, than because of any good argument by which I can support it. Germany may be much nearer the end of her staying power than available evidence shows, but on the other hand certain countries in the Entente are not much to depend upon, and America will require a long time (to make ready). Further, stagnation will destroy the country's determination. It is not easy to see through the problem, when present resources of both sides and hostile gains are considered.

Meanwhile the Flanders operations were being maintained under atrocious weather conditions, and in consequence the progress made was slow and costly. " For four days," wrote Haig in describing the operations early in August,

the rain continued without cessation, and for several days afterwards the weather remained stormy and unsettled. The low-lying clayey soil, torn by shells and sodden with rain, turned to a succession of vast muddy pools. The valleys of the choked and overflowing streams were speedily transformed into long stretches of bog, impassable except by a few well-defined tracks, which became marks for the enemy's artillery. To leave these tracks was to risk death by drowning, and in the course of the subsequent fighting on several occasions both men and pack animals were lost in this way. In these conditions operations of any magnitude became impossible, and the resumption of our offensive was necessarily postponed until a period of fine weather should allow the ground to recover.[1]

The month closed as the wettest August that had been known for many years, and although September was less bad the persistent continuation of wet weather in the early part of October " left no further room for hope that the condition of the ground would improve sufficiently to enable us to capture the remainder of the [Passchendæle] ridge this year." On the other hand, the

[1] Dispatch dated December 25, 1917.

Commander-in-Chief wished to maintain sufficient activity to assist indirectly the French operations to be carried out on October 23 in the neighbourhood of Malmaison, and also to hold the enemy fast in Flanders while completing his own preparations for the Cambrai offensive in the south, due to begin about November 20 and largely depending for success upon the element of surprise. Hence, although he decided " to maintain the pressure on the Flanders front for a few days longer," the scale of the fighting was reduced to limited attacks made during the intervals of better weather.

At a meeting of the War Cabinet on October 5 the Prime Minister had again urged the desirability of putting Turkey out of the war, and the General Staff were requested to consider the possibility of undertaking such an offensive in Palestine as would have that effect. This policy meant, of course, some, and perhaps a great, reduction in the resources available for use on the Western Front, a result totally at variance with the General Staff views. I had also to point out that account must be taken of the unsatisfactory state of the French armies and of the general political situation in France, which was still far from reassuring. For these and other reasons it would have been extremely unwise to slacken our efforts in the West in order to deal with a second-rate enemy in the East. Sir Douglas Haig also advocated, in a memorandum written at the Prime Minister's request, the continued concentration of effort on the Western Front.

Mr. Lloyd George then had recourse to Field-Marshal Lord French and General Sir Henry Wilson for advice. At the time these officers were holding respectively the posts of Commanders-in-Chief of the Home Forces and

Eastern Command, and therefore had no responsibility with respect to the general management of the war. In telling me of his intention to consult them, Mr. Lloyd George said that it implied no want of confidence in the General Staff, but that, in view of the very serious situation in which the country was placed, and the heavy loss of life that was being suffered, he felt it his duty to obtain a second opinion, just in the same way as a second doctor was called in when a serious case of illness occurred. He claimed, in fact, that he was following the precedent set by Mr. Asquith on August 5, 1914, when half a dozen or more Generals were summoned to meet the Cabinet in order to draw up the initial plan of campaign.

I was not impressed with the " precedent " argument as the circumstances were different, nor could I pretend to be satisfied that no lack of confidence was implied. The analogy of the two doctors was also rather far-fetched. When a second doctor is called in he consults with the first ; the two together decide on a method of treatment ; and the first then carries it out. Mr. Lloyd George's procedure was to be quite different. He was to call in not one additional doctor but *two*, and far from consulting with the first doctor (the General Staff) these new-comers were to keep severely apart from him. They were to prepare a joint-prescription of their own, and then Mr. Lloyd George, after comparing it with the prescription of the first doctor, would himself decide which of the two should be administered. As events turned out, the two new doctors differed in their views as to the treatment required, and accordingly they submitted separate prescriptions, thus making a total of three from which Mr. Lloyd George had to choose one.

It is not forgotten that Mr. Lloyd George was carrying very heavy responsibilities, and if he felt that outside advice would help him one may concede that he was entitled to have it, provided it was obtained in the right way. The outside advisers could not possibly be acquainted with all the details affecting their advice, and consequently unless, before being accepted, it was reviewed by those who had that acquaintance—the General Staff—it might be productive of more harm than good. I suggested this to Mr. Lloyd George, but he objected that he must have an opinion independent of the General Staff, and that it must be sent direct to the War Cabinet. The matter was discussed in Cabinet, and as my suggestion was favoured by most of the members a compromise was made, the two Generals being instructed to send their reports neither to me nor to the War Cabinet, but to the War Minister, who would transmit them to the War Cabinet after obtaining such comments as I might wish to make.[1]

In writing to Haig on October 11 I said :—

The War Cabinet met this morning and discussed general policy, French and Wilson being present. The Prime Minister made a speech, lasting for an hour, on the lines with which you are familiar. He said much the same as he said to you when he last saw you. . . . French and Wilson are to consider three alternatives :—

(*a*) Continuance of offensive on the West Front.

---

[1] In October, 1918, when affairs were serious on the German front, General Ludendorff had an experience similar to my own. Referring to a conversation he had with Prince Max, the German Chancellor, he says :—He " also wanted to hear the views of other high officers on the situation. Only G.H.Q., however, had a view of the whole position. The conditions were different with each army. It was impossible to generalize for the whole front from one army. I refused his request. The Field-Marshal [Hindenburg] and I alone had to bear the responsibility."

(*b*) Adoption of defensive on that front until the Russian army is reorganized and the Americans have put their full strength into the field.

(*c*) Knock down the German props, i.e. Turkey and Austria.

I do not much care what advice is tendered, as I shall not budge an inch from my paper and do not suppose that you will budge from yours. . . .

The following day, October 12, I wrote :—

We made a little advance this morning in that the Cabinet decided that the French-Wilson product should be sent to me in the first instance to be dealt with before it goes to the Cabinet. This is as it should be if the thing has to be done at all. The whole atmosphere is quite different to-day from what it was two or three days ago, and I think the Prime Minister has found out that he has not got the Cabinet with him after all.

The reports of the two officers were received in the last week of October, and neither gave definite backing to the Prime Minister's strategical designs in the East. The chief recommendation in both cases was the formation of some central Entente body to be charged with the general direction of the war—a proposal which had been discussed many times during the past three years without result. Sir Henry Wilson further referred to the important question as to when the Entente should attempt to obtain a final decision, in 1918 or 1919, and suggested that it should be settled by the new " Supreme Direction." Lord French recommended that we should "stand everywhere on the defensive, only resorting to such offensive action as would make the defensive effective ; await the development of the forces of the United States ; and in the meantime rely upon a drastic economic war to weaken the enemy." But neither officer explained the dangers which attached to a waiting policy. As I pointed out to the War Cabinet, if by some miracle we could smoothly pass over the next eighteen months, and in 1919 resume the war under present conditions, plus the reinforcement in France of a million well-trained American troops, there would be no question as to which was the best policy to adopt. But unfortunately we could not perform miracles, and therefore had to consider whether the Entente might not, despite American assistance, be weaker, and not stronger, in 1919 than in 1918.

Lord French devoted some twenty pages out of a total of twenty-six mainly to a criticism of myself and Sir Douglas Haig. According to his view, strategy and tactics had both been wrong, and the losses incurred could not be justified. Months ago, he argued, we should have recognized more intelligently the difficulties of the Western Front, and concentrated on destroying the Turks. That was now too late. I made no attempt to answer the criticisms except to remind the War Cabinet that the General Staff had, in fact, put before them in December, 1916, a project for an offensive campaign in Palestine.[1] At the time it seemed feasible, and the necessary preliminary action to give effect to it was taken. Later the situation had been changed by the collapse of Russia and the precarious shipping position, and the General Staff had therefore been obliged to advise against the campaign. It was not a question of being too late, but of new circumstances.

Three weeks afterwards, at the Rapallo conference, the establishment of a central authority was, as already recalled, agreed to in the shape of the " Supreme War Council." With this exception the reports of the two officers led to nothing tangible, the fact being that they contained nothing that had not been thought about and considered many times before. There had never been

[1] Of this Lord French knew nothing.

any difficulty in saying what would be a good thing to do. The difficulty lay in being able to do it.

It remains to be said that the Flanders campaign was brought to an end in the second week of November, its final phase being for the most part attended by the same vile conditions of ground and weather as had characterized it at the commencement.

It was the immense natural difficulties, accentuated manifold by the abnormally wet weather, which limited our progress and prevented the complete capture of the ridge. . . . They [the troops] advanced every time with absolute confidence in their power to overcome the enemy, even though they had sometimes to struggle through mud up to the waist to reach him. So long as they could reach him they did overcome him, but physical exhaustion placed narrow limits on the depth to which each advance could be pushed, and compelled long pauses between the advances. The full fruits of each success were consequently not always obtained. Time after time the practically beaten enemy was enabled to reorganize and relieve his men, and to bring up reinforcements behind the sea of mud which constituted his main protection.[1]

The decision to persist with the operations in the face of these disadvantages has been widely criticized, and it may be said at once that responsibility for the error, if error there was, must be shared by the Imperial General Staff, since it was their duty, in communication with G.H.Q. in France, to call a halt immediately that course became advisable. The original object of the campaign— the clearance of the Belgian coast—was seen to be doubtful of attainment long before the operations terminated, owing to the bad weather experienced and to the delay in starting caused by the change of plan earlier in the year. But, as already explained, there were strong reasons why activity had to be maintained. We must give

[1] Sir Douglas Haig's dispatch, December 25, 1917.

the French armies time to recover their strength and morale, make every effort to keep Russia in the field in some form or other, and try to draw enemy troops to Flanders which might otherwise be sent against Italy, especially after her defeat at Caporetto. All these purposes of distraction were achieved, and in addition heavy losses were inflicted upon the German armies.

Another reason for continuing the operations was the belief at G.H.Q. that the strain imposed upon the enemy was being so severely felt that it might soon reach breaking-point. To the Imperial General Staff this view appeared a little too sanguine, despite the intelligence received from G.H.Q. in confirmation of it, and, wishing to satisfy me that G.H.Q. were right, Sir Douglas Haig on one occasion asked me to interview his Army commanders and ascertain for myself whether they did not agree with him. That, of course, I could not well do, and he then invited me to meet them at a conference which he was about to hold on the matter. Whatever these commanders may have thought they certainly did not in the discussion which took place express an opinion contrary to his, or give any indication that they entertained one. Haig and his Army commanders being better judges of the enemy's condition than I could claim to be, I was not prepared to carry my doubts to the extent of opposing him, and of thereby obstructing the application of that little extra pressure upon the enemy which experience has so often shown may convert an inconclusive battle into a decisive victory.

It is difficult to deny that the campaign was protracted beyond the limits of justification, but a correct decision was not so easy to make at the time as it appears now, and, in fact, post-war information shows that G.H.Q.

opinion was very near to the truth.[1] Further, it should be remembered that from the first the prospects of success had depended upon the British armies being kept up to strength, whereas, owing to an inadequate man-power policy, they fell greatly below it.

[1] For example, Ludendorff says :—

" The fighting on the Western Front became more severe and costly than any the German army had yet experienced. . . . From July 31st till well into September was a period of tremendous anxiety. . . . At some points they [the German troops] no longer displayed that firmness which I, in common with the local commanders, had hoped for." For some time past he had been eager to launch an attack on the Dvina front " in order to bring about the fall of the Colossus," but it " had to be postponed repeatedly. Indeed, it became a question whether we could continue to bear the responsibility of retaining those divisions [for the attack] in the East. The Crown Prince was not alone in his anxiety ; several Chiefs of Staff of very cool judgment shook their heads. . . . .

" The troops had borne the continued defensive with extreme difficulty. Skulkers were already numerous. They reappeared as soon as the battle was over, and it had become quite common for divisions which came out of action with desperately low effectives to be considerably stronger after only a few days. Against the weight of the enemy's material the troops no longer displayed their old stubbornness ; they thought with horror of fresh defensive battles and hoped for the war of movement. . . . There had been incidents, too, which indicated that their cohesion was no longer the same."—" My War Memories, 1914–1918," pages 476–481 and 542.

CHAPTER XIII

PREPARATIONS FOR 1918

Examination of Situation by General Staff—They propose strongest possible Concentration in West and Defensive Policy elsewhere—Predict Enemy's intention to seek Final Decision in West before American Armies can arrive—General Staff Memorandum objecting to Offensive Policy in Palestine—War Cabinet refers Question to Supreme War Council—Central Powers' Bid for Peace at End of 1917—General Staff Opinion thereon—Again predict German Attack on Western Front about February—General Staff reply to War Cabinet Question as to the Entente Prospects of Victory —Technical Advisers of Supreme War Council recommend Offensive in Palestine—Results of Advice given to War Cabinet during previous Months—Events subsequent to the German Attack in March—Break-down of Executive Committee—Palestine Plan dropped—All available Troops dispatched to Western Front—General Foch appointed Generalissimo—Some final Reflections.

THE cessation of offensive operations on the Western Front in November, 1917, found the Entente without any comprehensive military policy or plan for the coming year—a state of affairs for which Britain was largely to blame. The task of co-ordinating the activities of the Allied armies, which for the first two years of the war had, by common assent, been entrusted to French G.H.Q., had, owing to the supersession of General Joffre and the failure of his successor, gradually fallen out of French hands, and no adequate substitute for the original arrangement had yet been provided. Having regard to the large contributions she was making to the war, not merely on the Western Front but elsewhere and in many ways, it was the duty and right of Britain to supply the element of direction which France had relinquished, and this she had done only to a partial extent.

She had been instrumental in assembling a number of Allied conferences for the discussion of various military matters ; and the " War Policy Committee of the Cabinet " had sat almost daily since its formation in June, calling for memoranda on a variety of subjects and taking " evidence " and " advice " from different people. But so far as future military policy was concerned nothing had yet been settled, Mr. Lloyd George on the one hand and the General Staff on the other holding, as they had done from 1914 onwards, diametrically opposite views as to what the policy ought to be. The General Staff continued to assert that the main road to victory lay straight ahead, across the Rhine, while Mr. Lloyd George insisted that that road was too hard, and that the best one lay, if not via Italy, Trieste, and Vienna, then via the Mediterranean, Jerusalem, and Constantinople. Throughout 1917 this dead-weight of disagreement had grievously hampered the management of the different campaigns in which we were engaged ; increased the difficulty of securing concerted action between the Allied armies ; and, as winter approached, prevented suitable arrangements being made to counter the arrival in France of enemy reinforcements from Russia—a movement which, as all the world knew, had already begun and would doubtless increase in proportion as Russia's powers of resistance continued to break down.

With the object, therefore, of trying once more to obtain an authoritative recognition of the importance of the Western Front, I submitted to the War Cabinet a general survey of the situation and the action recommended to meet it.[1] So far Mr. Lloyd George's strategy had received little positive support from his Cabinet colleagues, and it was hoped that, if a more or less definite decision on the lines recommended could be reached, an end would be put to the conflict of purpose which had hitherto prevailed.

The first question dealt with—one that had often been mentioned by Ministers after America joined the Entente —was whether we should aim at finishing the war in 1918 or defer the attempt until 1919. The answer was easier to give than to apply. Obviously we should, if we could, defer the attempt until America was ready. But could we defer it?

In Russia the Bolshevists had just seized the reins of power, and Lenin had proposed a three-months' armistice all round. It was premature, perhaps, to abandon all hope of Russia's recovery, but there was little chance of her doing anything useful in 1918, and still less of her continuing in the war until 1919.

In Italy the enemy had also been engaged in a campaign of peace propaganda which, owing to the lack of adequate counter-measures, had impaired the morale of the people and adversely affected a considerable portion of the army as well. Largely as a result of it the battle of Caporetto [2] had just led to the loss of about three-quarters of a million men, and the effects of this disaster, coupled with a not unnatural feeling of war-weariness, would be accentuated in the winter by the scarcity of food and fuel which threatened.

France, shaken by what had happened in Russia and

[1] General Staff memorandum, dated November 19, 1917.

[2] The defeat of Caporetto did in fact weld the country into closer union, but this result was not yet manifest.

Italy, was herself suffering from a series of acute political crises brought on partly by the exertions of three years of war and partly by pacifist and Socialistic intrigue and unrest, and no fewer than four different governments had held office during the last eight months. These symptoms of growing impatience and waning resolution are apt to be forgotten now, but at the time they were the cause of considerable anxiety, and the British military authorities dare not disregard the injurious effect upon the French mind which an indefinite prolongation of the war might conceivably have. Moreover, the effects of the mutinies that had occurred in the French armies in the summer had not entirely disappeared, and although the autumn campaign on the Aisne had shown that the fighting qualities of the troops were still of a good standard, the reserves of man-power were so depleted as to render a sustained offensive in 1918 difficult if not impossible.[1]

It is true that against these dwindling moral and physical forces the Entente could set off the acquisition of a new ally, America, but unless more shipping could be provided, and the British shipping authorities held out no hope that it could, only twelve American divisions would reach France by the summer of 1918, and twelve others by the end of the year.[2] These reinforcements might obviously not counterbalance the possible transfer

[1] Not once, but many times subsequent to 1916, it was said to me by persons in authority that circumstances might force France or Italy to drop out of the war before the end of another winter. However much or little one might disagree with such views, they could not be entirely disregarded.

[2] This was the accepted estimate at the time. Under the stress of circumstances far more shipping was provided in the spring of 1918 than the shipping authorities had considered three months earlier to be available. The result was that the number of divisions brought to France by July, 1918, amounted to twenty-five.

of hostile divisions from the Eastern to the Western Front, either in regard to numbers or time.

It was necessary, too, in making a choice between 1918 and 1919, to consider not only what would be best for the Entente but what would be best for the enemy. We might wish to defer seeking a decision in 1918, but the enemy might, and we must assume that he would, try to force one, for if it would pay us to postpone the main effort until 1919, it would pay the enemy to deprive us of that opportunity.[1] He would, if we were definitely committed to a defensive policy, be able to deal with us as and when he wished ; our armies would deteriorate in efficiency ; and the spirit of the nations, not excluding our own, would decline.

The conclusion which I reached, therefore, and laid before the Government was :—

That the campaign of 1919 may never come, and in any case we shall next year inevitably have to bear the chief brunt of the war. It is upon us that the burden of supporting the weaker allies will mainly rest. Instead, therefore, of voluntarily adopting a defensive rôle—and in this I include minor attacks and raids common to all defensive operations—it seems to me that we should, by our example, endeavour to galvanize into life the efforts of our allies. I can conceive no decision which is likely to prove more dangerous from a military standpoint, or more ruinous to the Entente cause in general, than for us to commit ourselves irretrievably to the defensive for the next eighteen months, and to neglect to make adequate preparations for attack if and when required and in the greatest possible strength.

If Russia makes a separate peace, or if the greater part of the enemy's forces now on the Eastern Front are able to come West, there may not be any adequate prospect of obtaining decisive results in the coming year. We may also find that the demoralization and losses of material in the Italian armies are so great as to make it impossible for them

---

[1] This view has since been confirmed by General Ludendorff. " The American danger rendered it desirable to strike in the West as early as possible."—" My War Memories," page 544.

to take the offensive in the first half of next year, and to throw a great strain upon us in the mere effort to assist the Italians in holding the enemy.

In these two events we must have due regard to economy of our resources, and may thereby be compelled to restrict the object of our operations to :—

(a) Keeping the initiative in our hands so as to prevent the enemy from attacking us at a time and place of his own choosing—that is, in circumstances in which the chances of victory are in his favour.

(b) Assisting our allies, directly or indirectly, if they are attacked.

(c) Continuing the pressure on the West Front which has hitherto had such good effect upon the interior condition of Germany.

The nature and duration of these operations would depend upon the situation at the time, but their object being primarily to prevent the enemy from attacking us, their scope would be entirely different from what it would be if we aimed at deciding the issue of the war.

If, on the other hand, Russia remains in the war and may be relied upon to keep a sufficient portion of the enemy's forces engaged, and if Italy recovers, is able to reorganize her armies and make use of her large untapped resources of man-power, then the prospect before us, in view of the increased number of guns and aeroplanes and the increased supply of munitions which we shall be able to put into the field, and the gradual increase of the American forces, might warrant our pressing the enemy to the utmost extent of our power and aiming at a definite decision in 1918. The wisdom of adopting this course would also depend upon the conditions obtaining in the enemy's armies and countries, and in the latter they may well be more favourable to us than we are now inclined to admit. There is no doubt whatever that Germany is greatly strained by the pressure which has been exerted upon her on the Western Front this year, and this strain, increased by cold and want during the coming winter, may well reach breaking-point before the harvest of 1918 if intense military pressure is resumed by us early in the spring. Further, we know that some of the other enemy Powers are as exhausted as are some of the Entente countries.

Which of the above two plans should be adopted next year it is at present quite impossible to say, as so much depends upon conditions which cannot now be determined. I therefore submit to the War Cabinet that the only practicable thing to do is to make ready to the full extent of our power by the early spring, and decide then to what extent we should fight.

In furtherance of this policy it was held to be " imperative that we should be prepared to concentrate our full strength in Europe, should economize in shipping so as to bring over all American troops available, and consequently that we should limit our outside commitments to what is necessary in order to defend vital interests. . . . Whatever may be the result of General Allenby's operations [1] . . . we should so act in Palestine as will best economize force for the benefit of the European theatres, as we cannot afford to lock up during the hot weather either in Egypt or Mesopotamia more troops than are necessary to enable us to hold our own." As to Salonika, it was recommended that " every man who can be brought away should be brought away, and be more profitably used elsewhere."

A defensive policy in the distant theatres was particularly to be desired because it would enable American troops to be brought to France with greater rapidity. A further recommendation made was that our remaining man-power resources should be immediately and drastically re-investigated, with the object of ascertaining what number of additional men could, by a maximum effort, be provided. The memorandum ended with the following statement :—

Quite apart from the question of deliberately aiming at a decision next year, it is probable that circumstances may be such as will compel us, for the purposes of self-defence alone, to fight our hardest.[2] I would therefore again emphasize the necessity of our being ready in all respects to anticipate the enemy in the greatest possible strength

---

[1] At the time these operations were being attended with conspicuous success, the object being the capture of Jerusalem.

[2] From the time that this memorandum was written to the date of my ceasing to be C.I.G.S., some three months later, this consideration was never absent from the minds of the General Staff, and it governed all the recommendations in regard to policy which they put forward.

and at the earliest possible date. If the War Cabinet accept this policy, and when we know what our resources in man-power will be, preparations to give effect to the policy can be proceeded with in accordance with definite military plans, which, when completed, will be submitted to the War Cabinet, it being clearly understood by all concerned that the extent to which the plans will be executed is a matter which the War Cabinet have reserved for subsequent decision. It will, of course, be necessary to decide one way or the other sufficiently early to give Sir Douglas Haig due notice, since to defer the decision until a few days, or even weeks, before the operations are due to take place, might have a bad effect on the troops and involve many other disadvantages.

The policy here recommended of the fullest possible concentration in the West proved to be as unpalatable to the Prime Minister as ever. He still maintained that an offensive in Palestine was the right strategy to adopt, and instead of troops being withdrawn from there to strengthen the West he would have preferred to see them reinforced. He appeared to regard the advice tendered by the General Staff as lacking in imagination, and it may have been so, but in any case it made clear to him the risks which his own strategy involved, and so prevented a repetition of the misunderstandings that had occurred between Ministers and their advisers in some of the earlier campaigns of the war.

The other members of the War Cabinet were not prepared to override the views of the General Staff, but neither did they wish to oppose those of the Prime Minister, and the result was that the policy recommended was neither approved nor disapproved. The question was merely referred to the new Supreme War Council, who at their first meeting at Versailles on December 1 instructed their " technical advisers " to examine and report upon a military policy for 1918 and on the situation in Italy, Salonika, and Russia respectively. Thus the British military authorities were left to continue their preparations for the coming struggle as best they could.

The only other action taken by the War Cabinet which need be mentioned was the formation of the " Cabinet Committee on Man-Power," and this was unproductive of any really useful results.

As already recalled,[1] after the occupation of Jerusalem in the second week of December, the War Cabinet directed the General Staff to consider the possibility of completing the conquest of the whole country, and, alternatively, of continuing the advance as far as Aleppo, 350 miles distant from where Allenby's army then was. The memorandum, dated December 26, which contained the reply, was to the following effect :—

During the five weeks that had elapsed since the submission of the memorandum of November 19, German divisions had constantly been arriving on the Western from the Russian Front, and as Russia had consented to an armistice and was now formally discussing terms of peace with representatives of the Central Powers at Brest-Litovsk, the transfer of force was bound to be intensified. Day by day it was becoming more evident that the enemy intended to try and snatch victory before the American armies could arrive, and the only effective counter was to meet him with every man, gun, and aeroplane that could be collected. Against this obvious conclusion no amount of rhetoric could prevail, and not unlikely its very simplicity was, in the Prime Minister's eyes, its chief condemnation.

The proposed advance to Aleppo was too fantastical to merit serious attention, and therefore the General Staff did not discuss it at any length. In the first place Allenby said that he would require eight or ten additional divisions

[1] *Vide* page 187.

and these could not be provided, and even if they could his communications would not be capable of maintaining them. Secondly, as he would not be ready to go beyond the Palestine border for another six months, no reliable estimate of the force which he might need could at present be made.

With respect to the less ambitious policy of occupying Palestine alone, the memorandum pointed out that although the Turkish forces recently encountered had been routed, had lost quantities of ammunition and stores which could not be readily replaced, and were said to be short of transport, Allenby, as shown by his telegrams, was not yet in a position to follow them up with any great vigour. Therefore they would have an opportunity to recover, while in rear of them would be considerable reserves whose numbers could not be determined but might eventually bring the total up to between 80,000 and 100,000 men.

The advance from Gaza–Beersheba to Jaffa–Jerusalem had cost us 19,000 casualties, and if the advance was to be continued to the northern borders of Palestine—100 miles from Jerusalem—the drafts required to make up existing deficiencies, and to replace future battle casualties and sick wastage, might amount during the next four months to 90,000 men. It was not possible to find these without depleting the Western Front beyond the point of safety. Already the armies there had fallen so much below strength that infantry brigades were being reduced from four to three battalions each, or a reduction of 25 per cent., and the Government had just informed the War Office that the estimated requirements of men for 1918 could not be met.

Again, although fighting in Palestine might be less severe than in France, conditions in some respects were more arduous, and no troops could be expected to go through a hot season without a rest. Consequently, as the country was to be held " for the remainder of the war," two or three additional divisions might be needed for relief purposes.

A large and immediate increase in railway material and rolling-stock would also be necessary, and this was awkward because since Caporetto the Italian situation had made such demands upon French railway resources as seriously to impair our own and the French power of transportation on the Western Front. It was important that this state of affairs should be remedied at the earliest possible moment.

Lastly, there was the shipping difficulty. The submarine menace had been brought under better control, but sunken ships take a long time to make good and the tonnage available was still far below requirements, not the least of which was the conveyance of American troops across the Atlantic.[1]

Summed up, my advice was :—

Having regard to all the above, to the present state of our man-power, to the general military situation, and to the naval and shipping position, it is for serious consideration whether the advantages to be gained by an advance to Dan (northern Palestine) are worth the cost and risk involved. The answer depends to some extent, though by no means entirely, upon whether the conquest of Palestine would put Turkey out of the war. As to this there is a scarcity of foodstuffs, but even

---

[1] It is strange that the seriousness of the shipping position did not serve to check the Prime Minister in his insistence to develop operations in the East, where the amount of tonnage needed per man was so much greater than in France, to say nothing of enemy submarines in the Mediterranean. Speaking in London about this period, Mr. Lloyd George said : " Victory is now a question of tonnage, and tonnage is victory. Nothing else can defeat us now but shortage of tonnage."—*The Times*, December 15, 1917.

if peace were made with us we would be unable to do anything to relieve the food scarcity, though doubtless the distribution of the food actually in the country would be facilitated by the cessation of military traffic on the railways.

I do not claim any special qualification to speak on the political aspect, but it would seem to be very difficult for Turkey to shake off the German grip—even if she wished to do so. The Turkish General Staff and War Office are largely in the hands of Germans ; Turkish armies and minor units are commanded by German officers ; German machine-gun units and artillery are to be found in all Turkish theatres ; Germany is the source of Turkish munition supplies ; and several thousand German and Austrian troops are in Constantinople, which is at the mercy of German warships, the *Goeben* and the *Breslau* anchored in the Golden Horn.

As to the general military situation I can say little to help the War Cabinet beyond what has been said in my memorandum of the 19th ultimo. The opinion of the General Staff is that we should incur a grave risk by increasing our liabilities in secondary theatres in the present critical circumstances, and that we ought to cut down our commitments in those theatres to a defensive minimum and concentrate all other resources in the West. General Allenby should be able to exploit his success in the direction of the Hedjaz railway, and generally to make the Turk very uncomfortable, with a less force than he will have when the division arrives from Mesopotamia.

The vital point to remember is that the conquest of Palestine requires men and material which can be provided only at the expense of the Western Front, and I would submit that the War Cabinet should, before deciding to extend the Palestine campaign, consider carefully the probability of the enemy attempting to force a decision on the Western Front, including Italy, early in 1918, and the possibility of his succeeding in doing so if we do not concentrate our resources there.

I asked that the matter might be settled at once, as it was essential that if Allenby was to continue his advance the requisite arrangements should be commenced immediately, so that advantage might be taken of the cool season. If, on the other hand, a defensive policy was to be adopted, I wished to give priority as regards drafts to France, to withdraw one division from Palestine and send it to France, and to arrange for the dispatch there of such further reinforcements as could be spared. A delay in giving a decision might mean that later on we would have troops and guns on the move taking no active part in the war either in Egypt or France. No decision was reached, however. The War Cabinet, or Mr. Lloyd George, were determined that the Palestine project should proceed, and as they could not induce the General Staff to agree with them they turned for the second time to the "technical advisers" for the professional backing of which they stood in need and asked them, on December 31, to report on the "Military and strategical situation in the Turkish theatre and South Russia as a whole."

About this time, Count Czernin informed the Bolshevists at Brest-Litovsk that the Central Powers were ready to assent to a peace without indemnities or annexations, provided the Entente Powers would accept these conditions and agree to join in the negotiations. On being asked by the War Cabinet for my views on the offer, I suggested [1] that although it ought not to be peremptorily turned down it did not necessarily imply that the object for which we were fighting had yet been achieved. The Central Powers would naturally seek to utilize the situation in Russia to increase pacifist tendencies in enemy countries, and to induce their own people to continue fighting, on the plea of self-defence, if peace could not be obtained on their own terms. It was the more easy for them to create an atmosphere favourable to these ends because the so-called war aims of the Entente, being a little conflicting as well as somewhat selfish, had usually been stated in rather vague terms and so lent themselves to misrepresentation. I therefore recommended, as on

[1] General Staff memorandum, dated December 29, 1917.

some previous occasions, that the Entente Powers should publicly announce at least what they did *not* want even if they had a difficulty in agreeing upon a definition as to what they did want.

The Central Powers doubtless desired an early peace, and would probably accept terms more favourable to the Entente than those just announced. On the other hand, there was no sign that the German authorities were as yet prepared to abandon the doctrine of the " mailed fist " which had brought on the war, and until they were it would be foolish to suppose that trustworthy guarantees of future peace could be obtained. To promise not to annex territories conquered during the war might not prevent the Central Powers from acquiring by peaceful persuasion those which they desired to possess, such as Courland, Lithuania, Poland, and Macedonia, while the Entente would be compelled to return to Germany the colonies which she had lost, and restore Mesopotamia and Palestine to Turkey, who would, in effect, become a German vassal. Peace would thus find Germany in a stronger position than ever, and free to exploit her Eastern policy to the full. She was, in short, probably not seeking a peace so much as a truce, which, while dispersing the Entente forces to the four quarters of the globe, would enable her to organize a fresh attempt for securing that world domination which she had failed to obtain in the present war.

Leaving aside the ambitious territorial benefits which certain members of the Entente hoped to acquire, the questions to be answered were, could we outlast Germany in our endeavour to secure the future peace of the world ? Were Austria and Turkey more likely to drop out of the war than some of the Entente nations ? Could we resist whatever attack the enemy might make while America was preparing ? To none of these questions could precise answers be given since they were affected by many political, social, and economic conditions of the different Entente countries, about which no one could make a reliable forecast. The naval and shipping situations were also beyond the power of the General Staff to appreciate. The one certain thing was that, when the enemy found his offer to negotiate rejected, he would redouble his efforts to gain a decision before America could intervene. There was no other way by which he could hope to avoid defeat if the Entente countries remained firm in their determination to win, and he could not assume that they would not do this.

The *time* when his great bid for victory would be made was fairly obvious. It had to be

assumed that the enemy is reasonably well informed of America's preparations, and will know that she may be expected to begin to make her weight felt in the field in the autumn of next year. Under modern battle conditions it takes a long time to obtain even a partial decision, and therefore it is in the enemy's interests to begin as early as he can. It is not probable that he will be able to begin in the immediate future, that is within the next two or three weeks, for he has had to fight very hard throughout the year on the Western Front and has lost heavily in men and material. His troops require a rest, his drafts require training, and he has to assemble his forces, to replace his guns, and accumulate supplies of ammunition. As far as these various factors are concerned we may expect him to be ready from about the middle of February onwards, and as March and April will be the months during which the shortage of food and fuel in Germany will be most acute, it seems probable that, having regard to the necessity for sustaining the morale of his people, he will not defer his attack till after February.

With regard to the *place* of attack, it was pointed out that the enemy's

three main objectives are the Channel coast, Paris, and Northern Italy, and he has on the Macedonian front a subsidiary objective with which he may make play. Wherever he may elect to strike his main blow we must assume that he will pave the way for that blow by threats elsewhere.

Italy is the most tempting bait, as quite apart from her military weakness at the present time, she has been throughout the war, and still is, in a false strategical position. Her armies are deployed in a great salient and a successful attack delivered from the mountains against the flank of this salient may bring disaster. Having failed to foresee the Italian collapse the enemy was unable to follow it up, but for the past month he has probably been endeavouring to exhaust the Italian armies as much as possible so as to prepare for a greater blow next year when his preparations, particularly as regards transportation, have been completed. On the other hand, unless the climatic conditions next year are abnormal, it is unlikely that a great attack will be made from the mountains before the end of April or the beginning of May, and if it is not, the Italians, with the British and French support they now have, ought meanwhile to be expected to hold their own.

If, as suggested above, the enemy so acts, by feints and spreading false information, as to induce us to disperse our reserves, so that they cannot be used against his main effort, the *Salonika Front* will offer many attractions. The climate there about the end of February or early in March should be favourable for operations on a large scale, and he will know that any troops we send there could not be made available on the main fronts for many months. On the other hand, Bulgaria is weary of the war and may take a great deal of persuading to attack, while the enemy will realize that we can reckon on some reinforcements from the Greek army and would not in any event require or be able to send large forces to Macedonia. Still, an attack on this front is an eventuality for which we must be prepared.

As regards the *Franco-British Front*, the state of the ground and the climatic conditions are not favourable for attack early in the year on the northern part of the British portion of the line, but south of Arras conditions become more favourable and it will be remembered that in February of 1916 the enemy was successful at Verdun. The conclusion is that we must be prepared for a great battle, or rather series of battles, early in the coming year which we shall have to fight defensively ; that, being on the defensive, we shall have difficulty in deciding where the enemy's main attack will fall ; that we must be prepared for losses of ground, prisoners and guns ; that we must have the largest possible number of reserves ready to move at the shortest notice in any required direction ; and that until we can define the enemy's intention we must resist appeals for help which are certain to be made and avoid frittering away our reserves to meet what may prove to be subsidiary attacks. In fact we shall require to be always on the alert, to keep cool heads, and when we act to act quickly. . . .

If we defeat the enemy's offensive, as we may reasonably hope to do if we make suitable and adequate preparations and do not send our reserves off in wrong directions, how much nearer shall we be to getting a favourable peace ? This depends not only upon ourselves but also upon the extent to which the other members of the Entente keep in the field, and upon when America can enter in force. . . . The moral and physical effect of the intervention of an entirely fresh and enthusiastic army at a late stage in the struggle cannot fail to be of the greatest possible value, and we need to do everything we can to expedite and assist in the preparation and dispatch of this army. If we do this, and if we determine to endure, and if our Allies do likewise, until America is ready, we may hope to get eventually a favourable peace.

Shipping and men, in adequate quantities, were, as they had for long been, the main essentials needed to enable us to endure, and it was for the War Cabinet and not for me to say whether they could be produced. But I suggested that they could, and added that if they could not then, " militarily, there seems to be no alternative but to accept peace on Germany's terms, and these I fear would sooner or later be disastrous to the British Empire."

This concluding note of warning was no exaggeration, and it was intended to force the Government to take more effective steps for the provision of men—a matter that had been seriously neglected throughout the year. It was also meant to convince Mr. Lloyd George that there was more to be gained by employing our ships to bring the American armies to France than by using them for the prosecution of a campaign against the Turks in Palestine. Neither object was achieved.

Mr. Lloyd George's attitude at this period was difficult to understand. He continued to dally with the man-power question ; persisted with the desire to undertake extensive operations in Palestine, in disregard of the daily increasing danger on the main front in France ; and yet he appeared to doubt our ability to bring the enemy to terms. This inconsistency of mind was shown at the commencement of the New Year, 1918, when the War Cabinet put to me the following questions :—

Can the General Staff foresee a victorious ending to the War ? If so, when and under what circumstances ?

Do the General Staff foresee such an improvement in the future military situation of the Allies as would induce the enemy to assent to peace terms more favourable to the Allies than those offered, or likely to be obtained, at the present moment ? If the answer is in the affirmative, will the improvement be on such a scale as to justify the sacrifice involved in continuing the struggle ?

Can the General Staff foresee, either in 1918 or in 1919, a reasonable probability of the infliction on the enemy of a defeat that would not leave the military domination of Prussia successful and intact ?

That these questions should be asked was, perhaps, only to be expected, for the war severely tried the resolution of those responsible for its management, and there was nothing to wonder at if some should occasionally falter and give way to depression. On the other hand, the questions were practically the same as those already examined in the memorandum of December 29, less than a week before, and in the one dated November 19, and there was nothing new to be said about them. They were, it may be further observed, much the same as the question which the General Staff had been called upon to answer at the end of 1916 and which Mr. Lloyd George (then War Minister) had so strongly condemned.[1]

[1] *Vide* Vol. I, page 280.

In my replies [1] I submitted that it was essential to
look on both sides of the picture. The Entente side,
owing to the final collapse of Russia, the defeat of Italy,
heavy shipping losses and consequent shortage of certain
supplies, general war-weariness and shrinkage of man-
power, especially in England and France, might appear
black, but the enemy's side was not wholly bright. Had
Germany foreseen a speedy end to the war by the complete defeat of her enemies, no feelings of humanity
would have induced her to propose a peace which was
certainly not the one which she set out to obtain.
Hence we might safely assume that the German authorities did not see their way to victory, but felt that if they
did not take steps to stop the war they might themselves
soon be devoured by the forces of anarchy which they
had stirred up in Russia. Another possible motive in
making the offer of peace was, as already suggested,
that in the event of its being refused the people of
Germany, Austria and Turkey could be told that the
Entente were still bent on their destruction.

It was necessary that our answer to the offer should
be so framed as to leave no loophole for any allegation
of this nature. We must make it clear that we had no
quarrel with the people, and the latter would then know
that it was not England—as they were told—or any of
the Allies that stood in the way of peace, but only the
Junker Government. For the moment they might not be
prepared to throw over that government, but the further
heavy losses that might be suffered on the Western Front
in 1918, coupled with the continuation of economical
pressure, might bring about its downfall before the year
was out. If that happened we could certainly expect to
obtain more favourable peace terms than at the present

[1] General Staff memorandum, January 3, 1918.

time, and in submitting these observations the opinion was expressed that, " having regard to the intolerable position in which we should be placed if peace were made now, the sacrifices involved in continuing the struggle would be justified, provided we can achieve the necessary military successes. The question is : Can we hope to achieve them ? "

As to this I could only repeat that it depended upon a variety of factors beyond the power of the General Staff to calculate, and say that if we were engaged in a war in which the British armies alone were fighting a single belligerent, and in which considerations other than those of a military character were of no account, it would be possible to give an opinion with some pretence of accuracy.

But nothing resembling these conditions obtains in the present stupendous struggle, which is not a war merely of armies but of some twenty or more nations, and draws into its vortex every branch of national life. The chief factors about which I am necessarily ignorant, and which prevent me from being more explicit, are the extent to which the Royal Navy expect to cope with the submarine menace and generally to secure our sea communications, the shipping position, the rate at which American troops will be put into the field, the staying power of the Entente, and the number of men to be supplied to the British armies during 1918.

As to the latter point, it was clear that the armies would become weaker month by month and not stronger, unless far more men were provided than those foreshadowed in the draft report just furnished by the Cabinet Committee on Man-Power,[1] and I again urged

that although we must have shipping and also a Navy adequate to our needs, it is certain that we shall never get a satisfactory peace unless and until we exert such pressure on land against the enemy's armies as will show to Germany that it is useless to continue the struggle. Insufficient shipping and an inadequate Navy may cause us to lose

---

[1] *Vide* Vol. I, page 317.

the war, but neither shipping nor the Navy can ever win it. The question is, therefore, are we making the best distribution of our resources as between the different services which are contributing to the prosecution of the war, and are we getting the maximum value in return? I cannot say, as I do not know what calls are made upon our shipping or whether they could be reduced. Nor do I know what personnel the Navy requires, what it has got, how it is employed, what number or class of ships are needed, what are being constructed, what labour is required in the shipyards, and whether it could be diluted. Nor do I pretend to know the possibilities of offensive and defensive naval action, but it is a disappointment to me to find, especially as we now have American naval assistance, that the Admiralty regard it as not improbable that an invading force of 70,000 German troops could be transported across the North Sea to our shores. I suggest, with every respect and deference, that the allotment and employment of our resources of all kinds merit further investigation. When this has been made it will, I think, be possible for the War Cabinet to reach a safer and clearer conclusion as to our prospects of winning the war than they are able to reach from the restricted and indefinite replies I have been compelled to give.

On the whole question I feel, most strongly, that notwithstanding our difficulties and the many uncertainties with which we are faced, we can win if we will but determine to do so and act accordingly. We cannot expect to win without making the greatest possible effort, and enduring a far greater strain than any which we have yet felt. With the vast potential supply of men in America there should be no doubt of our winning. Our task is to do our utmost to ensure holding our own until America arrives, and meanwhile make every endeavour to expedite her arrival.

Two days later, on January 5, the Prime Minister supplied a statement to a Trade Union conference in London defining what the British war aims were and what they were not, and on January 8 President Wilson issued his celebrated Fourteen Points of a similar character. These announcements were satisfactory enough in making known that there was a wide gulf between the peace conditions proposed by the enemy and the terms which the Entente were prepared to accept, but the means of enforcing these terms, namely more ships for the American armies and more men for the British armies, still remained to be provided. The prospects of obtaining the ships were no better than before, and the position in regard to men was, if anything, worse.

Nothing specific having yet been heard from the " technical advisers " in answer either to the question of general military policy or to the question of Palestine (referred to them for report in November and December respectively), I again urged the War Cabinet, on January 14, to decide the Palestine matter themselves. The other and more general question had by now been determined for us by the diminishing strength of the French and British armies, the tardy arrival of the Americans, and the constant transfer of enemy divisions from the Eastern to the Western Front. There, as in 1914, and whether we liked it or not, the great struggle would have to be fought out.

Unfortunately, while the General Staff were anxious to assemble as large a force as possible in the West, so as to be able not merely to parry the blow which there threatened, but to hit back the moment an opportunity of doing so offered, some 760,000 troops were being retained in the East. Of these a considerable number could have been spared, but could not be moved pending a decision as to whether the primary object was to be, as the War Cabinet desired, the defeat of the Turks, or, as the General Staff desired, full concentration against the Germans in the West. The War Cabinet would decide nothing until the " technical advisers " had reported to the Supreme War Council. This was not done until the end of January—that is, ten weeks after I had first asked for instructions regarding general policy, and five weeks after the Palestine project was similarly submitted for decision. Than this no more serious delay occurred during the war, and it was due not to any fault of the " technical advisers," who at first differed in their views and also lacked knowledge of the general position, but to the unworkable system of which they were the instruments.

At a meeting of the Council on February 1 the " technical advisers " recommended that, subject to the Western Front being made secure, " a decisive offensive should be undertaken against Turkey, with a view to the annihilation of the Turkish armies and the collapse of Turkish resistance." What forces were needed to give the security mentioned the advisers omitted to say, and therefore their recommendation was not of much value.

Though eloquently supported by Mr. Lloyd George, who repeated all the old arguments in favour of fighting elsewhere than on the Western Front, the recommendation found little favour in the eyes of the French, and M. Clemenceau, who presided at the meeting, spoke strongly against it. He referred to the constant arrival of additional German divisions in France, to the fact that several rich French provinces had been in German possession for more than three years past, and he asked how was it possible, while French soil remained violated, and the French capital in danger, for him to regard with approval the dispatch of Entente troops to fight against Turks in another continent ? Operations in Palestine were, he did not deny, a matter for the British Government to decide, but he pleaded that at least the Western Front should not be made weaker than it then was.

Before putting to the meeting the resolution proposed by Mr. Lloyd George for giving effect to the technical advisers' recommendation, M. Clemenceau asked if anyone present wished to offer any further observations upon it. I felt it my duty to say :—

It is not for me to approve or to oppose any resolution of the Council as I am not a member of it, but as I have been summoned to attend I feel compelled to submit, in view of the state of the Entente's resources, especially in men and shipping, and of possible events on the Western Front this year, that the Council ought to adopt a defensive policy in all secondary theatres, and to keep no more troops there than are necessary for that purpose. I am also of opinion that to undertake the campaign in Palestine as recommended by the " technical advisers " of the Council is not a practical plan, and to attempt it will be very dangerous and detrimental to our prospects of winning the war.

Sir Douglas Haig, who was present, said nothing, to the best of my recollection. He probably regarded Palestine as being no business of his, as in a sense it was not, although indirectly it had an influence upon his operations. General Foch also remained silent, having apparently nothing to add to what had been said by his Prime Minister, M. Clemenceau. So far as I remember nothing was said by the Italian or American representatives, who no doubt regarded the question as one mainly for the British Government.

M. Clemenceau then suggested that the Council should take note of the objections which I had raised, and asked whether they involved any modification of the resolution. Mr. Lloyd George said that he still adhered to it, and as no one else made any further remarks it was accepted.

Immediately after the meeting I apologized to the Prime Minister for having opposed his plan before the foreign delegates, and explained that, if I had said nothing, they might have thought I had no objection to offer. He angrily disagreed, saying that, as I had already acquainted him with the General Staff's views, there was no necessity to repeat them before the Council. This, I may observe, was quite a different attitude from the one he had taken

up when giving evidence before the Dardanelles Commission a year or so earlier. He then agreed with
the Commissioners that if naval and military advisers
present at Ministerial Councils did not express dissent
it was legitimate to assume that they agreed with what
was being done.

The Palestine and Dardanelles cases taken together
furnish an instructive example of the dilemma in which
a naval or military adviser may find himself when
Ministers are bent on forcing through plans of operations
of their own, knowing that the professionals do not
approve of them. If the adviser, believing a plan to be
bad, remains silent, as Lord Fisher did at the War Council
when the Dardanelles project was being discussed, the
result may be disaster and he will be blamed for not
having pointed out the danger. If he protests, as I did
at Versailles, his relations with Ministers may become
impossible, as mine did, and he may still fail to prevent
the objectionable plan from being carried out, in which
case the result may again be disaster, as happened on the
Western Front in March, 1918.[1]

It is submitted that naval and military officers holding
the position of professional advisers to the Government ought not to be deterred by these or any other

[1] Referring to the pressure which he put upon Lord Fisher in order
to secure his concurrence in the naval attack at the Dardanelles, Mr.
Churchill says : " Was it wrong to put this pressure upon the First
Sea Lord ? I cannot think so. War is a business of terrible pressures,
and persons who take part in it must fail if they are not strong enough
to withstand them. As a mere politician and civilian, I would never
have agreed to the Dardanelles project if I had not believed in it. . . .
Had I been in Lord Fisher's position and held his views, I would have
refused point blank. . . . First Sea Lords have to stand up to facts
and take their decisions resolutely at the moment of choice."—" The
World Crisis, 1915," page 166.

considerations from plainly stating what they think. Of course, they must do all they can to cultivate good relations with their ministerial masters, and endeavour to meet their wishes, but when a state of war exists, and men's lives are at stake, they will be disloyal to their country if, knowing that a plan is bad, they do not speak out and condemn it.[1] My experience is, that if officers act in this manner, it will be seldom that Ministers will either wish or dare to override their opinion. They may, for reasons of policy, quite properly negative proposals which their professional advisers put forward, but that is quite a different thing from insisting upon the execution of military operations which those advisers pronounce to be militarily unsound.

At the same meeting of the Supreme War Council the question of British man-power was raised, General Foch alleging that we had not called up nearly as many men for military service as we might have done. Mr. Lloyd George replied that if he were asked to produce more men there might be a revolution in the country, and he protested against the actions of the British Government being criticized by an officer of another nation. He pointed out that the disposal of British man-power was the business of the British Government alone, and declared that he would withdraw from the conference if the presiding Minister, M. Clemenceau, allowed General Foch to interfere when he had no right to do so. Although entirely justified in making the protest Mr. Lloyd George had only himself to blame for what had happened. As

---

[1] Napoleon is credited with having said : " *Tout général en chef qui se charge d'éxécuter un plan qu'il trouve mauvais, est coupable. Il doit réprésenter ses motifs, insister pour que le plan soit changé, enfin donner sa démission plutôt que d'être l'instrument de la ruine de ses troupes.*"

already explained,[1] he had only a few weeks before disputed the accuracy of the War Office calculations in regard to wastage, and had requisitioned the services of a French officer to advise him thereon. While in London this officer necessarily gained a good deal of inside information about British man-power, which he doubtless passed on to the Chief of the French General Staff, General Foch, by whom it was utilized in support of the allegation just mentioned. It thus came about that Mr. Lloyd George, after employing in London a French officer to disprove the calculations of the War Office with respect to the number of men needed, found himself obliged at Versailles to call upon a member of the War Office to disprove the calculations of the French with regard to the number of men that could be produced!

It was further decided at the same meeting that the " technical advisers " should become an " Executive Committee," under the presidency of General Foch, vested with powers to determine the strength, dispositions, and employment of the allied strategical reserves, and to issue orders thereon to Commanders-in-Chief. The Committee was made, in fact, to constitute the High Command of the Allied armies.

The general results of the advice given to the War Cabinet during the previous three or four months in regard to preparations for 1918 may now be summarized :—

(*a*) The warnings with respect to the continuous arrival of German reinforcements on the Western Front, and the prediction that a desperate attempt to snatch victory would probably be made by the enemy on that front not later than February, were, for all practical purposes, disregarded.

[1] In Chapter VII.

(*b*) The reiterated recommendation to bring away from Eastern theatres all troops not required for defensive purposes, so as to meet the impending attack in the West in the greatest possible strength, was similarly ignored, and an offensive campaign was to be undertaken in Palestine against the Turks.

(*c*) The requisition for 600,000 men for the Army during 1918 was rejected by the Prime Minister's Man-power Committee as being both impracticable and unnecessary ; impracticable owing to the more pressing demands of other services, and unnecessary owing to the defensive policy that it was proposed to pursue on the Western Front.

(*d*) The decision to vest control of the allied reserves in a French-British-Italian-American Executive Committee made the Allied system of command more unsatisfactory than ever, in that it increased the number of superior authorities already existing and divided the armies into two portions—one being left under the orders of Commanders-in-Chief; while the other was to be controlled by the Committee. The confusion thus introduced was aggravated in our case by the British representative being made entirely independent of his own General Staff—a hopelessly vicious method adopted by no other Government.

Why the British preparations were not more in accord with the situation can be understood from what has already been said. The principal reason was that Mr. Lloyd George insisted upon the policy of defeating Germany by the process of " knocking down the props." He seemed entirely to overlook the fact that Germany herself constituted the props, and that the moment she weakened the Central Alliance would fall to pieces. He thought that the attempt to seek a decision on the Western

Front could safely be deferred until 1919, when the Americans would have arrived in full strength, and he made insufficient allowance for what the enemy might do in the meantime, being of opinion that we were " over-insured in the West." He knew little about the importance of good organization, and seemed to care equally little for military method of any kind. He had a profound belief in his own strategical conceptions, and in his zeal to see them adopted was more eager to procure evidence in support of their merits than to listen to criticisms which exposed their defects. Sometimes he was inclined to go farther than this, and, like Ahab of old, to display a distinct antipathy towards those soldiers who, mistrusting his strategy, dared to " prophesy evil" concerning it.

With the consequences of this unfortunate state of affairs I had no dealings, having ceased to be C.I.G.S. on February 19, but the chief events that followed the Versailles conference referred to above may be recapitulated so as to complete the narrative.

The " Executive Committee " called upon the British, French, and Italian Commanders-in-Chief to allocate a certain number of divisions for the general reserve. Sir Douglas Haig, having largely extended his front in relief of French troops, and having good information to show that the main attack would probably be directed against his Third and Fifth Armies, declined to furnish the quota demanded. The matter was then referred to an Allied conference which met in London, on March 14, and Haig's refusal was upheld. That, in effect, put an end to the Executive Committee as an organ of command, for as no general reserve was constituted the Committee was left with no executive functions to perform.

The Prime Minister's nervousness as to the ability of the Entente to defeat the Central Powers was not lessened, apparently, either by the creation of the Executive Committee or by the appointment of a new C.I.G.S., for about the middle of March he asked the latter whether, in his opinion, a favourable decision to the war could be obtained in 1919 or later—a question similar to the one which the General Staff had already answered three times during the past few months. Both the War Cabinet and the new C.I.G.S. seem to have thought that the war could not possibly be decided in 1918, and preparations were accordingly directed towards making the main effort in 1919, or later. The C.I.G.S. deferred for the moment giving a complete reply to the question put to him, but he said, what had been said many times before by me, that a favourable decision could only be obtained by defeating the main German armies, that that could only be done on the Western Front, and that man-power was the crux of the whole problem. As already told, he asked for 46,000 additional men with which to man the tanks he proposed to build for 1919, and stated that the possibility of keeping the infantry divisions up to strength in the meantime depended entirely upon whether heavy casualties could be avoided. Within three days of this statement being made the German attack began, casualties on an unprecedented high scale were suffered, and the legislative measures recommended by the Military Members of the Army Council sixteen months before were then taken.

With regard to Palestine, although the " technical advisers " had by their recommendation at Versailles given to Mr. Lloyd George's enterprise the professional legitimacy which he could not obtain for it from the General Staff, they were not able to provide him with

the additional troops needed to carry it out, and at the
same time comply with the conditions which they themselves had laid down with respect to the security of the
Western Front. The two things were, in fact, irreconcil-
able, and the " advisers " probably felt them to be so
or they would have rejected the proposal outright. When
the German attack on the Western Front was launched
the situation arose which the General Staff had foreseen
four months before and tried to prevent: a large
number of troops had to be transferred to France from
Palestine, and so found themselves out of action for
several weeks just at the time when every man should
have been fighting. They consisted of two complete
divisions, twenty-four other battalions, five siege batteries,
and other details.

Troops from other Eastern theatres, as well as from
England, were hurried to France at the same time as the
withdrawals from Palestine were ordered, and, in general,
the crudity of British strategy in persisting in the Eastern
adventures collapsed like a house of cards. From the
first these schemes had, in so far as they exceeded defensive requirements, been devoid of any sound military
basis, for we never possessed the surplus of troops or of
shipping to justify them. The right course was, as
events now proved, to make sure of victory in the West.
If we won there we won everywhere, and if we failed
there we lost everywhere.

The provision of a military authority superior to both
French and British Commanders-in-Chief, as recommended by the military authorities at the Versailles conference, similarly proved to be indispensable as soon as
the fighting began. Sir Douglas Haig, being unable to hold
his ground, asked General Pétain for assistance, and the
latter, for perfectly good reasons from his point of view,

did not supply it as promptly and as liberally as the former desired. Sir Douglas Haig therefore appealed to his Government and the outcome of his appeal was that, at Doullens on March 26, the Governments of France and Great Britain decided to appoint General Foch " to co-ordinate the action of the Allied armies on the Western Front." Three weeks later he was made Generalissimo.[1]

Different opinions have been expressed as to whom credit should be given for securing this result, and, amongst others, it has been variously assigned to Sir Douglas Haig, to Lord Milner, and to Mr. Lloyd George. A moment's reflection will suffice to show that it was due to no particular individual—unless it be to General Ludendorff—but to force of circumstances. It had been open to anyone at the Versailles conference to suggest that a Generalissimo should be appointed but no one made the suggestion, nor was the appointment seriously discussed. M. Clemenceau would, I have no doubt, have been glad to see General Foch in the position, and may have hoped that his selection as President of the Executive Committee was a step in that direction. But there was nothing to indicate that Mr. Lloyd George would have been equally glad, for he had no high opinion of any of the senior allied Generals, General Foch not excepted.

Italy was more or less ready to fall in with any arrangement, but the American authorities, though desirous of meeting the wishes of their Allies, did not give the impression that they would go so far as to allow their armies to be commanded by an officer of another nation.

[1] The functions of General Foch were, it will be observed, considerably, and rightly, circumscribed as compared with those which it was proposed to confer upon General Nivelle at the Calais conference —*see* page 206.

As to Sir Douglas Haig and General Pétain, they were no exception to the general body of commanders, who invariably like to retain full control over all troops serving within their sphere, and, so far as I could judge, both were desirous that the existing system should remain undisturbed.

As to my own attitude in the matter, I would have preferred any system of command to that of the Executive Committee, for nothing could have been less suitable as an organ of command. At the same time I was not in favour of handing over the British armies, upon whom the brunt of the fighting in 1918 must rest, to an officer of another army if that course could possibly be avoided. My views were hardened by what Lord Kitchener had often said in 1916 when we were discussing operations on the Western Front : " Never allow your armies to come under French command, but keep control of them in your own hands." His desire always was that we should aim at having the strongest army in Europe when the war came to an end, and so be able to ensure that suitable terms of peace were exacted.

I submit that, except in very special circumstances, the placing of armies permanently under the control of a foreign General, having no responsibility to the Parliament of the country to which they belong, can never be a measure that any soldier will recommend, or any Government will sanction, without reluctance. The presumption is that armies fight better under a Commander-in-Chief of their own than under a foreigner, and there are other obvious objections to the latter in respect of such questions as casualties, discipline, and appointments. It is essential, too, before trying to establish " unified command " that the allied Governments should be agreed amongst themselves as to the general policy to be pursued, and be satisfied that the agreement will not be disturbed, since without unity of policy unity of command may lead to the operations being conducted in the interests of one ally rather than of the others, and so defeat its own ends. On more than one occasion unity of policy as between some of the Entente Governments was far from being either definite or stable.

Again, while we may acknowledge with gratitude the services rendered by General Foch at a most critical period, and admire the ability and tact with which he eventually restored the situation, it need not be taken for granted that his appointment at some earlier date would have made any material difference to the course of the war. He took up the post of Generalissimo at a moment when Ministers were at their wits' end to know what to do, and he was accorded a much freer hand than any Commander-in-Chief had previously enjoyed. The plans of operations were *his* plans, and they were not, as sometimes in the past, a compromise between what the soldiers wanted and what Ministers allowed them to have. Not only so but he was able to keep his plans to himself. They were not, as before, liable to be bandied about at conferences attended by numerous Ministers, secretaries, interpreters, typists, and other people of several different nations. Even the War Cabinet were not always informed of his intentions, and the military representatives attached to his head-quarters well understood that they would incur his displeasure if they disclosed them.

The position of General Foch would have been quite different a year earlier, for instance, for he had then recently been removed from the command of the French Northern Armies and was practically put on the shelf for some five months afterwards, while Mr. Lloyd George would certainly not have granted to any General in 1917 the freedom of action which circumstances compelled him to concede in March, 1918. As it was, Sir Douglas Haig was officially instructed in the middle of June that if any order was given to him by General Foch which, in his opinion, appeared to imperil his troops, he had full liberty to appeal to the British Government before executing the order. A month later, when the French were threatened with an attack at Rheims, and Foch called upon Haig to supply certain divisions as reinforcements, the War Cabinet, not approving of the measure, sent one of its members, General Smuts, to see Haig and inquire whether they ought not, as a Government, to intervene. Haig's reply was to the effect that having appointed Foch Generalissimo we ought to support him, and no doubt that was the right view to take. The fact nevertheless remains that, Generalissimo or no Generalissimo, a Government cannot absolve itself from responsibility for the welfare of its troops.

The question may be asked at this point how it came about, in face of so much mismanagement, that we emerged from the war victorious and not defeated. As a partial answer I may explain that in dealing with the different campaigns I have purposely emphasized the things that were wrong rather than dwelt upon those that were right. Moreover, mistakes in management are to be found in all wars as in every other kind of business, and having regard to the length of the one here described, to the disadvantages under which we began it, and to the intense strain imposed upon those charged with its conduct, the wonder is that the mistakes made were not more numerous and the friction set up not more acute. In both respects the Entente had a better record than the Central Powers.

As to the troops themselves I need only recall that the

indomitable spirit which carried us safely through the autumn of 1914 was displayed to a no less eminent degree in the spring of 1918. Then, as in 1914, the errors of the past, ministerial or military as they might be, had to be redeemed by the fighting ranks, and, as usual, the penalty exacted was very heavy. By the end of April we had lost, roughly, 70,000 prisoners, 750 guns, and 4,000 machine guns. The total casualties, killed, wounded, and missing, amounted by the end of May—a period of seventy-two days—to 343,812 officers and men, or about 80,000 more than in the last hundred days of the costly battle of Passchendæle in 1917.

One of the most praiseworthy features of the war was the solidarity with which the allied countries, Russia excepted, continued to stand together through long years of difficulties and disappointments. Conflicting interests, jealousies, and national pride, made themselves occasionally felt, as they were bound to do, but it still seems true to say that in no previous war were the relations between allies more unselfish or mutually helpful than in the war of 1914–18. Between officers and men of the various armies a feeling of good comradeship everywhere prevailed, while in matters connected with concerted action the respective authorities invariably displayed every consideration towards each other—not an easy thing to do when dealing with people whose language, customs, and temperament are entirely different from one's own.

To conclude. The events which I have attempted to describe were so stupendous that any ordinary narrative of them must necessarily have in it many gaps, many imperfections. My endeavour has been to show how the duties and responsibilities of the soldier on the one hand and of the statesman on the other were interpreted and carried out, and it will have been observed that methods varied considerably from time to time. For the first year or so the War Minister, Lord Kitchener, assumed control of the military as well as the ministerial business of his department, and the military chief, the C.I.G.S., being thus overshadowed by the ministerial chief, and ignored by the Cabinet in general, became little more than a cipher. During 1916 the division of duties was differently and more usefully adjusted, with corresponding benefit to both parties and therefore to the State. Following the change of Government at the end of 1916 the position again became unsatisfactory, more so, even, than in 1914–15. The constant aim of the new Prime Minister was to take the military direction of the war more and more into his own hands, and to have carried out military plans of his own devising, which, more often than not, were utterly at variance with the views of his responsible military advisers. The great reverses consequently suffered by the British armies on the Western Front in March, 1918, compelled a return to the principles of 1916, and to a better, if belated, recognition of the fact that military work is best left to military people to do.

Regarded as a general proposition, there can be no question that, with us, whatever may be the case with other countries, the supreme control in war must be civil, and since no one department of State should be allowed to wage war on its own account as was too frequently permitted in 1914–15, there must be within the Government machinery a central point of union from which authority can be exercised over all departments alike. That point must be the Cabinet, or such portion of it as may be determined, or the Prime Minister himself—this latter probably being the best system of the three. A Minister of Defence, whatever his value may be in peace, has no place in the organization of the Government for war. The fact that this appointment continues to be suggested indicates that even yet people suppose that war is a matter solely for armies and navies, and that ministerial duties are connected almost entirely with those services. Nothing could be further from the truth. The activities of war embrace every element of the national life, and upon the Cabinet devolves the responsibility for combining the whole military, naval, diplomatic, financial, and economic forces of the nation for the defeat of the enemy. This is a formidable duty, and cannot be properly discharged unless those holding ministerial office have, by previous study, made themselves acquainted with the principles upon which the business of war should be conducted, and have a correct knowledge of the way in which the use or misuse of Armies and Fleets may affect the welfare of the State.

The function of the civil chief, the Prime Minister, is to appoint the naval and military chiefs, avoiding like the plague all idea of balancing suspected inefficiency in these officers by seeking a second opinion from others. If they fail to retain his confidence they should be replaced, not supplemented, by those who have it. Lord Grey puts the case very well, in referring to our waste of effort in secondary theatres :—

The moral for civilians in the future is to ascertain what the best and most responsible military opinion holds to be the central and cardinal point of the war, and, having ascertained it, to keep within the narrowest bounds everything that will divert strength from that point. The highest military authority cannot be divided. The Government must choose someone to command. If they cease to trust him, they must change him ; if military opinion be incompetent and wrong, no Government can save the country from defeat.[1]

It is, further, the business of the civil chief to formulate policy ; to call for military plans to be made to suit the necessary variations of policy ; and to ensure that the policy laid down and the means for carrying it out are kept in harmony. But it is no part of a Minister's duty to frame military plans for himself, as was sometimes done during the last war, and once a plan has been approved Ministers should think twice before interfering with its execution.

As to the military chief—the professional adviser of the Cabinet—he should realize that, owing to the extensive ramifications of modern war into the life of the nation, the days are gone for ever when, on the outbreak of hostilities, Ministers handed over almost entire control of the operations to the military authorities and afterwards withdrew from the stage until the time arrived to negotiate terms of peace. The real head-quarters of armies in these days are to be found not in the field abroad, but at the seat of Government at home, and plans of campaign are, and must be, now analysed and criticized by civilian Ministers at the Council table in a way quite unknown a few decades ago. The military chief must accordingly be prepared to expound and justify, lucidly and patiently, the plans for which he seeks ministerial sanction ; and he must also be able to explain and substantiate his objections to such alternative plans as Ministers themselves may suggest, and, perhaps with much persuasion and dialectical skill, try to get adopted. Public opinion is more vocal in these days than it was a hundred years ago, and therefore Ministers are now peculiarly liable to be swayed this way and that by

[1] " Twenty-five Years, 1892–1916," Vol. II, page 74.

interests that are not only inconsistent with those of the Army but in direct conflict with them. It follows that soldiers who exercise high command should, without in any way becoming what are termed political Generals, know something about politics and try to understand the way in which Ministers look, and must necessarily look, at political things. This is easier said than done—the readiness of both parties to make concessions notwithstanding—and for a modern Chief of Staff to keep on good terms with his civil chief during the stress of a great war, and at the same time avoid transgressing important military principles, is very difficult indeed. Often, in order to save his plans from being rejected altogether, will he be tempted to agree to compromises and half-measures, knowing full well that, though harmless in appearance, they will sooner or later drag him down to perdition.

Finally, as a result of improved means of communication, ministerial intervention in military affairs is not now confined to the high direction at Government headquarters. It may extend to the battlefield itself, as, for example, when French Ministers assembled certain of their Generals to consider Nivelle's plan of campaign for 1917, and when the British War Cabinet questioned the dispositions of General Foch in July, 1918.

These new methods of conducting war cannot be viewed without a feeling of apprehension, and in order to avoid the danger with which they are fraught, and the discord between policy and strategy to which they may give rise, it is essential that responsible soldiers should correctly adjust their ideas to the more difficult conditions under which they now have to work, and redouble their efforts to give effect to the wishes of Ministers whom they serve. Ministers, on their side, should concede to military requirements the full consideration they merit, remembering that bad strategy can never be good policy ; and they should be careful to recognize the point where, in the nation's interest, their control over military affairs should intervene and where it should be withheld. If, in this way, the functions of both parties are defined and understood—a form of war preparation which costs nothing, and to which no objection on the grounds of militarism can be taken—the position will be infinitely better than in 1914–18, and by means of it much money and many lives may one day be saved.

INDEX

INDEX

INDEX

INDEX

INDEX

INDEX

INDEX

INDEX

INDEX

INDEX

INDEX

Robertson, Sir W., conversation with Mr. Lloyd George after Versailles conference, ii. 287

defends army against Mr. Lloyd George, i. 177

disagrees with Sarrail, ii. 144

discusses Nivelle's appointment with Mr. Lloyd George, ii. 210

instructions to Maude *re* occupation of Baghdad, ii. 77

interview with Gen. Pershing, i. 327–30

interviews Nivelle, ii. 208

letter to Kitchener from, on C.I.G.S., i. 168–71

letter to Lord Grey on Rumania, ii. 120

letters to Sir D. Haig from, i. 255–7, 270, 271, 294–5, 313, 322–4 ; ii. 16, 17, 204, 215, 220, 229–30, 247–9, 250–1, 253, 254–5, 258–9

memo. by, on conduct of war, i. 196–206

memo. on co-ordination by, i. 193–5

memo. to C.I.G.S. on necessity for concentration on Western Front, i. 196, 241–5

memo. to Lord Salisbury on invasion of Belgium, i. 44, 45

note from, to Mr. Lloyd George, on possibility of winning the war, i. 286–9

offered post of C.I.G.S., i. 164

offered post of War Minister with seat in Lords, i. 284

on air raids, ii. 16, 17

on appointment of War Committee, i. 161–2

on Army requirements for possible European War, i. 29 (note)

on difficulties of proposed conquest of Palestine, ii. 165

on duties of General Staff, i. 165

on effects of Russia's collapse, ii. 282 *et seq.*

on Germany as potential enemy, i. 20–23

on his appointment at Versailles, i. 234–6

on mission of Mesopotamia Expeditionary Force, ii. 73

on need for unified military control in Persia and India, i. 173–4

on need of centralization, i. 173

on possibilities of " knock-out " blow, i. 280–3

Robertson, Sir W., on probability of heavy German attack in 1918, i. 323

on question of Generalissimo, i. 223–4

on strategical reserves, i. 222–3, 225, 230

on tendency of War Cabinet to direct military operations, ii. 203, 204

on war policy for 1916, i. 253

opinion of " technical advisers' " recommendation, ii. 287

opposes Balkan operations, ii. 88, 92–3, 99, 111, 112

opposes Rabegh project, 156 *et seq.*

presides at Paris conference (May 4, 1917), ii. 234

presses for decision on Dardanelles, i. 139

proposals by, for future conduct of the war, ii. 56

recommended by Sir J. French as Commander-in-Chief, i. 71

recommends defensive policy in Palestine, ii. 179–81

recommends evacuation of Gallipoli, i. 132–4, 145

recommends placing Mesopotamia operations under General Staff, ii. 58, 59

replies to a charge by Mr. Lloyd George against General Staff, ii. 243–7

report of Calais conference furnished to War Cabinet, ii. 214

report to War Cabinet *re* Palestine campaign, ii. 179–81

reports to War Committee on Rabegh project, ii. 161–2

resigns from C.I.G.S., i. 331

strictures on Salonika Expedition, ii. 146

suggests earlier use of American troops, i. 327 *et seq.*

suggests more prominent part for Britain in war policy, i. 208–10

supersession of, i. 232–3 ; ii. 292

telegram to Allenby from, ii. 187

telegraphs Commander-in-Chief in India *re* mission of Mesopotamia Expeditionary Force, ii. 73

threatened resignation of, as C.I.G.S., i. 187

tribute to the troops, ii. 298–9

urges War Cabinet to decide Palestine matter, ii. 275, 285

INDEX

INDEX

INDEX

INDEX

Butler & Tanner Ltd., Frome and London
F.50.926